# ASPIRE

## DARE TO DREAM

Dr. William Andrew Boyle

WALTON
PUBLISHING HOUSE

Walton Publishing House
Houston, Texas
www.waltonpublishinghouse.com
Printed in the United States of America

Library of Congress Cataloging-in-Publication Data under
ISBN: 978-1-953993-70-0

# DEDICATION

*I wish to dedicate these writings to my heroic Mom, fabulous children, terrible (in a nice way) siblings, and the late Dr. Collin M Boyle (Balram).*

*You all are my inspiration!*

# Preface

A spire: Dare to Dream captures the life story of a very positive and persevering young man from Haraculi, Berbice River, Guyana, South America. Growing up in the jungle of the Amazon, it was a very underprivileged and difficult environment but didn't seem so for this young lad and his siblings.

He prevailed despite the odds and became an example to his Guyanese and Caribbean citizens. It is an almost fictional journey that was filled with many dangers but also fun and laughter.

His school days, both primary and secondary, were filled with mouth-watering adventures. His later life is rewarded by deserving successes and achievements.

Andy's life journey is exceptionally inspirational; it is one that should be emulated.

*Dr. W. A. Boyle BSc, MBA, Dr. Hc, A. A*
*Anthony Sabga Caribbean Laureate (Entrepreneurship) 2018*
*Honorary Doctor (Letters) University of Guyana, 2022*

# Foreword

*By Joseph G. Singh*

In the closing chapter of this autobiography titled *ASPIRE: Dare to Dream,* Dr. William Andrew Boyle A.A. writes to his readers: "I would like to expound on a few areas which I think can serve as catalysts for a better life. They have served me well, and I'm certain they will similarly affect you. I am not perfect, but I feel satisfied that I'm living a good and fruitful life. If these writings resonate with you, I will have accomplished one of my many goals. That is, to positively influence you."

I have little doubt that readers will not be inspired by the life and philosophy of Dr. Boyle. You will learn how he evolved from a barefoot child, born into a loving, caring, and hardworking family from Haraculi, Berbice River, into an accomplished microbiologist, respected high-flying professional, visionary entrepreneur, dedicated family man, philanthropist, and exemplar, who has been accorded due recognition by his motherland, Guyana, with the award of a national honor – the Golden Arrow of Achievement; by the A. N. SABGA Caribbean Awards for Excellence Programme as the Laureate in 2018 for Entrepreneurship; and, by the premier tertiary education institution in Guyana – the University of Guyana, with the conferment on him of an Honorary Doctorate of Letters in 2022.

Andy's journey began in the small riverain community of Haraculi where, as a child, he enjoyed an idyllic lifestyle with his parents and siblings - milking cows, swimming in the placid and encouraging black Berbice river water, eating a breakfast of fried green plantain and saltfish "which were and still are the most delicious components for breakfast in the world," and paddling for an hour "the two arduous miles of meandering, awesome black waters to get to school for 9:00 a.m."

But, as he pointed out, "it was a very picturesque and amazingly beautiful trip to school." He reminisces about the teachers who impacted his life "one way or the other" and recalls the use of slates before the transition to exercise books. His description of life and experiences at school and in the community includes the memories of the 'wild cane' used by the teachers to keep order, the trapping of wild birds such as the maam and wild pigeon for the weekend bush cooks, the use of kerosene lanterns, gas lamps, chopping fish by torchlight, and falling asleep at night to the "pleasant and soothing sounds of the night."

His account of Sundays at Kimbia Reformation (Lutheran) Church, the partaking of the 'goodies' such as salara, sponge or fruit cake, ginger beer and swank (lime juice), the family get-togethers and social gatherings including a good 'name-talking,' was the glue that kept the family and community together "and should be cherished and encouraged."

His boyhood experiences of having to walk for hours across the savannahs to seek medical attention, the reliance on bush medicines such as the juice from the 'wild cane' and the manicole palm to "stop wounds bleeding," and the regular "cleaning out" using laxatives such as sweet broom, crabwood bark, and grated greenheart seeds, boiled together, would have influenced his decision "one day to investigate the effects of these common herbs to probably discover and identify the active ingredients within."

Andy points out that "while bush medicines do work, more comprehensive studies need to be done to establish clear guidelines on dosages and specific usages." He proudly states, "Eureka is currently undertaking studies to detect the anti-fungal and antibacterial properties of the herb locally known as 'house corner' or 'ants bush.'"

Bragging rights for landing prize catches of Rockhead Basher, Laow Laow Law, and Tiger Fish gave Andy status as an expert fisherman. Encounters with deadly snakes such as the Bushmaster, the accounts of incidents and experiences of friends and family, the paddle boat races with boats with such names as 'Miracle' and 'Take It Easy,' the greasy pole and cricket competitions - such as Sand Hills vs. Juliana All Stars, and the reason for 'burning feathers' will give you, Dear Reader, an insight into the vibrant community life experienced by young Andy and his siblings.

His life took a profound turn when William Andrew Boyle topped all the students who sat the National Grade Six Assessment and was awarded a place at the prestigious New Amsterdam Multilateral School. Realizing that he (and his older brother Collin) would find living in New Amsterdam, away from home in Haraculi, "extremely challenging and difficult at times," he states that with these negatives came the positive thoughts - "we consoled and reminded one another that we were there for a purpose, a much bigger one, i.e., to get an education and that come what may, we were determined to excel, we were determined to."

This phase of young Andy Boyle's life prepared him to exercise self-discipline, to apply himself to his studies while demonstrating prowess in sports, and develop lasting friendships. There are accounts of learning to ride bicycles, managing the crush of the fairer sex, and the hilarious account of watching his first movie. He writes nostalgically of home and of his much-welcomed holiday visits to Haraculi. He writes emotionally of the importance of family and of the nurturing and mentoring he received from his parents – his 'phenomenal' father - William Fitzgerald Boyle, and his 'super-Mom' - Claudia Antoinetta, his grandmother (Gamma) - Eloise; his nine siblings and of their progress in life. His distress at the sudden loss of his brother Dr. Collin could therefore be understood and appreciated.

After secondary school, his working life commenced with preparation for training as a marine pilot, but this was not his calling, he was elated that his application for a Public Service Scholarship was successful, and he was selected to study microbiology in Cuba. Fortuitously, his older brother Collin had also been accepted to go to Cuba to study Veterinary Medicine.

Andy's account of the early years in Cuba, the benefits of the study, challenges faced by foreign students, and short visits to the USA to reconnect with family members who were living and working there culminated in 1989 with his achieving and accomplishing his goal, a BSc in Microbiology, cum laude, and his return to Guyana. His placement at the Central Medical Laboratory of the Georgetown Public Hospital and his teaching assignments as a part-time lecturer at the

Health Sciences Department of the University of Guyana, not only prepared him for his own career but also facilitated his relationship with Karen, whom he courted and married. He gained not only a wife but a devoted mother-in-law, Princess May Gordon, and a supportive father-in-law, Colonel (Retd.) Clarence Gordon.

Marriage, the traumatic passing of their firstborn child, the completion of his contract with the Government, and the decision to venture out on his own with the establishment of Eureka Medical Laboratories (EML) in 1995, are emotionally and candidly reported on in this autobiography.

The challenges and opportunities with EML and eventual recognition and international certification opened doors to other opportunities and other business ventures – Caribbean Wind and Sun Inc. (CWS), focusing on renewable energy from solar power; Amazonia Farms Inc, a business dealing with egg production; and Eureka Atlantic Offshore Medical Services Inc. (EAOMS) - providing occupational Health and Safety to clients in the Oil and Gas Sector. Andy's mantra is to "never depend on single income, make investments to create a second source." It is this entrepreneurial spirit, drive, and enthusiasm to successfully manage this cluster of businesses with his family, staff, and co-workers. The community in the Berbice River, that stamped Andy as a pioneering, successful, and philanthropic person of excellence and his selection as an A.N. SABGA Caribbean Awards for Excellence Laureate. Not surprisingly, Andy has set no limits on his ambition, the desire to be the best he can be, and an exemplar to young professionals and businesses. His vision is "of Eureka being the Caribbean's leading chain of Accredited Laboratories with values of being Caring, Innovative, and Courteous."

He has not become so engrossed in his businesses that he has cocooned himself in his own world and dreams. On the contrary, he and Karen have played essential roles in mentoring their three children – Tony, Andrew Jr., and Keziah- and he writes with deserving pride about their achievements. He is also committed to membership in Service Organizations and the Lodges, in which he has held leadership positions, being involved in support for disadvantaged individuals and communities. His remarkable list of accomplishments, achievements, and contributions are inspirational.

Andy Boyle's journey through life demonstrates the power of imagination and positive thinking. Still he also cautions "that life is surely not about dreaming but to work diligently to achieve your goals." I have had the good fortune of my own life and career intersecting with Andy's at distinct phases. He was a student at the Kimbia Primary School in the 1980s, and I, as Director General of the Guyana National Service, would have had occasions to interact with his parents and extended family of the Berbice River and students of the Kimbia Primary School.

His father-in-law, Colonel Retd.) Clarence Gordon, was a close colleague and friend of mine in the Guyana Defence Force, and he and his wife, Princess May Gordon, would have brought the young Karen to family-oriented activities. She has blossomed into a senior medical professional in her own right.

When the Kidney Foundation of Guyana, which I had the honor to co-found and chair for a decade, required a place to hold meetings with the executive, and a mailing address, he unhesitatingly offered his facilities at EML. As a Member of the Eminent Persons Selection Panel for the A.N. SABGA Caribbean Awards for Excellence, then chaired by Sir Shridath Ramphal, my regional colleagues and I selected him from among several eminently qualified candidates from the Caribbean, as the Laureate for Entrepreneurship in 2018. And, as Pro-Chancellor of the University of Guyana (2018-2021), the University Council of which I was a member, took the seminal decision to support the then Vice Chancellor's recommendation for the University to honor deserving persons with Honorary Doctorates. Andy is one of the deserving persons honored in 2022.

It is with great admiration and pleasure that I pen this foreword at Andy's request and urge readers, and especially young professionals, to seek, to emulate his example. and follow his credo: "Don't just go where the path leads but create your own path and leave a trail for others to follow. ASPIRE and DARE TO DREAM."

*Joseph G. Singh*
*Major General (Retd.)*
*February 2023*

# Foreword

*By Paloma Mohamed Martin*

I have known Andrew Boyle for the greater part of my adult life. It has been an inspiration and a joy to see him and his partners innovate and respond proactively to bio-medical needs in Guyana over these decades. However, though I knew he was talented and multi-faceted, I never had him in mind as a writer. So, I was very surprised and deeply honored to be asked by Andy to contribute the foreword to his first book. His autobiography "Aspire: Dare to Dream."

I am delighted also because I have been calling consistently and stridently for more autobiographical and biographical works of successful people, especially in business, and in other areas in the Caribbean for some time because this is the way we get to study their cases and learn from both their successes and their challenges. "Aspire" is a delightful, unexpected chronicle of Andrew Boyle's personal journey. It is welcome for many reasons.

First, it adds to the small but growing canon of autobiographical writing from people of note in Guyana and the Caribbean, providing a rare insight into the formative drivers of his business acumen and success. It also underscores how leaders such as these actually address adversity and turn challenges into their chariots for celebration.

Secondly, "Aspire" might be amongst the first autobiographical books by a Guyanese of Indigenous descent who has attained the pinnacle of business and social acumen. Many might perhaps be surprised to learn that Andrew Boyle proudly identifies as an Indigenous person. In this regard, it assumes even more significance to students and members of those communities as to what they can achieve. This is an example.

In his account of his life as a child in Haraculi, also known as Good Hope, an obscure village in Berbice in Guyana's remote region 10, we can learn something about the geography, social relationships, and life there through the memory of a man who grew up there as a poor and preconscious child, who vowed to look up at the skies as he rowed his canoe to school every day. He believed that "the sky was the limit."

The third reason this book is important is the central theme of love and family that flows throughout the book, from the early values instilled by his Gamma and parents, his days with his siblings, to his personal affairs of love, and the financial contributions of his own parents and in-laws, to the seeding of Eureka Medical Labs.

Andrew's strong focus on his family is endearing. It is also instructive in a world where family structures and values seem to diminish since he places his familial relationships with Grandparents, parents, uncles, family friends, and teachers to siblings, significant others, and offspring as central in his arsenal for success. This is in keeping with the work of Guyanese sociologist Professor Ken G. Danns' whose early work on the "sociology of enterprise" at the University of Guyana placed strong families at the Centre of economic prosperity.

On the business side, we are delighted to welcome this account of Mr. Boyle's life and to be afforded a quick insight into how he and his partners were able to build a company that is now a household name synonymous with medical laboratory testing in Guyana. This account is only one of perhaps five known works of its kind by Guyanese and others in the region in recent times. In this regard, it is invaluable.

He walks us through the early days in 1994 when he and then wife, Dr. Karen Boyle, decided upon the name "Eureka," to the struggle for formal funding, their resilience, and the input of many family members both in moral, technical support and in financial contributions to their dream. Andrew Boyle candidly reveals the frustration overcome by mental fortitude, grit, resilience, innovation, and dogged determination that it would take to build the Eureka empire over these almost 30 years! What a vision, a journey of aspiration, and what brilliant execution to actualize it. For this, he has been variously honored by national and international organizations, most recently with a Sabga award and an Honorary Doctorate from The University of Guyana in 2022.

Moreover, for many whose major pathway to progress in science, the reconciliation of a spiritual life or belief that there is a chief heavenly architect with their training and learning about how science works can sometimes be difficult. Not so for Andrew Boyle. What was also relatively unknown, but again not very surprising as the accounts of many other successful people go, are the accounts of his spiritual life embedded in this book. This strong sliver of sinew runs through his entire life as he accounts for his upbringing in the Reformation Lutheran Church at Kimbia, near his home village. Though many, through worldly success, would tend to abandon, occlude or even deny their strong beliefs in God, Andy Boyle does not do that. Instead, he places God centrally again in his life. "Train up a child in the way that he should go, and he will not depart from it." Andy Boyle's early life story significantly underscores this. In his words "Thank you, God; You have blessed this poor river boy beyond measure."

Andy, of course, has also shared his blessings. He has been extremely generous to those in his life and community. Regarding the University of Guyana, his contributions to teaching, provision of technical services, materials support, internships, and employment for graduates have been steady. However, Andy and Eureka's rapid response to COVID-19 testing at a particularly turbulent time in Guyana might have contributed significantly to the successful management of the virus in Guyana. I can attest that for the University, while some of us kept working during the lockdown, Eureka's ready response to our requests for testing and re-testing of suspected cases on staff helped us to keep our UG Community spread at zero during those trying times.

There is so much more to this multifaceted son of Guyana's soil of which we can speak, but one would need to read the book since forewords are intended to be cogent comments on the work and author, meant to whet one's appetite and to encourage prospective readers to dive in, so I will stop soon.

Andy Boyle's, *Aspire: Dare to Dream*, is a candid, hilarious, personal, and racy read from a man who is still relatively young and who, God willing, still has much more growth left in him.

Thank you, Andy, for taking the time to give us this important book full of wisdom and hilarious dry humor, which helps us understand how you arrived at where you are today.

I was profoundly touched and honored to be asked to write the foreword for this first book. I was very glad to be a tiny part of this journey. May the work and life of this indigenous son of Guyana, who has touched so many in positive ways, continue to be blessed, "for he who does good and trusts in God lacks no good thing."

*Prof. Paloma Mohamed Martin, Ph.D. Vice Chancellor, XI*
*The University of Guyana February 14, 2023*

# Table of Contents

*Map of Guyana, showing the Berbice River.*

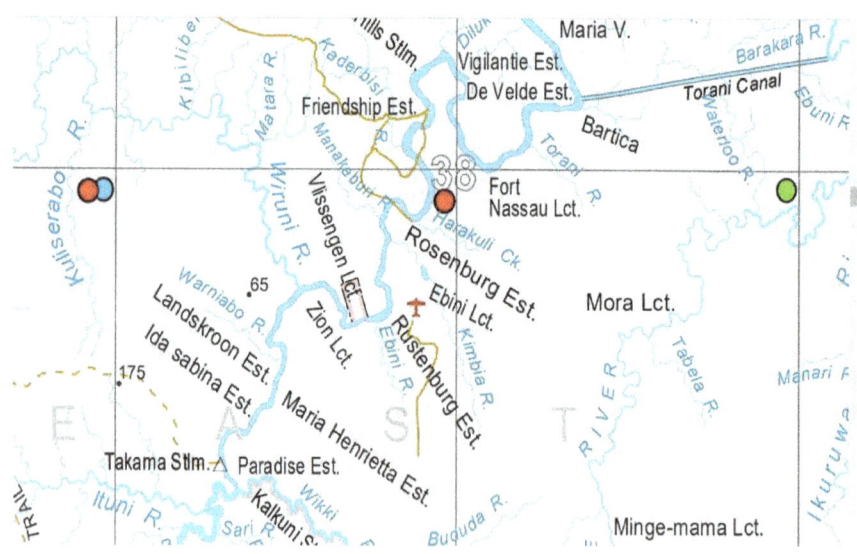

*Map showing Haraculi*

*(Compliments of Bro. John Piggott)*

# CHAPTER 1

# It's A Boy!

I t was eight o'clock on that bright and sunny May morning; the sun was up in all its glory. In addition to being bright and sunny, the general surroundings were pleasant, with the fresh, sweet, rose flower-scented and cooling breeze occasionally blowing over the almost placid and black water of the lovely Berbice River.

A striking yellow plantain canary sang cheerfully in a luscious flamboyant tree with all his might, as if he were making a colorful announcement. Blue Sakis chirped happily in the Buruburo (Solanum stratmoniifolium) bush nearby. A perky hummingbird tasted the succulent nectar from the Hibiscus flowers of the garden and seemed to linger on each multicolored beauty a little longer than usual. It was a fantastic and joyful morning at Haraculi (also called Good Hope), Berbice River.

It had all happened in our wonderful family home, which stands on the right bank, looking eastwards towards the mouth of the black and meandering river. This tiny village is situated precisely two miles from the Kimbia Primary School and Reformation Lutheran church. Only a mere seven homes are situated along the river on both sides, making up the total Haraculi village.

*Sunset at Haraculi*

*My childhood home*

Home deliveries were regular occurrences in those parts of the world. Cousin Kathleen Lindie nee Gladstone, who lived just about five hundred yards away, obliquely from my home, was the "local midwife." After an arduous night of labor, Mom had given birth to her third baby boy, weighing six pounds eight ounces. I'm told that I was a sight to behold. My head was a tuft of long, curly hair, and my skin was light brown, much like my grandmother's (Gamma). Yes, I had arrived in this fabulous world. My birth was signaled by some annoying crying, which, though very typical of newborn babies, was quite significant in my case. Master William Andrew Boyle, aka Andy, was here to stay on that fantastic morning of Monday, May 11, 1964.

I'm also told that my maternal great-grandfather, Mr. Henry Phillip Bender, was still alive at that time. He was born on December 1, 1882, and died the year after I was born. In actuality, I have no recollection of any encounters with my nineteenth-century ancestor. Nevertheless, I find the reality of a family member from that era being alive at the time of my birth intriguing.

I was told that Ole Henny, as he was familiarly called, was a farmer. In fact, I was born into a lineage of farmers on both the maternal and paternal sides of my family. In addition to farming, my great-grandfather and grandfather also owned small clothing shops. Farming, owning shops, and logging were, and still are, the main economic activities in the Berbice River. It should be no surprise that I, too, was expected to carry on the family legacy of farming and operating a shop in the Berbice River.

From a tender age, it was instilled in my siblings and me the importance of being a leader and being independent. It was very revealing when

Mom once told me that I was the worst-behaved of her children while growing up. She probably meant that I was no peach, maybe because I got into lots of scuffles with my peers, was persistent, had a terrible temper, and was always involved in arguments. The first recollection of my naughtiness occurred when I was about one year old.

It was narrated to me that Ole Henny used to sit with a tiny whip in his hands. As soon as I approached and reached to pull down the decorations and other tempting ornaments, he would give me a gentle but firm switch with his whip. This was done repeatedly until I understood that I was not allowed to touch those prized embellishments. When I was a toddler, Papa worked far away from home and would visit on average once per month. Because he was not a regular occupant of my mother's bed, I was told I wouldn't allow him to share it with us. It was also relayed that I would even bang my head against the wall in protest. He would have to squeeze into the bed, but not until I was fast asleep before attempting to do so. Despite this supposed resentment while I was a toddler, Papa was most amused and joked about it. Papa thought it was a good thing for a child to exert dominance. This trait contributed to minor conflicts with my siblings, as they were also strong-willed and loved to dominate.

During that same stage of my growth, I was told that my older brother Collin would pinch me under the table and ask straight-faced if I had been bitten: "Something bite you?" He would do that repeatedly until I cried. On another occasion, we picked Padoos or Whitees, as some people named the fruit. It was heavily overcast, and we were engrossed in picking and enjoying the goodies on top of the tree. Collin, who had noticed that it was going to rain, started to climb down hurriedly. I had also seen the rain falling in the distance and asked my more experienced brother if it was raining. While scurrying down the tree, he repeatedly answered that it was dew.

Before I noticed what was happening, he had already descended and run towards our home while I was alone in the tree. I cried bitterly and received a good drenching from the rain. He had repeatedly outsmarted me, making me resent him temporarily and further compounding my innate ability to fight back.

*Little Collin and Andy*

One day, maybe when I was about five years old, I saw Collin sucking a lollipop. It appeared succulent and inviting as he latched on and closed his eyes. He, being the sneaky and naughty lad he was, instead of giving me a taste of the goodies, knowingly dipped another lollipop into some pepper sauce and handed it to me with a big, friendly smile. As soon as I delved into consuming the sweet, supposedly succulent candy, I realized what a terrible thing he had done. It was too late! I had already placed the pepper-laced confectionary into my mouth.

I then let out a blood-curdling scream and threw myself on the floor while pretending to be struggling to draw my last breath. Papa, who was fixing an outboard engine under the house and in close proximity to where we were, reacted angrily and gave him a sound spanking which immediately stopped my crying. This incident caused Mom to be extremely upset with Papa because of how badly Collin was inflicted with intense corporal punishment.

I was timid, especially during my preteen years. Some of the bigger girls in our community enjoyed chasing me down to solicit a little hug, and they would also kiss me. Though I might have enjoyed the attention and show of affection, I often ran away on the pretext that I didn't want them to kiss me. In reality, I thrived on that strange attention and relished the experience.

Growing up with many siblings and being one of the older ones might have boosted my confidence. The role of being a natural leader may have been automatically thrust upon me. Naturally, the younger members of the Boyles' clan expected us, the older ones, to deliver, and we did. I was extremely playful during my childhood, as was expected of children. Later, when faced with tough living, I became more responsible. John F. Kennedy once said, "When the going gets tough, the tough get going."

# CHAPTER 2

# Yuh Think It Easy?

"Come on, children. It's school morning; time to wake up." These were Mom's gentle but firm utterances, as was the usual occurrence. It might have been about 5:45 a.m. on that cold and cozy Monday morning. Obviously, this was our first warning. Collin, the obedient one, immediately heeded that first call, but Glendon, my smaller brother, and I continued to enjoy another bit of slumber. This, in my opinion, was the sweetest part of sleeping. I'm unsure if five minutes had elapsed because I was caught up in chasing my elusive dreams when the second warning came. This time, it came with threats of lashes and a barrage of insults. Papa also chimed in from downstairs. Apparently, he had just returned from milking his set of cows.

He was no ordinary man. He got up at 5:00 a.m. every day, maybe even earlier sometimes. Somehow, he expected his children to be early risers as well. He often said, "Early to bed, early to rise, makes a man healthy, wealthy, and wise."

I used to say, "Let me remain so," because I simply couldn't seem to muster the strength, will, and energy to get out of my cozy, spring-filled paradise. As a result, this comfortable nook would often be soaked with urine in the mornings. It was a sad occurrence that took me years to get over. I would dream that I was urinating and sometimes realize midway in the process that, oops, it was in my bed. This was very embarrassing and a source of ridicule from my parents and siblings.

After several threats, we hastily got up and proceeded disgruntledly to do our chores. These were already clearly outlined and pre-planned for the entire week. By this time, Collin had already milked his cow and proceeded to dip in the river with a silly smirk on his face. Milking my cow was quite a routine and relatively easy task. My problem was garnering the courage and strength to rise early. The cows selected for us were tame and relatively easy to handle. They were eager to feed their penned young ones after spending the entire night away from them.

Milking actually requires that the cows are put into a V-shaped structure and tied to prevent them from kicking and to avoid injuries. The calf is brought to taste the milk from her teats and to initiate flow. The teats are then washed using a bowl of clean river water, and the manual process of milking commences, one teat at a time. Each cow produced about one to two gallons of milk, quite a significant amount. After the exercise is completed, the cow is usually left to nurse her hungry calf.

*Cows Grazing*

Getting ready for school was fairly routine; it meant completing our chores and getting dressed. Swimming in the placid and encouraging black Berbice river water often seemed to get the better of us, though. After a few fleeting minutes, Mom, like a drill sergeant, ordered us out of the water. It appeared she had anticipated us to be irresponsible and overstay our welcome in the water. Glen and I would have easily stayed in the water swimming all day if given the opportunity. Strangely, these waters are known to be infested with Perai or Piranha (Serrasalmus rhombeus) that are capable of biting off one's toe. Several of our natives have unfortunately lost several of their toes due to encounters with these dangerous fishes. We thought that we were invincible, or maybe stupid, is a better description.

This is a classic example of why children need to be guided and not left on their own because it takes a while before one becomes responsible like the way normal adults are, most of them. After taking our bath, it was time to feed our hungry mouths.

Fried green plantain and salted fish were and still are the most delicious components for breakfast in the world. This tasty menu was routinely provided almost on a daily basis, and we relished those occasions. Homemade bread and eggs were also quite commonly eaten, but fried green plantains were considered to be a particular treat to our little mouths. It was very much like the revered Jamaican meal of Ackee and saltfish.

Mom had already done our lunch basket simultaneously while doing the morning delicacy. She must have been a superwoman as she multitasked and skillfully sent us off to school daily, well-fed, tidy, and organized. After consuming the sumptuous meal, it was time to get ready.

We are ten siblings. The six youngest siblings came much later, and I don't remember actually growing up with them. When they came along, we were already "grown." Then, just before we became teenagers, we were shipped off to New Amsterdam to attend secondary school. My eldest sibling Ken lived with Mom's parents (Daddy and Gamma), two of the nicest people I have ever come across in my life. Daddy, as we would call him, from listening to how Mom called him, was always full of good advice and life lessons. Gamma was loving, gentle, and never, ever seemed to get upset. Collin, the second child, was a very compliant and exemplary brother who, because of his orderliness, always got us in trouble.

"Why can't you be like brother Col?" they would often say. I was the defiant and rebellious one, and Glendon, aka Glenny, the fourth sibling, was not much different from me.

We were expected to leave home at 8:00 a.m. to get to school by 9:00 a.m. During "against" tide, it was generally suggested that we leave home fifteen minutes earlier. That was when the tide flowed in the opposite direction to our travel route, and it was more difficult to paddle against the tide since it was literally moving in opposition to the normal flow of the river. On the other hand, paddling with the tide, or while the water flowed in the direction of travel, was like sweet music to the ears. The boat moved forward easier, and it was less stressful to maneuver.

Children from seven different homes, well dressed in our school uniforms but shoeless, were all bundled into a huge canoe. Shoes and Yachting boots were only used for going to church or, in some instances, to go downtown or to the occasional party.

The bigger children were tasked with ensuring that the smaller ones were protected. Ken was designated as the captain of the craft, while Danny and June Gordon, Verna, and Juliet Watson, our neighbors /cousins, automatically assisted to keep us, the little ones, in line. We kissed Mom goodbye, and we were on our way.

No matter how busy she was, she invariably found time to give each and every one of us a little peck on our little cheeks. Those fleeting hugs came with some bit of pep phrases: "Be a good boy now; make mamma proud." We, in return, always looked forward to those hugs and words of encouragement. She must have felt empty during those long days, but then again, she always seemed to have a little toddler or two to contend with.

The journey to school was relatively routine, two arduous miles of meandering, awesome black waters. It was a very picturesque and amazingly beautiful trip to school. Canje pheasants or Hannah (Opisthocomus hoazin), vultures, parrots, or various species of colorful birds, monkeys of varying descriptions, sloths, and snakes of diverse types all added to the excitement.

The journey to school was more purposeful, and there was no "wasting of time," quite unlike the trip back home. Even though we were focused on getting to school on time, we did engage in healthy, intermittent chats. The entertaining conversations mainly revolved around what was done over the previous weekend. Sometimes the discourses centered around discussing the exploits of one of our parents' fishing expeditions and obviously an exaggerated version of the event. I find that children, in subtle ways, try to boast and impress their peers. Our interactions were lively, but we didn't stop paddling.

The homeward-bound trip was a more relaxed and savoring one, especially if the weather was pleasant and we were moving in the same direction as the silent, streaming tide. On rainy days, it was a rush to get out of the adverse weather, and the journey was more purposeful. We would don our raincoats and reluctantly make our way through the murky weather. The use of umbrellas was not very practical in those instances because of the occasional high winds that we usually experienced during those times.

During these periods of inclement weather, it tended to be scary. We thought about and would have heard stories of persons being chased in their canoes by caimans. This fear was compounded by the older children who made us afraid by relating these stories so that we didn't linger on the journey.

I was never a fan of paddling; as a matter of fact, I vehemently disliked it, but a periodic shout from Ken or one of the bigger ones kept us all in perspective. We drank water by cupping our hands and dipping into the flowing river, joked, chatted, argued, or quarreled as we paddled, sometimes in unison, along the way. There were times when we traveled with other similar vessels, carrying children from other villages along the way. Sometimes we raced with these other boats along the way and this was a source of excitement.

*Children paddling (Rowing)*

After what seemed like a never-ending boat ride, we finally arrived at the Kimbia Primary school. We were all dripping with perspiration, but that was the order of the day. All students paddled to school; it was a way of life; that's all we knew, and it was expected of us. We didn't see anything wrong with this mode of transportation. It was much, much later that I saw children, in some instances, traveling to school using small outboard engines. This was unheard of during my time.

Someone once asked me about the possibility of relieving oneself while on those canoe journeys. The simple answer is to lean over the boat to perform those urgent duties. This strange exercise, though, is normally reserved only for urination.

I really can't recall my first day at school. Who remembers what happens at four years, nine months, the age when most of us started? I, however, have a recollection of several primary school teachers who impacted my life in one way or another. Messrs. Rampersaud, Victor Kersting, Dennis Chandan, James France, Tamesh Singh, Harry Saywack, Edward Sewdatt, Terry Kissoon, Robert Thom, and Mrs. Joyceline Lindie, to name a few.

As a disorganized youngster, I might have been lackadaisical, but I was eager, keen and quick to learn. Slates were used during my early years in primary school. These were framed, blackboard-like writing devices. Erasing was easily done using a damp cloth, but students spat on their fingers and often rubbed out their erroneous writings. This reminded me of the Stone Age, Fred Flintstone era. I might have broken quite a number of those antiquated slates during my primary school tenure. It was so exciting when my first exercise book was given to me. Really, I was from that era that transitioned from slates to conventional exercise books.

Now, I wouldn't say it was easy, but these experiences helped to mold me.

*Kimbia Reformation Lutheran Primary School*

*New Kimbia Primary School*

*Andy in a canoe*

# CHAPTER 3

# Shittabatty

School was fun; I mean, lots of fun and fights too. I practically grew up sheltered to some extent, especially with my two bigger brothers for protection, just in case. Ken was somewhat a father figure to me. Even though he is only four years my senior, he was always there to lend a helping hand and to rescue me from fights and other mishaps.

My mind runs back to when I was probably about five years old. It was a real disaster; a very embarrassing one. Milk powder and biscuits were shared out to students in those days. We mustered every possible container to collect those 'goodies.' Some of us even made funnel-like containers using the paper of the multi-layered milk powder bags. I must have had too much to eat that day. Even after those many years, I can still taste the milk powder on my lips. I clearly remembered moving quickly to the toilet but in a manner that minimized the possibility of me spilling prematurely. I held my breath while walking quickly, barely wanting to inhale or expire forcefully or spread my legs too far as I shuffled toward the school's washroom. Oh, how uncomfortable I felt. I can't remember if I had an audience. I guess I was too preoccupied with my ordeal.

Those facilities were in plain sight for all to see. It meant that every time someone used the so-called outhouses, the other students would be entertained. "Toilets," as they were called, were pit latrines. Pit latrines were and still are the order of the day in the hinterland regions of Guyana. These were little house-like structures built over a five to six feet excavation in the earth. The seats were constructed for relative comfort and ventilation provided by the open spaces at the top, near the roof.

Every home in our area had one of those outhouses, which were often situated just about one hundred yards away from the homes. Our primary school was equipped with two of these separate structures: one for males and the other for females. They were often strategically placed downwind, to prevent unwanted and fetid fumes from returning to one's domicile or school. Some were even done to accommodate two people at the same time. This meant that a conversation could be easily struck up during that period of engagement between the two occupants. Only adults were allowed to use those facilities as it was not safe for children to do so. The children were potty-trained, but it was not uncommon to see a naughty child easing his/her bowel somewhere in the yard, thus fertilizing the earth. This unhealthy and unsightly practice can enhance the spread of parasites. Hookworm larvae can penetrate the naked feet. In some cases, dust infested with ova (eggs) of Ascaris lumbricoides (roundworms) can be inhaled, thus propagating parasitic infections. These intricate details were never ever on our young, innocent minds nor those of the adults in those days.

*Pit Latrine*

During my tenure at Haraculi/Good Hope, we might have changed three to four latrines. This phenomenon occurs when a desperate need arises. This can result from the overuse of the toilet facilities, causing them to fill to the brim. Erosion is also a major contributing factor that can cause a collapse of the pit, forcing one to abort its uses. Changing latrines was done by simply covering up or just abandoning the original structure and moving on to use of the newly constructed place. Drums were used to combat erosion and caving in those cavities. These, however, had to have the tops and bottoms removed to prevent the banging sound of fecal matter hitting the bottom of the drum. Toilet tissue, being a luxury in those days, was made available only when important visitors were expected.

There was then a mad scramble to outfit the facilities accordingly if the visit was unexpected. Newspapers nicely cut in one-foot squares, used exercise book pages, dried corn cobs (the cob after the seeds were removed), or leaves (there is a very special fig leaf with a rough surface that's quite useful for this purpose) were used as substitutes for toilet paper. The presence of maribunta (wasp) would occasionally hinder the smooth flow of this daily routine. Every household had one, and its sophistication said a lot about the family's economic stature. Whether they used leaves or corn sticks, care had to be observed to ensure these implements were free from red ants and other irritating termites. Corn sticks may seem very crude and primitive, but they were quite useful for the designated purpose, and this, too, was disposable. A guarded roll or two of conventional toilet tissue was kept strictly for visitors.

*Toilet Tissue Plant*

*Inside Pit Latrine*

It so happened that I, in haste to speedily relieve my extremely urgent call of nature, managed to have a minor accident just before reaching to perform the actual process of offloading myself. Even though I had exercised absolute caution and care, I spilled in my pants, and a bit of the excrement ran down my legs. In the haste to relieve myself, to add insult to injury, my little already soiled short brown pants and briefs fell into the latrine pit.

Oh, what a disaster! At that moment, I was more concerned about taking care of the immediate business. Afterward, I desperately tried to reach for the fallen trousers to no avail. I tried reaching with my little feet by stretching them after hanging with my hands from the latrine seat. Good lord, it was barmy of me to have attempted that ridiculous stunt!

Clearly, I was way too short to reach it and also suffered the danger of falling directly into the heart of the smelly pit that was half filled with decaying waste matter. That would have been a dreadful and certain death. Having eventually successfully relieved myself, I was now faced with the herculean task of leaving the facility very indecently attired. The mere thought of me, yes me, coming out with my private parts dangling for all the girls to see was unbearable and unthinkable.

I embarrassingly remained there in the smelly latrine and would not leave. Who in their right mind would do such a horrible thing? I just stood there and cried. Ken, my caring big brother, like the very responsible brother he is, searched and searched until he eventually found me. He couldn't even dream of going home without me, either. At one moment before I was found, I noticed him in the vicinity, and I tried whistling discreetly so as not to gain the attention of a potential audience. It didn't work, or perhaps it did. He quickly organized a towel, soap, and a pair of trousers from one of the teachers' children and then took me to the river, where I was washed and clothed. I was probably only five years old, or thereabout, but it was one of the most humiliating experiences of my life. It was the subject of much ridicule and the reason for many taunts and fights. The boys around my age called me all kinds of names related to the rear anatomy and excrement (Shittabatty).

# CHAPTER 4

# Typical Afternoon After School

O ur first day back at school was relatively uneventful. Except for the smell of new clothing and catching up with new and old friends, it was as routine as usual. From my recollection, the sessions were all situated in one big, open area. The classes were crudely divided by blackboards. It must have been difficult to concentrate while sharing the same space, with chatting students and teachers trying to effectively share much-needed knowledge. Order was kept during those 'arduous' sessions by the use of the 'wild cane.' When anyone was disciplined in school, it was like performing in front of an audience of about 80 students. I vaguely remember witnessing a student being 'benched' practically in front of the entire school. Benching is a local term used for flogging in the rear while bending over a table or bench. Some of the problematic and spoiled students would wear two or three pairs of trousers to negate the effects of the blistering lashes of the wild cane. Oh, that must be so humiliating and belittling, perhaps even reminiscent of slavery days.

The journey home, likewise, was a smooth and relaxing one. We couldn't wait to get home. Reaching home early meant getting two to three hours of playtime. One of our pastimes included the setting of traps for wild birds, especially the bush pigeons and other species of ground-feeding forest birds, Trumpeters (maam), and Pale vented pigeons (weeruu), which, when caught, served as ingredients for our impromptu weekend bush cooks.

As soon as we reached home, we changed into our rags or house clothing and then went off to check up on our bird traps. But before leaving, Mom would have our afternoon snacks ready and waiting. This often included warm cows' milk and pancakes with syrup and sprinkled brown sugar, and sometimes pumpkin fritters or other tasty, freshly baked pastries. Mom always insisted that we ate properly.

Our traps were located in the back dam, probably half a mile into the forest, somewhere along the old tractor road.

Earlier on, Daddy (Grandad Menzo) was involved in a bit of logging. He supplied Dally, a species of softwood used in the furniture industry. The old tractor road was used to haul those logs from the back dam.

We always traversed those areas together: Ken, Collin, and I at first, then later on, Glendon, and then much later on, our other siblings. Ken always had more than one trap, and so did Collin. I remember owning a few, but that was much later, perhaps when I was around nine or ten years old. The fun and excitement accrued from these adventures were priceless. The traps had to be checked very early in the morning as well as during the evening. We were quite disciplined in this regard; perhaps this was so because of the expected benefits. In retrospect, these routine exercises helped us to develop a sense of responsibility and maturity to some extent. We had fun while carrying out these projects, which commenced from the building of the traps to the capturing of the prey, but we were motivated to excel. Oh, how our little hearts pounded when our sights beheld a surprise catch fighting frantically to escape! On the other hand, it was very heartbreaking to find a set of feathers and or a shattered cage. This surely meant that the prize was stolen by a wild animal or that the catch was too strong for our fragile and crudely constructed traps.

Sometimes the wild birds were bruised and had to be treated. Collin probably practiced his veterinary skills since those childhood experiences; he used ashes on their wounds, not before clipping their wings to prevent them from flying away. Our prized possessions were then placed into another crudely made cage. This five-by-four-foot cage was made with cleverly interwoven sticks. See illustrations of the crude and primitive traps and holding cages that we used in those days. These were crude but innovative technologies that were passed down mainly from Daddy Menzo.

*Wild Bird Traps*

*Pale vented Pigeon (Weeruu) (Patagioenas cayennensis)*

*Trap Setting*

Our routine chores of penning the calves were clearly understood and executed without fuss or resistance.

Failure to comply with these tasks would have surely been rewarded with a spanking coupled with some form of punishment, including being deprived of a valuable activity. During the fading light, we might have played a game of police and thief or maybe a dog and the bone, all depending on the number of kids who happened to be in the vicinity. Mom always, yes always, had trouble pulling us away from whatever game that we happened to be engrossed in. Then it was shower time or bath time again, in the inviting black water, where another session of playing was initiated.

We were required to do whatever school work and maybe assignments aided by the dim lights of lanterns. These were kerosene-lit devices that provided very poor lighting, clearly inadequate for reading and studying. Mom would have about four lighting implements ready and refueled just before nightfall. It was not until sometime later in my childhood days that we acquired a very bright and effective gas lamp, much to our delight. This was a very luminous lighting fixture that was hung in the middle of the hallway and attached with a rubber tubing that connected the 20lb propane gas bottle from within our parents' bedroom. It was particularly interesting to see Mom or Papa change the mantles of the gas lamp. A sock-like mantle was tied over where the propane gas exited into the lamp. This mantle was first burned by lighting a match under the device before being ready to be finally lit using propane gas as the fuel. Many years later, we acquired a one-cylinder Lister engine and generator. This made us feel as though we were living the best life ever.

Every family used torch lights to illuminate their paths, even if it meant walking down to the peaceful waterside to take a dip in the cold and inviting water. This form of lighting is also used to 'chop fish.' Fishes tend to lie asleep in shallow waters along the water's edges. Natives hunt these fishes by using spears or cutlasses. Patwa (Cichlasoma Bimaculatum), Lukanani (Cichla Ocellaris) or (Peacock Bass), Hoplias Aimara (Hymara), are all known species of fish that are snared this way.

At the end of our usual days, which would be roughly between eight and nine p.m., we would fall asleep to the pleasant and soothing sounds of the night. Crickets, sometimes frogs, especially during rainy weather, and the occasional screeching of night birds would dominate the strange, sometimes scary (usually for children) but characteristic evening sounds of the Berbice River.

Children should be allowed and encouraged to play. It helps with their physical and social development. Wherever and whenever possible, youths should get involved in sports and other healthy extra-curricular activities. It keeps them out of trouble and helps to groom them into becoming valuable and responsible citizens. It may not prevent them from being called false names; actually, false names may develop during these activities, but it's worth the effort.

# CHAPTER 5

# Sundays In Haraculi

I loved Sundays. It was the day that allowed us to sleep until a bit later than usual. The cows had to be milked as per norm, but we were given maybe an extra hour of sleeping time. Church commenced at 11:00 a.m., and we didn't have to paddle, that is, as far as I can remember. Papa drove us to church, all well-attired in our Sunday best, in his speedboat. It was required that we wore shoes, and this proved to be a very uncomfortable experience for me personally. As the third child, I was subjected to 'handed down' footwear (and other clothing) which was most awkward and embarrassing sometimes.

My mind goes back to the time when I had forgotten to put on my shoes while on a trip to New Amsterdam. It was the moment we came off of the steamer that it was realized that I was shoeless. I don't remember who had accompanied Mom and me on the trip. She quarreled with me for not remembering to put on my footwear. *Really, how can you blame an eight or nine-year-old child who is not accustomed to wearing shoes?* Mom seemed more embarrassed than me as she fretted and scolded me along the way. We quickly reached the nearest store, where she bought me a pair of rubber slippers (rubber dinghies or flip-flops, as they are sometimes called). It was then that it was sadly discovered that I couldn't walk with slippers. I tried to grip the footwear with my toes instead of relaxing and walking normally. This seemed so difficult and awkward for me that they ended up bursting. Mom fretted and fretted and tried using a large safety pin, which she surprisingly retrieved from her undergarments, to prevent further damage to the slippers. Unfortunately, it did not work because, after a few steps, they broke once again. That day, I eventually got my first brand-new pair of sneakers. Sometimes there are silver linings around dark clouds.

We attended the Kimbia Reformation Lutheran Church, which was situated in the same compound as my Primary School. Papa or other lay preachers would bring the message in the absence of the visiting pastor, who preached on the first and third Sundays. Papa was a good preacher who, in his own way, skillfully linked the message with practical lessons of life.

Going to church at Kimbia was relatively solemn for the most part, and Sunday school was held just before the actual church service. Children were kept in check from their usual outbursts except for the occasional crying of the babies in attendance. The crying babies were immediately temporarily removed by grownups until their crying subsided before returning to hear the one-hour message.

Daddy Menzo, on the other hand, attended church at Sandhills, some ten to fifteen miles down the river, in the opposite direction. He drove a launch, and he, Gamma, and Ken would normally leave during the early morning hours. Gamma would wake up early in the morning to cook and prepare for the journey. Daddy stopped along the way and picked up friends and family. These persons included uncle Henry, aunt Mickey, cousins Dorric, Berl, Esther, Edward, their children, and the Patoirs (cousins Terence, Emily, Vernon, Wesley, etc.). The Sand Hills Anglican Church was even more solemn than our church, and their congregation was much larger.

After returning from church, we visited Daddy and Gamma during those cool afternoon hours. It was customary and something we looked forward to. Mom would practice her skills on the organ, and Dad would likewise lead us in singing well-known hymns. Gamma always seemed to have some goodies in store, whether it was Rolly Polly (a common name for Salarra), sponge, fruit cake, bread, jam, or nut butter. 'Cassiree' (a drink made from potato), good old ginger beer, swank (lime drink), or maybe aerated drinks (usually for special occasions, like Christmas, Easter, etc.). Oh, what a joy it was to listen to the older folks share their wisdom while they discussed topical issues.

*Daddy's House*

Daddy operated a small clothing store but refused to open its doors on Sundays, his rest day, until much later in the afternoons. It was only in dire emergencies that he would be convinced to sell and in cases where the shoppers might have journeyed (paddled) from afar.

The Sunday afternoon outing would end with us walking through the pathway that linked our two houses, just about 400 yards away. On one such evening, little Joshua, who was probably four or five years old, pretended to be asleep when we were ready to go home. Mom kindly asked me to lift him because the 'poor' baby was sleeping peacefully. He was placed on my back, and I struggled as he 'jockeyed' me through the road. On arrival at our house, he came off my back and said, "Thanks for the ride." Yes, it was a nice free ride. I just smiled and said that there was going to be another time.

After dinner and minor chores, we would usually sing praises and say prayers. Papa's guitar playing was not as good as he thought it was, but he accompanied the songs that we sang nevertheless. We were allowed to select songs from our local hymn book. I remember choosing my favorite ones, "Love Divine All Loves Excelling" and "Oh For A Heart To Praise My God" by Charles Wesley. I will forever remember and treasure those moments.

Family get-togethers, other affairs, and social gatherings should be cherished and encouraged. Further, it is said in Proverbs 15:29 (KJV), "Family that prays together stays together."

# CHAPTER 6

# The Fight of The Century

Over the years, I've come to the realization that my fuses were extraordinarily short, and as a kid, I was extremely intolerant of taunts and criticisms. Despite being relatively 'small-boned' and puny, I never ever backed down from a challenge. My temper was short, and it was so overwhelming that I could easily grab the nearest tool and use it without thinking about the consequences.

When cornered, it was also not uncommon for me to use another efficacious method of defense, a somewhat effective one at that. This was used to the detriment of the bigger opponents, especially when they had the upper hand, like during a chokehold. Like a rabid Pitbull, I would sink my teeth, very much like the Mexican footballer Luis Suarez or the famous boxer Mike Tyson, into the closest body part and never let go until the chosen flesh was removed entirely.

Vin Gordon, my neighbor who lived opposite our house on the other bank of the river, was born just a matter of hours before I was. He was born on May 10, 1964. We were very good friends whilst growing up, but our friendship was more like a roller coaster. One day we were the best of friends, and the other, we were like bitter enemies. He was much bigger in stature than I was during our childhood, and he might have thought he could have taken advantage of me.

One day, when I was probably around seven years old and known for having fights over trivial matters, I was sitting quietly, minding my own business, when Vin came up behind me and gave me a slap. I can't seem to remember what might have caused this seemingly unwarranted onslaught. Young boys and men generally love to extol themselves, especially in the presence of the opposite sex. It's a trait shared by the male species; maybe it massages our fragile ego. Vin might have had all of the above in his thoughts and probably never expected me to react as violently as I did. The stinging slap ignited a fire within my head, and what made matters worse was the fact that Marcia Agard, Pearl Flemming, and other girls were around and clearly saw me receive the act of humiliation.

How dare this young bully do this to me, especially in front of girls? I aimed a packed punch straight at his nose. I'm not sure if he expected a retaliation because he was caught off guard. The 'Mike Tyson' punch floored him, and almost immediately, the appearance of blood from his nostrils was evident. We began to tussle, and it was a brawl. Suddenly, I was caught in a debilitating chokehold.

He was much stronger than me, and I found it extremely difficult to break free from his vice-like grip. It was at that moment that my defensive instincts got the better of me. I, with all of my might, bit him on his biceps. That was no ordinary bite, one that caused him to scream out aloud and immediately release the choke hold. I vividly remember biting and holding until parts of his flesh were literally completely bitten off.

It was only when he slammed my forehead against a 'Kokerite' or 'Cocerite' (Attalea Maripa, a palm-like tree) that I released my massive canine grip. At that time, curious onlookers who probably thought that we were obviously going to kill each other hurriedly separated us while we hurled insults at each other. By this time, Vin's nostrils and arm were covered in blood and parts of his flesh hung limply. A huge, very painful bump (bungee) appeared on my forehead, at the point where my head was forcibly hit against the tree.

Later that afternoon, Vin's mommy paddled over with her wounded son to complain to my mother about her 'rabid' son's handy work. My bump (bungee) was then shown to cousin Shirley's (Vin's) mother, and this gave her some consolation that Vin was not the only one who was wounded. We were forced to apologize to each other and made mutual promises to never repeat that nonsense.

We didn't fight ever again; I guess we might have learned our lessons. We became really good friends afterward and clearly respected one another. After the repeated use of Iodex rub, the huge bump on my forehead eventually subsided. Vin's wound on his arm also was patched up nicely. My advice to youngsters is to avoid situations that can lead to violence. Why fight? We are not animals. Conflicts can be resolved using dialog or simply walk away; it works.

# CHAPTER 7

# The Unholy Communion

Kimbia Reformation is a Lutheran Church and is situated a 'stone's throw' from our primary school, literally. The windows were dangerously positioned very low down on the walls of the church, and this allowed for easy and unimpeded access into the vestry. From the ground to the windowsill was a mere two feet high.

Most of my family members are Lutherans, and we worshiped practically every Sunday at Reformation Church. The routine saw the smaller children attending morning Sunday school at 11:00 a.m., one hour before the regular service. The resident pastor would usually schedule visits once per month to each of the four parishes within those districts in the river. My father, or other self-proclaimed community leaders, frequently took up the slack and presided over those church services when our pastor was unavailable.

As a boy, going to church at Reformation was something to look forward to. It was a joy listening to Cousin Josephine Agard and her husband, Cousin William, aka Git Agard, leading in the singing of hymns. Cousin Shirley ably accompanied the lusty singing with sweet and melodic organ music. Papa sang as if no one was listening and did relatively well, even sometimes in the absence of instrumental music.

*Kimbia Reformation Lutheran Church*

Afterward, the community would come together and talk about common issues like the weather, sometimes politics, or general discussions and seldom informal discussions about strengthening the Lutheran Church to prevent members from jumping ship to join the Adventist church nearby. A good name-talking would not be uncommon during these random sessions. This practice of 'name-talking' is an agenda item at 'country' or rural people's gatherings.

"You hear cousin Jane sick bad, bad?"

That would be the opening statement, and others would chime in with their versions or interpretations. At the end of that discussion, Cousin

Jane's story will be amplified with numerous additional opinions and diagnoses. Then it's quite possible for one of the participants of that "name-talking" discourse to join another subsequent group discussion with a totally different opening line:

"You hear Cousin Jane dead?" This can then be swung according to the next 'name talker.'

On communion Sundays, the third one every month, the visiting pastor shared communion. The wine used for this symbolic feast was stored in the adjoining vestry. This vestry chamber was considered to be revered and totally out of bounds. Certainly not as restricted as the biblical Sanctum Sanctorum. Only the visiting preacher and maybe some of the elders were allowed to enter that holy room.

During one afternoon recess period at school (it might have also been after lunch, or perhaps during the lunch break, the class teachers were either not on duty or were probably involved in other extra-curricular activities), Desmond Gladstone, Wade Carter, Keith Boyle (all my cousins), and I climbed into the church vestry via those low-lying windows. I can't remember if Vin Gordon was also a participant in that exercise. He vehemently claims that he was not involved with us. It was speculated that I may have been the "ringleader" or the chief cook and bottle washer during the horrible adventure, but no one could substantiate this to date. I have strongly denied being the person who initiated this heinous act. It is also not clear how we decided to climb into the vestry. Did we actually break into the window? Was one of the windows left ajar? All that is remembered is that we ended up in the sacred room where we shared the spoils of our labor.

After our disgraceful break-in, we did the most atrocious deed one could ever imagine: we drank every last drop of the very delicious and sweet-tasting red church Cherry Brandy wine. We were all about seven to eight years old and supposedly well-behaved kids. It was inconceivable to think we would have dreamt of committing such a horrendous act. Oh, how embarrassing that must have been to our poor parents. Could you possibly imagine four drunk boys going back to school and then after to their respective homes?

We were ridiculed during the journey home. I distinctly remember making ridiculous and funny jokes in my drunken state, like falling down and accusing Desmond Gladstone of pushing me down. I don't remember the classical flogging I received afterward, but I could clearly imagine how severe it must have been. Some of my siblings later jokingly opined that the blessings that we received from drinking the church wine were enough to last a lifetime.

# CHAPTER 8

# Spare The Rod and Spoil the Child

The licks, lashes, whippings, 'cut-tails,' whoopings, wallopings, hidings, or beatings I was given after drinking the church wine paled in comparison with others I received over the course of my lifetime. Mom later confessed repeatedly that I was an exceedingly difficult child and that harsh beatings might have helped to reform me. She further believes that corporal punishment works and that I'm an evident testimony of this. I imagine that today, the more modern days, Mom could have easily been prosecuted for child abuse, and in the more developed countries, she would have long been placed behind bars. Some may actually debate the efficacy of corporal punishment in keeping children along that straight and narrow path. The more liberal and modern parents believe in talking to children and treating them like adults and not in beating and other harsh punishments. It is believed that the origin of this proverb is the holy bible. Proverbs 13:24 states in the New International Version, "Whoever spares the rod hates their children, but the one who loves their children is careful to discipline them." New Living Translation: "Those who spare the rod of discipline hate their children."

Belts, branches from the "Queen of flowers" (a flower plant with straight, long, and flexible branches, very suitable for whipping), shoes, wild canes, or the hands all served as tools to unleash hefty blows of correction. I got licks for fighting in school and with my siblings, for not complying with my duties, and for disregarding orders. Simply put, I was a rebel and one with a temper, too. I may not have been at fault for initiating the various conflicts, but it was my vigorous and compulsive reactions that caused me to be rewarded with flogging. I would strike out with the nearest available device. A wooden rocking chair in the form of a horse was broken into pieces as it was aimed at Collin, barely grazing his head before being smashed against the wall. It was as if I felt something snapping in my head when provoked, and I would unleash the wrath of my anger on the guilty perpetrators, no matter their sizes. Over the years, I have learned to count to ten and to be more measured in my retaliation. I've become so docile and peaceful; it's truly remarkable indeed. Perhaps, it was the extensive beating that caused me to be so subdued, but only God knows. Mom was known as the disciplinarian, and Papa allowed her that luxury. He was always out on the farm or timber grant, so his active time at home was relatively limited. When he did, though, it was done with brutality as he did so in anger.

Despite being subjected to various whippings, I have not done similar to my children. Yes, in extreme cases, I was forced to use the rod, but very rarely so because I firmly believe there can be other forms of punishment, like depriving them of various privileges instead of beating them. I do, however, understand and agree with my being reformed the way I was.

When Tony, our eldest son, was just around two years old, we all made a trip to St. Vincent and the Grenadines. It was our first trip as a family. My wife Karen, Tony, and I were required to stop over in Barbados. Our in-transit period at the airport was only about two hours. Now, during that waiting time, we walked around, grabbed a snack, and did a bit of window shopping. At that time, we were not financially endowed or 'loaded,' so window shopping was basically all we could have comfortably done.

While walking around, admiring all of the glamorous items in the various showcases, Tony got a glimpse of a luxury watch and, like most kids, said that he would like us to buy it for him. At first, he insisted gently by tugging my hand, insisting that he wanted the watch. We ignored his overtures and pretended to look at other interesting items. It was at that point that all hell broke loose! Tony hurled himself backwards, his left hand slipped out of mine and he let out a piercing cry as if he had been hurt by a flying object. With super swift movements, I managed to prevent his little head from hitting the ground. Karen, who was probably around seven months pregnant with Andrea, was not in any position to subdue this little man as he displayed his colorful tantrums.

Had it been my dear Mom, I'm sure that a few stinging slaps would have immediately ended the scene and drama. I felt like unleashing similar clandestine ones but was inhibited because of the large audience of tourists who, by then, had gathered around. It appeared as though my gentle methods of cajoling him seemed to have fueled his ridiculous behavior. The more I tried to calm him down, the more he cried and screamed. I gripped him firmly on his arm and whispered between my teeth that he should stop this right now or else. He screamed even louder, indicating that I was now squeezing his arm. Our flight was announced, and we had to rush to board our connecting LIAT flight. I lifted the almost three-year-old little fighter, and we ran to board the flight. It was indeed an embarrassing occurrence. Would a few tight lashes have helped the situation? He then slept throughout the journey and later acted as though that incident had never happened. As he grew older, I let him know that that kind of terrible behavior was not acceptable. It never ever happened again. Strangely enough, as a fully matured young man now, he loves to collect watches. At this very moment, I assure you that he has more than ten fully functioning wristwatches in his possession. Quite an irony, don't you think?

So, in reality, I have experienced/seen both sides of the coin, and in my opinion, extreme acts of corporal punishment against children are inhumane and should not ever be used. Again, this is my opinion, and I firmly believe that children should not be brutalized but spoken to instead. Perhaps, as pointed out earlier, inculcating other forms of punishments, like deprivation from fun activities should be used.

# CHAPTER 9

# Bush vs Traditional Medicine

I'm told that my Papa's eldest sister Jean, the first of his seventeen siblings, had died during childbirth a very long time before I was born. It compounds the fact that living so far up in the Berbice River, away from hospitals and regular medical care, was not only horribly inconveniencing but literally a threat to one's existence. It's almost inconceivable to comprehend what happens up there during an emergency. The fastest boat takes exactly two hours from my home in Haraculi to New Amsterdam. The rigors of the journey can be extreme, especially if it is unplanned. It is suggested that one usually leaves when the tide is quite low in order to arrive in New Amsterdam when the tide is nice and full. If the trip were made in the reverse, that is, leave instead during the high tide, then it is expected that the rough waters accompanying the low tides, would make the speed boat ride very uncomfortable.

With emergencies, one cannot predict when they will occur, whether it's during the night or day, heavy downpours or bright sunny weather or if the tide would be low or high. Transportation difficulties are compounded by the high cost of fuels and lubricants in those areas.

This is coupled with the unavailability of suitable water-plying vessels. I must say, though, that over the past few years we have seen an augmentation of those fast boats.

Today, in each village, there are small health centers that cater to persons with minor illnesses like hypertension, diabetes and coughs and colds, these clinics invariably suffer, time to time, from various shortages of medication. When I was a young boy, health outposts/centers existed only in the three villages of Sandhills, St. Lust, and Ida Sabina. St. Lust was probably the one closest to my village and could be accessed via the river or by land. The journey by land meant walking or driving across the Wiruni and Kimbia savannahs. A speedboat took less than half an hour and paddling would take in excess of three to four hours.

I had made the journey across the savannah when I was forced to seek medical attention. Glenny and I had been involved in a silly scuffle that resulted in me receiving a huge gash on my head. It was extremely painful as blood gushed out of the massive cut on my head. Daddy used the juice from a freshly cut 'wild cane' (Gynerium) (a thin cane-like plant that grew in the wild) to stop the bleeding and immediately encouraged us to make the trip across the seemingly non-ending savannah. These indigenous, emergency 'blood clotting' practices can be vital life-saving measures, particularly in areas where conventional medical care is scarce or practically non-existent. I'm also told that the juices from the top of the wild Palm plant (Euterpe edulis), commonly called the Manicole Palm, can also be used to stop wounds from bleeding. These are the same palm trees that produce the manicole brooms used to beat "Ole Higues," a creature of local folklore.

Very early on the following day, we commenced the journey on foot and it took us roughly one and a half hours of walking. It is recommended to take such a journey early in the mornings or perhaps late in the afternoons when the severe effect of the sun is not a factor to contend with. Papa knew the way to St. Lust very well and walked with me as we prodded shoeless through the barely visible pathway of tall grass and savannah shrubs. In my agony and discomfort, it was very difficult for me to appreciate the surrounding beauty and awesome wonders of nature in its fullest glory. I felt the throbbing pain of the deep two-inch gash on my head, which was covered crudely by the inexperienced hands of my doctor Mom but strangely enough, it did not bleed. Maybe the effects of the fresh 'wild cane' juices had long-lasting effects. Even though the actual taped wound didn't bleed, bloody sweat from my head trickled down my face. The pain was severe but we kept going on what seemed like a never-ending trek. Papa walked quickly and had to slow down his pace so I could keep up with him. While keeping in front about seven steps ahead, with his brisk walking, he would glance backwards to see if his son was okay. A few times during this arduous journey, I felt as though I was going to faint and. On those instances, Papa slowed his steps and inquired if I was okay.

I remember nodding under my broad-brimmed felt hat without answering because I was terribly exhausted and didn't want to waste my energy to answer. At one point, he headed off path and walked towards the bushes; there, we reached a spring that was hidden under the trees. He obviously knew the terrain very well. The shade and coolness felt heavenly and when I followed his lead and splashed cold spring water on my sweaty and salty face and neck, it gave me a feeling of revival. We had been walking for what might have been an hour or perhaps even longer. The water was fresh, cold and tasty. We sat on two old logs near the spring and Papa offered me a bake and saltfish, made by my super Mom. This was the perfect break which I absolutely needed and the rest was graciously welcomed.

Clearly, Papa knew it; he probably saw the tired look on my face. It was torturous having an eight-year-old walking barefooted for so long through the savannah with thick grass taller than himself. *What if there were rattlesnakes?* Papa again took the opportunity to scold me for fighting with my brother but was not too harsh as he noticed that I was still in agony despite us taking that well-deserved break. We took what seemed like a mere ten-minute break then he suggested that we get going before the sun got too hot.

Further along in our journey, we were startled by a flock of frightened birds that darted out of a clump of bushes near where we were walking. My little heart leaped and pounded in my chest, but Papa didn't seem shaken or concerned. We walked and walked until the vegetation changed from savannah grass to regular bushes, and the track became more defined. Papa indicated that we had arrived at the hospital, which was situated across an empty field. It was simply an ordinary health center manned by one live-in nurse and a handyman. Somehow, I felt an adrenaline rush and quickened my steps. We had arrived, oh Lord. I wasn't sure I ever wanted to do that marathon again.

Auntie Girlie, Papa's sister and a qualified practicing nurse, was stationed at the health center in St. Lust at that time. She scolded me for having fought with my brother as she skillfully stitched my raw wound without local anesthesia. It was excruciatingly painful, but I didn't want to appear like a crybaby. Remember, I was only about eight or nine years old at the time. Auntie Girlie was amazed that the bleeding had been stopped after the juice from a local herb was applied.

Papa had briefed her and explained everything that had happened. After being nicely patched up, we were offered some of her delicious lunch, and then we hit the arduous trail once again for our return trip. She gave Papa some tablets and instructed him to take two immediately, along with others with special written instructions for later. This time it seemed to be much shorter and the fact that I was nicely patched up made me feel more comfortable and at ease. The pain was no longer there; perhaps I was given painkillers. The arduous journey gave me bragging rights on my return home. The tales of the trek through the savannah included how beautiful the area was and that it was a 'piece of cake.' That the suturing was not painful and that the general experience was mind-blowing. Nowhere was there any mention of how I almost died of exhaustion and pain.

Another frightening experience that proved the efficacy of wild cane in stopping severe bleeding was when Collin accidentally hooked me with a fishing hook. We were happily fishing when he swung his rod that was attached to a line and fishing hook. It seemed as though my hand, just above the wrist, was in the way and the sharp hook penetrated my skin and flesh. It bled profusely and Daddy, in his wisdom, quickly squeezed the juice of wild cane that almost immediately arrested the bleeding. With a brand-new razor blade, he made a lightning-fast incision to remove the barbed fishing hook. No sutures were necessary and my hand miraculously healed in a few weeks.

At the end of our August holidays, we were all required to take a "clean out." This custom of giving laxatives to children was thought by our elders to have been a very effective way of preserving our health. These 'medicines' included 'senna' pods (pods from the Senna alexandrina plant), castor oil (Ricinus communis), and Epsom salts (Magnesium sulfate), followed by daily 'bitters.' These were a mixture of herbs that had a sharp pungent and bitter taste. It is believed that those laxatives cleaned the impurities and detoxified our little bodies. The funny-tasting brews also served to open our appetites and 'purify' our blood.

I really didn't mind using bitters which usually consisted of herbs like 'sweet broom' (Scoparia dulcis) crab wood bark, grated green heart (Chlorocardium rodiei) seeds, 'cotton bush,' 'piabba' (Hyptis pectinata), amongst others. These bushes were then boiled together using water from the last of the falling tide (water from the lowest tide, just before it changed). Oh boy, how they opened our appetites! Senna pods tasted horrible and getting me to drink took some doing. All my other siblings drank it with little or no fuss. Whether it was nicely made as a beverage like tea or served unsweetened and black, it certainly did not matter to me. I would vomit my little heart and soul out on each and every occasion. The only way that I was able to ingest this awful-tasting laxative was to drink it spoonful by spoonful and with the assistance of a bit of lime or lemon after each spoon.

Later, Mom shared that this was exactly how she was given the medicine when she was younger. My siblings would quickly consume their dosages and run out to play, leaving me in agony. Actually, a belt or whip was waiting to strike me if I dared to vomit. Each and every session, through tears, sweat and extreme courage, I managed to prevail, vowing never to subject my children to this inhumane punishment. I simply couldn't stand the scent of senna pod tea, I abhorred it.

This reminds me of my experience in Cuba when I tasted ice tea for the first time. Ice tea, because of the lime flavor, simulates somewhat to senna pod beverage and lime. When I took my first sip of the ice tea, I spat it out, much to the embarrassment of my friends. It took me right back to those glorious senna pod childhood days. Senna pod tablets and PL pills (another laxative) were available but Mom thought it best to have us drink the 'real thing' to give us a 'proper work-out' or tummy gripes and diarrhea. In her opinion, the griping pains were good, and it showed that the medication was working. We even sometimes pretended to be in a lot of pain, much to her liking. On other occasions, there was no need to fake it because the griping pains were real.

It was later discovered that young guava leaves or green guava fruits somehow alleviated those pains and caused a cessation of the diarrheal condition. Oh, what amazing effects bushes have on common conditions. I vowed, one day, to investigate the effects of those common herbs, and to identify the active ingredients within. During those times, Piperazine citrate, an awful-tasting worm syrup, was also given regularly. This clearly meant that the 'out houses' were used with extreme frequencies throughout the day and sometimes in the evenings. Some siblings were even forced to seek refuge in the bushes because of simultaneous use of the facilities.

Unfortunately, three peers my age tragically died when a grandmother in our village mistakenly gave them and several others caustic soda to drink instead of Epsom salts. Some were thankfully saved because they had not taken full doses. It was truly a horrible tragedy causing the entire village to mourn the deaths of these youths. Could you imagine how that poor grandmother must have felt? Thankfully everyone understood that it was clearly an accident and there was no willful act of homicide on her part. Alvina, Dennis and Kenny lost their little lives all because of a terrible mix-up of chemicals.

Several years later, a very strange incident occurred when I had taken Karen to visit my homeland, Haraculi, and to meet my folks. Very much like new couples, cystitis, more so honeymoon cystitis, was not uncommon among them. This phenomenon is very prevalent in similar persons because of the minute cuts and bruises that are derived from repeated and frequent sexual activity. (Conventional medication is usually prescribed after performing a urine culture and sensitivity or simply by using a sufficiently broad-spectrum antibiotic). As soon as we arrived, she sadly noticed that she had developed a urinary tract infection. We were not prepared for this disaster and there is no way we could have procured suitable antibiotics. It is said that cranberry juice usually works relatively well in alleviating similar conditions. *Where in the heavens would we find Cranberry juice up in the lovely Berbice River?* The other option was to return to Georgetown to relieve her of the pain and discomfort. Oh, what a predicament!

By breakfast time she seemed to be getting worse by the minute. I tried to lighten the moments by making jokes and distracting her from her ordeal. By then she had already visited the outside latrine maybe about four times during that morning. UTIs cause frequent urination, pain, burning and discomfort, which is surely not something you would want to have when you are far away from medical care.

I guess Karen was ashamed to tell Mom what was happening to her for fear of being ridiculed during her first time meeting her mother-in-law. Mom had planned for us, not with senna pod beverage but with her concoction of bitters. She encouraged us to each take a glass full of the horrible-tasting brew. I gleefully obliged and Karen too, probably for the first time in her life. We both drank every drop of the 'bush' and consumed ourselves with making Karen feel at home and, of course, answering searching questions from the ever-vigilant Mother in Chief; she was very protective of her children.

Little Felecia, our baby sister, was about seven years old and so excited and happy to meet her new sister-in-law. We chatted and laughed for several hours and surprisingly Karen did not go to the latrine, not even once. *Was it the concoction that knocked out the cystitis?* It was concluded that there must have been some antibacterial substance in the brew. Bush medicines do work, but more comprehensive studies need to be done to establish clear guidelines on dosages and specific usages. At the moment, the use of bush medicine is a lot of speculation and guesswork. It wouldn't be strange to hear an unqualified voice saying.

"Bro, you should eat parched jamoon (Syzygium cumini) seeds to cure your diabetes," simply because he had heard it being mentioned somewhere.

During infancy, especially shortly after birth, children born to mothers with vaginal yeast infections may develop a condition called thrush or oral candidiasis. They can also acquire this illness from the environment, dirty cutlery, hands etc., simply because their immune systems are not geared to be fully protective and they are very vulnerable to these external attacks and many others. Thrush is, therefore, more pronounced in undernourished and malnourished babies and also in those with other debilitating conditions like AIDS etc.

Our Mother in Chief is able to quite easily detect whether or not babies, especially hers, have thrush. She can look at the macroscopical characteristics of their fecal samples or at skin texture and walls of their mouths and detect with a high degree of certainty whether or not the child has thrush. She would ground the carefully washed leaves of an herb locally known as "house corner" or "ants bush" (Struchium sparganophorum). This purée is then mixed with a little salt and given to the affected babies orally before feeding. In extreme cases this is syringed through the anus with amazing effects. It should be noted here that Eureka is currently undertaking studies to detect the anti-fungal and antibacterial properties of this effective herb.

What would you do if you were ever stranded in the forest without food and water? Some people would sit, cry and await help, while others would get busy and hustle to find a way out while consuming the edible plants that exist in lovely nature. They can also drink water, yes, very pure water from a particular 'water rope' or vine. This vine, when cut, can immediately fill a few glasses of healthy and pure water. The water fizzes as it pours out from the vine whenever it's severed. The diameter of this rope-like vegetation can reach about six inches, but the sizes that are normally seen are in the vicinity of two to three inches thick.

As mentioned earlier, I have witnessed bush medicines being used to stop wounds from bleeding. One example is simply squeezing the juices from a freshly cut wild cane or wild cabbage, which is also called the heart of palms and can be extracted from the top of a manicole Palm. This wild cabbage is quite edible and can be eaten raw or cooked like regular cabbage.

I was about eight years old when I had a very painful ulcer in my head. Mom shaved around the area and placed a piece of Elastoplast to cover the open abscess (ulcer). This seemed to make things worse. It felt as though something was biting inside of the sore. This excruciating pain, though intermittent, was almost unbearable. Papa took one look at it and said that it was a 'mosquito worm.' Being an experienced 'bushman,' he was able to discern its origin. They then applied wild gum (somewhat like chewing gum) to cover the wound. A similar gum is also used for hunting birds like the very popular Finches (locally known as Bastards or Towa Towa). This is done by covering a slender stick with this wild gum and attaching this gummed stick near a cage with a whistling 'caged' bird. Later during my studies in Cuba, I learned that this parasite is called Dermatobia hominis. Strangely, the eggs are laid on leaves or branches. When an animal (or human being) happens to touch those areas where the eggs are laid, they are attracted to the warmth, become larvae and burrow into the skin of the warm-blooded creature. These larvae then feed and eventually grow into adults and are dropped out of the wounds. During their growth and development, they cause tremendous discomfort and pain. The treatments are to have the larvae surgically removed or to have the oxygen supply cut off by the application of impermeable gum. The latter was exactly the method used in my case.

Can you imagine what life would have been like without the use of these crude bush medicines? With proper studies and effective trials, it is believed that bush medicines could have more widespread usage. Even though there are clearly numerous benefits that can be obtained from bush medicines, steps need to be taken to conduct more studies for their current and future uses.

*Ants (house corner) bush - Struchium sparganophorum.*

# CHAPTER 10

# Fishing: The Christmas Catch

Catching fish is an extremely enjoyable experience; it's relaxing and personally rewarding. It takes me into another realm and temporarily dissolves my preoccupations. Therapeutic is a single word that can be used to encompass the peaceful and orgasmic feelings that this exercise brings.

It also might have been the tale of that Christmas Day fishing experience that may have influenced my love for catching fish. Daddy, my maternal grandfather, told me of his incredible fishing encounter. According to him, he grew up relatively poor but was content and happy. He had been married only for a few months and it was Christmas Eve and there were no fancy foods to eat. He ventured out that evening to 'chop fish' because at night, fish would rest near the shores, on flattened areas, during the low tides to sleep. By quietly approaching these sleeping creatures, one can snare bucket loads with the aid of a cutlass, spear, arrow, or bow.

Daddy had been out practically all night but didn't manage to encounter any fish sleeping along the river banks. Maybe the fish themselves were caught up in the festive season, or the moonlight was too bright. Fish do not rest well during moonlit nights; they are usually scared away as soon as the hunter's torchlight is beamed on them.

It had been an extremely frustrating and disappointing exercise for him; he was sleepy and tired and wanted to call it a night. *Could he possibly go home without a catch, especially on Christmas Day?* He was about to turn his canoe around and return home, when he decided to shine his light one more time into the shallow waters. To his surprise, he noticed a massive Hymara (Wolf fish) (Hoplias aimara) resting between some submerged brambles (dead tree branches). Sitting at the bow of his canoe allowed him to strategically move his craft silently so that the prey was not easily disturbed. He said that his heart had started beating so loudly that he was afraid that it might have awakened the sleeping monster. He quickly and silently grabbed his arrow and bow and took aim at the resting beauty. There is a very clever way of holding the drawn arrow next to the cylindrical flashlight. He took aim and quietly let the deadly arrow fly. The well-aimed arrow reached its target and he was able to capture a huge twenty-pound prize. That early Christmas morning, he returned home with a huge Hymara to Gamma. Oh, how excited she must have been. Daddy was so elated that he excitedly repeated his exploits over and over to my siblings and I as we grew up over the years. Don't ever give up; yes, sometimes the catch is closer than you think.

# CHAPTER 11

# Innovative Fishing Methods

One Saturday, the elders of Good Hope came together and decided to "beat Haiarri" in the upper Haraculi creek. This was a perfect display of teamwork. I was probably only six or seven years old and was very impressed with the way in which members of the immediate community came together. We were about five strong canoes, and seemingly all the elders knew their roles. We paddled for quite a bit up this tiny branch of the river.

As the creek narrowed and allowed for effective blocking, the older team players placed a wall made of sewn-together manicole palm barks that allowed water to pass but stopped fish from traversing the barrier. This was done in two places, allowing an area of about 60 feet to be harvested. Later, it was explained that the barriers were placed to prevent the indiscriminate killing of more fish than needed, essentially preventing wastage. These temporary barriers were also effective in preventing the affected fish from escaping the "treatment" area.

Cousins Lawrence, Clifton, Verol (Flash Gordon), Grandpa Menzo, Papa, some of our workers and respective families were all geared to get immersed in our fishing expedition. Two-feet lengths of Hairarri vines (ropes) were distributed to various family heads and they, in turn, began pounding or mashing them before trashing them on the surface of the water. These thick vines are poisonous plants used very effectively to capture fish in the indigenous communities of Guyana. These ichthyotoxic plants contain rotenone, a chemical compound that stupefies fish but is harmless to humans.

This was done strategically upstream so that the 'juice' of the crushed vines could properly circulate downstream. This seemed to be an exercise in futility since we, the youngsters, were clearly unaware of what would happen next.

It might have been about half an hour after initiating the trashing that we began to reap the dividends of our labor. Suddenly, a massive Hassar (Hoplosternum littorale) leaped in the air, landed in the water, and then leaped a few times before floating up. What seemed like at least 100 fishes joined in the frenzy and did similar acts. Before we knew it, fishes of all types and sizes were affected by the Haiarri poison. Every man jack from the five groups became involved and either pointed out a floating fish or collected them as they became incapacitated. This form of fishing was not encouraged to be done on a frequent basis as it markedly depleted the fish population. In fact, this method of fishing is illegal but that does not stop natives.

This strange and archaic mechanism of fishing is hardly ever practiced and is thought to be a dying art. It could be that the new generations have not learned the techniques well and may not even recognize the Haiarri vines in the forest.

During my younger days, we used another interesting fishing system using natural herbs. The wild form of tobacco called 'Kanali' or 'Cunally' is also used effectively to poison and snare local fish. The leaves of this wild plant are collected and pounded to form a purée of pulp and juices. These are then mixed with grasshoppers, parts of the nests of wasps (maribunter) and flour. It is said that the grasshopper would cause the fishes to jump around and the wasp's nests would increase their buoyancy and force them to float for easy retrieval. I'm almost 100% sure that the wild tobacco would have a similar effect on the fishes and induce them to jump and float, very much like the other suggested ingredients.

These various components are kneaded together and then made into little 10mm sized balls which are thrown into areas suspected of having fishes. Amazingly, in as little as fifteen minutes, the fish, as big as one foot in length, will begin to jump and float. These are then collected using quakes (basket-like receptacles), because it's sometimes not easy to comfortably hold on to the still relatively active fishes.

Conventionally, we used hand hooks for relatively small fish. These are lines with little hooks attached to a simple fishing rod. This type of fishing can be done in shallow waters e.g., close to river banks, ponds, trenches etc. The baits used can be simple flour mixed with water (flour bait), worm baits (earthworm) (Lumbricina), Macaro, a worm taken from the seed or banga of the kokerite or cocerite (Attalea maripa) (a palm-like) tree.

But come to think of it, these are extremely innovative ways of using natural herbs to fish. These strange procedures need to be studied with the hope of improving their efficacies. Fish pens, as they were called, were very ingenious contraptions used to trap fish. The bark of the manicole trees were used to create an enclosure along the bank of the river. This enclosure was built to allow water and small fishes to 'filter,' leaving trapped fish to remain in the pen for retrieval during the low tide. A heavy door that slides down and closes at one's whims and fancies. This is tied to a rope which is pulled when it's perceived that there are enough fish swimming inside of this pen. Wild soursop, roasted corn, the guts of calabash fruit, termites (wood- ants) nests (filled with live termites), rice brand, amongst other materials, were used to entice fish to enter. This was quite a clever and relatively inexpensive way to catch fish. My siblings and I enjoyed checking to see whether there were fish "playing" in the pen. Several times we were misled into thinking that there were schools of fish, only to find at low tide that there were only a couple of Dary (Leporinus granti) or other common species of local fish.

On other occasions, we managed to pull the string that triggered the door to fall and made bumper hauls. I'm told that naughty individuals would defecate in those fish pens to further entice gullible fishes to enter. This fish pen could also be set so that the fish themselves could trigger the heavy door to close. Hymaras were the elusive types of fish that were usually caught in this system. This automatic contraption is usually done at night to snare those monstrous beasts. Sadly, these fishing techniques are becoming extinct as our villagers become more urbanized.

# CHAPTER 12

# Rockhead Basher Expedition

Rockhead Basher (Plagioscion auratus) (Basha) fishing at the mouth of the Haraculi creek, was, and still is, being practiced frequently. This type of fishing is usually done in the dry season, particularly during the months of July to October. The helicopter-like blossoms of the majestic Long John trees are telltale signs that it's Basha season. In order to fish for these silver monsters, we had to gather live fish bait. The baits used were pond fingerlings of the species of Hassar, corrubiero, yarrow, etc. The common silver dollar or Serebeh from the river could also be used as bait.

I remember my first time fishing for Basher. We had our full complement of live fingerlings to serve as bait. Ken, Collin, the late Christel Lindie (a cousin from across the river, cousin Kathleen's daughter) and I left around mid-morning with the tide falling, which might have been midway through the lowering tide. It was said the Basha would graze (feed) just about at the end of the falling tide and then later during the middle of the high tide. We finally reached the mouth of the Haraculi creek after paddling for about half an hour or so. We were all armed with 2" hooks that were strapped onto coarse polyethylene twine with lead sinkers to assist in keeping the hooks close to the bottom of the river. We settled and drifted quietly in front of the creek around where Christel suggested would have been a suitable area. We then selected baits for our respective hooks and commenced pumping our lines. Apparently, this pumping action (movement of the hand with the line up and down in strokes of twenty inches, in an up and down movement) attracted those beautiful silver prizes and simulated the little fishes swimming up from the floor of the ground and then back to the floor again. It should be noted that the depth of the water in front of the Haraculi creek was in the vicinity of only between twenty and thirty feet.

It was not long after we had thrown our lines into the dark, seemingly frightening black depths of the Haraculi creek that it happened. I felt a surge of firm pulls on my line and immediately reacted by jerking in return. My little heart was pounding non-stop as I felt the uncontrollable resistance in my fish line. This must have been a big one! I screamed out loudly,

"Gat a big one hay bai!"

I felt the sting in my delicate little hands as the huge fish struggled on the far end. All this time, my heart leaped uncontrollably and the rush of adrenaline gave me the strength to fight back. This feeling is what drives fishermen from all walks of life to pull in their catch. It's the reason why sports fishing is so intriguing. Christel blurted out a laugh and said,

"Boy you gotta be joking, stop your nonsense."

By the time I was about to let go, another squeal of excitement when I was immediately joined by my two older siblings. With our bare hands, we fought with my big catch, pulling and muttering amongst ourselves. Ken acknowledged that indeed it was a huge monster. The strength of the fighting fish moved our boat about 50 feet from our original position. Teamwork is fabulous; it must have been about five to ten long minutes before we caught a glimpse of the fighting beauty. This time seemed like forever as we fought this supposedly huge river monster. She was almost in the boat, then somehow, the fish mustered some more energy to stay in the cool black water for a few moments longer as the line stung our little fingers. The stinging fingers caused by the friction of the taut polyethylene twine and the tugging and struggling fish were almost unbearable.

"Pull nuh man" shouted Ken, and Collin retorted, "We pullin'!"

Finally, the beautiful beast seemed to have expended all her energy and we managed to, with one heave, lift her into the boat. Oh, what a massive beauty she was! It was not a Basher as was expected but a huge unscaled monster. Some called it Manari, Blinker, or Loaw Loew (Brachyplatystoma filamentosum). It was my first extraordinary catch, one that I will never forget. It might have weighed around 130 pounds, just a bit less than our combined weight. My face shone with excitement, and I had bragging rights for supposedly snaring one of the largest fish of our time. The bruises and burns we received while struggling with my catch didn't matter; they were minor compared to the glee and satisfaction we felt while watching the gray and black monster's gills open and close, as she blurted out a regular, coarse grunt, "Hmmm, hmmm, hmmm."

This amazing experience gave us a valid reason to be boastful for years later. We were branded as expert fishermen, even though this exercise might have been a fluke. Sometime later, a few weeks after this grand phenomenon, we were fortunate to experience another breathtaking encounter.

"Long lines," as they were called, are two to three hundred feet long heavy polythene cords (locally called calf ropes) tied to strong and flexible branches, and like Basher lines, were strapped with 4" hooks and connected to sinkers (iron bolts, lead, or anything preferably made of metal) to keep the baited hooks on the riverbed in the middle of the river. Another interesting feature added to this device was to have two empty glass bottles tied to the same branch where the end of the fishing line was attached. When a fish was caught on this line, the struggling fish would cause the two bottles to cling and make sounds, warning us of the prize.

One day, early afternoon perhaps, we caught a beautiful tiger fish, also called the "Cullity" fish (Pseudoplatystoma fasciatum). It was only about two to three feet in length. This was a routine catch and by now, nothing to get too excited about, after all, by now, we would have had much bigger encounters. My little brother, who is only two years my junior, didn't want us to harm the beautiful tiger-looking fish. He shed bitter tears and begged us not to harm the very attractive creature. Since then, he has been furnished with the name 'Cullit' named after the 'Cullity' fish.

Funny enough, false names are easily derived and placed appropriately on the guilty perpetrators. Names like Roast Daawg, Pumpkin Belly, Bat Ears, Nancy, Tootumbrook, Git, Rat, Corroba, Bucky, Dank,

Cappai, Fan, Boyee, Girlee, Baba, Monkey, Balgo, Pado, Mother BT, Lydia, Wiggers, Moon, Gramp, Blackman, Panther, Soldier Bread, German, Cutass, Teddy, Bouncy Luncy, King Buck, King Hawk, Ganny, Buddy J, Snake Eye, Green Pine, Bony Lala, Egg Head, Red Sweat, Glue Face, Red Man, Mannish Puppy, Force Ripe, Leapfrog, etc. are some of the false names of persons in the village. False names are meant to be funny and not to annoy the perpetrators. Often there is a hilarious story behind them. In the case of Buddy J, which really meant Buddy Jackass, He would purchase items for $200 and resell them at $150. Clearly, he was being silly and extremely ignorant of business transactions, hence his colorful title.

*Andy & Colwyn Boyle – Massive catch*

# CHAPTER 13

# Abby Macedo

We were both around seven years old and the best of friends. He was a gentle soul and a very positive, well-spoken individual. Abby and I were also relatives. My grandmother, Gamma, and his grandfather were Gladstones and first cousins. Sometimes I used to think that he was beyond his time. This was owing to the fact that he gained a lot of knowledge from his dad, Frank Sr., and Uncle Victor Macedo, who were well-read and had seemingly endless ideas on almost everything. Abby soaked it all up and would demonstrate his expertise in class where even some of the teachers were at sea, especially in the areas of current affairs and world geography. I learned from him that Hungary and Turkey were two countries. I used to marvel at this youngster from whom I learned a whole lot. Abby was the last child of several siblings and we all grew up quite close. His big brother, John Macedo, is currently the Honorable Mayor of Lethem in region nine.

It was vaccination day at Kimbia Primary School. The visiting nurses appeared to be friendly and relatively accommodating. Our teachers had sent consent forms to our parents and all was ready; permission was granted and we made every effort to be emotionally prepared. In my opinion, no sane child could be ready to be pierced by those sharp, frightening, and shiny needles. We were told that vaccines were necessary and that we had to get them. Later in my life and as an active Rotarian, we strove to promote vaccinations, especially in a quest to eradicate the deadly polio virus from the face of the earth.

As we prepared to receive our shots, I noticed the horrible smell of medications which made me sick. Later in my life, when I went to visit my cousin Michael Brutus, who was a patient in the hospital, I almost fainted. Maybe it was a combination of the "hospital-like" scent and the fact that we were going to be injected that made me reluctant to proceed. It was a similar scary feeling to when we were required to visit Doc Edwards, the dispenser who worked on the medical boat that traveled the river.

Abby was the first in the line to be vaccinated, followed by yours truly. Later I figured that they were working according to the alphabetical order of our names, Abby and Andrew. The intervention was not as bad as was anticipated. We had oral poliovirus vaccine drops and probably booster tetanus shots. We were far too young to even comprehend what vaccines were being administered to us. Up to the end of that vaccination day, all was perfect and without any incidents whatsoever. It was until the following day we received the horrifying news that my pal, Abby, was rushed in a speedboat down to New Amsterdam to seek urgent medical treatment.

We later learned that when he woke up on that gloomy morning, he was completely paralyzed. Was it related to the polio vaccine we had all received the previous day? Was he allergic to some of the vaccine's components? Was it contaminated with the polio virus? Did he receive an overdose? Was he given the right vaccine? Did he have polio before the vaccine? These were all burning questions asked by the adults.

During that prolonged day of speculations, practically nothing was done in school. Living in the riverside villages, we were at a tremendous disadvantage, unable to communicate effectively with external societies. It was as if we lived in another world, one excised from regular civilization. This was the harsh reality of living so far away from developed cities and towns.

It came as a huge surprise and tremendous shock. No, this couldn't be true; something must have been horribly wrong. My best friend had died. Abby had died from a supposed overdose of the polio vaccine, according to his family members. His parents, siblings, and the entire community of Kimbia were torn to pieces. It was one of the saddest days of my life.

His body was flown to Kimbia in a red, white, and blue amphibious aircraft (seaplane). It was also my first time seeing such a marvelous flying device that landed on the river in front of the school. The smartly dressed American marines shared sweets with the eager children. I clearly remembered receiving cigarette-shaped candies (sweets). It was a solemn occasion, but the sharing of sweets made the burden lighter, especially for the kids.

# CHAPTER 14

# My First Sister Has Arrived

O h, how my Papa wanted a baby girl! He confessed this several times among his siblings and friends. He was particularly close to his older brother, Brindley (Brother Brinds, Uncle Brinds). Brinds frequently bragged whenever their mates got pregnant. It was a mild competition between these two buddies.

Papa would say, "Bro. Brinds, I gat one coming deh."

He would answer, "Papa, you late, I done gat one in the breach," referring to their newly pregnant wives. Clearly, their chatter was not meant in any way to denigrate women, but simply to lighten the moment. Uncle Brindley was a very jovial individual, who loved to make jokes and tantalize. It really didn't matter to us whether or not we got another sister or even a brother. We, the four musketeers, were quite happy with our wild and carefree lives. Whenever Mom became pregnant, she never displayed her preference to have a boy or girl. She is not a very predictable individual and was able to easily mask her feelings.

One early afternoon, there seemed to be an abnormal hustle and bustle around the house. The late Cousin Kathleen from just across the river seemed very concerned about something. She kept walking briskly back and forth, seeming to be organizing something. Gamma had a purposeful, sort of worried, and maybe excited look on her face. Mom, who was usually in the thick of things, was confined to her bedroom. Something strange was about to happen and we didn't have the slightest clue. It was probably around 5:00 p.m., usually, the time when we made sure that our chores were completed so that we could do our homework and school assignments. This was so that these tasks could be finished before nightfall as it was extremely difficult to ably do them in the dim lantern light.

"Come on children, please stay outside, your mother is not so well," Gamma gently cajoled. Now, my Mother is a superwoman and no ordinary one too. She could shoot a shotgun and some of her targets included chicken, hawks, Lukanani fish, and any predators that ventured near her children. I remembered a few times when she shot a huge Lukanani and Glenny and I jumped into the water to retrieve the injured fish. It so happened that she shot two at the same time, she was a markswoman. I couldn't bring myself to imagine that she was incapacitated in any way. My Mama is the one who had endless energy, the one who always made sure that her little ones didn't even have a scratch. She took out thorns (plimplers) from our little feet. Sometimes she scratched off "Bete rouge" (red grass lice) (Trombiculidae) on our arms and genitals. Mom not feeling well? Unheard of! Daddy and Papa were also out of the house, but they excitedly chatted in codes and we were too young to decipher what was really happening.

It may have been about three to four hours of this never-ending, strange evening. Even though we were all happy with the additional play time, we began to worry that something was wrong. Then suddenly, we heard the cry of a baby!

"It's a girl! Papa, you finally got your girl," announced Gamma. Daddy and Papa had bright smiles on their faces and shook each other's hands as they seemingly congratulated each other as if they had both done some spectacular feat. Daddy patted Papa on his back and said, "Well done." We were much too young to understand what had just transpired. Mom had just given birth and it was only several years later when I came to understand that cousin Kathleen was the midwife who was ably assisted by Gamma. Tales like, the baby came in an airplane were told over and over; we actually believed them.

We were finally allowed inside and told to tidy up and wash our hands before being allowed close to our newly added baby sister. Later that same or might have been the following night, Papa had a few drinks, or maybe a little more than a few, and began shouting out to our neighbors,

"Ah gat a girl! Claudia just gat baby, she gat a girl!"

He was extremely happy and couldn't contain himself. Valerie (aka Dath, Mother B) was born! During the ensuing days, several visitors claimed that she was exceedingly gorgeous and pretty. I was nervous to hold her and Mom gave us all a chance to lift her while she lay harmlessly in her blanket, but I was not old enough to lift without assistance.

At 7:00 a.m. on the ninth day of her birth, daddy came over to preside over a brief religious ceremony. "Oh God, our help in ages past, our hope for years to come," by Isaac Watts, were lyrics from the signature hymn that was sung. Prayers were said, along with words of blessings and encouragement. Apparently, this was a regular occurrence to welcome the newborn babies in our family. It was a wonderful tradition, one that gave us all a great start in life. It's a common traditional belief that visitors are not usually allowed to see the newborn children until after nine days. Such a practice is quite understandable since little babies are very susceptible to external infections.

During the ensuing days, several visitors (aunts, uncles, cousins, or persons with inquisitive minds) all agreed that she was an exceptionally beautiful baby. All of this added ammunition to Papas' cannon; after all, she was the apple of his eye. Val grew up with her four older brothers and was influenced by us in every possible way. She learned to climb regularly up coconut trees; and ran, jumped, and swam like her older brothers. Never one day did we ever treat her differently because of her gender; she was simply a little Tom Boy. So, my sister V did arrive and it was an immense pleasure having her as our dear little sister.

# CHAPTER 15

# Cardy and the Bushmaster

During my many amazing childhood years at the Kimbia Primary, I really don't recall being serious about my studies. It was a carefree, wonderful life. Why worry when you have parents and big brothers to take care of you? School, in my opinion, was just a place to catch up with friends. We had morning, midday, and afternoon breaks. The minute the bell rang signaling the end of one of those sessions, it was a mad rush to exit the school building. Sometimes, it was a challenge to live up to, maybe a race to pick up fruits from the nearest tree that was in season.

Cardy Peters was obviously the fastest runner in the school and would easily outrun us with little or no effort. As kids, we raced every day as if we had hoped for a miracle to one day beat him. There was and still is a huge silk cotton-like tree that's situated to the left of the church landing. That would be on one's right hand when facing the church from the riverside. This gigantic tree bore cashew-like fruits called Hoobudee. There may be some sort of relationship between the cashew and the Hoobudee trees because their fruits are very similar with simulating stain-like tastes and both have external seeds. It wouldn't be wrong to classify it as a wild cashew.

The red, ripe, and luscious fruits would be available to the first one who managed to get there. That sad day, as usual, Cardy out-ran us and managed to get there first. At the same time, he arrived, a few of the ripe Hoobudees fell but dropped close to a massive drain that was covered with weeds and bushes. Cardy darted down close to where he saw the goodies fall. Vin, Brian, Keith, and I were not too far behind, but just near enough to see him crouching to retrieve the elusive fruits. It might have been only seconds later when we heard him let go an earth-shaking yell:

"Ouch, a snake bite me!"

He held up his right hand and back peddled while pointing towards the dark area where the dreaded snake was. He had dropped the coveted fruits on the ground while we all stood motionless and in shock. Cardy's right wrist had two telltale, bleeding fang marks. The snake bite marks were about two inches wide, thus indicating that it was a monstrous creature. Without explanations, I immediately ran with all my might to get Ken and the bigger boys. These were the times when the big ones took over.

"Quick, quick, a snake just bite Cardy!"

I hurriedly managed to finish before my tears began to flow; after all, I was still a little nine or ten-year-old boy. Before you knew it, he and practically the entire school converged near where the horrible incident occurred. By then, the teachers had taken control of the proceedings. Roger and Oscar Peters, two of Cardy's cousins, went cautiously looking for the snake.

"Take him to cousin Menzo," suggested Verna.

By that time, Cardy's right hand had become quite swollen and he was weeping uncontrollably, probably because of the pain and obvious fear. He claimed to have seen the brown, gold, and black reptile just before being struck. That it had all happened so suddenly and without warning.

Very quickly, a team of four strong young men, along with a couple of the bigger girls, started their journey to reach my grandfather, Menzo, the snake doctor. Shortly after they had left, Roger and Oscar found and killed the snake. It was the dreaded and extremely venomous five feet three inches Bushmaster snake (Lachesis muta) (silent bringer of death-in Latin). What a beautiful snake it was. It had irregular black markings that were superimposed on a yellowish-brown body along with pinkish-white spots/lines on some of those black markings. It was a gorgeous-looking reptile but a frightening sight to behold. It was around 12:30 p.m. and school was prematurely dismissed for the rest of the day.

I'm told the paddling team took merely forty minutes to get to Daddy, but he was not at home. It took another hour and a half to get him from his farm, which was roughly two hours away, before Cardy could be treated. Luckily, his arm, just below his elbow, had been tied to prevent the venom from traveling into the rest of his body. Daddy Menzo was known as the local snake doctor, who learned his expertise from his forefathers and then passed the knowledge down to Mom.

People would travel from miles away to seek his intervention. He would carefully shave the area, apply his medicine topically, and then also give the patient medicine to take orally. He had treated many individuals for snake bites and had a success rate of 100%. On this occasion, though, he seemed worried and kept muttering that he hoped it was not too late. Cardy's hand had now swollen completely out of proportion and had turned black and blue. Regrettably, there were no painkillers available, only raw high wine to negate the effects of the agony. According to Daddy, he did all that he was capable of doing, but conventional medicine needed to take over. He had recently undergone cataract surgery and had some difficulties doing a proper job.

The patient was subsequently taken down to the New Amsterdam hospital for follow-up treatment. That meant securing an appropriate speedboat, fuel, and the gamut of arrangements to make that urgent journey. This, once again, was another clear example of the terrible lack of readily available healthcare facilities in the Berbice River. Thankfully, he made it down to the New Amsterdam Public Hospital.

The intervening doctors sang praises to Daddy for his initial intervention, which most likely saved Cardy's life. According to reports, they did absolutely nothing further. After a few days, Cardy's arm began to rot and the stench was unbearable for him and his fellow patients. His parents were urged to take him to another bush doctor, there in New Amsterdam. The elderly traditional medicine woman explained that parts of the shell from the teeth of the bushmaster were still left embedded in the wound. His hand, from the wrist, fell off while she was performing treatment. Later young Cardy was referred to have his arm, just below the right elbow, amputated. In total, he might have spent more than six weeks being treated, including having his right arm amputated. When the news of him losing his arm was announced, the entire school wept. It was very sad, but then again, he could have been dead. The headmaster, Mr. Chandan, sought the assistance of members of the community to have the bushy areas cleared of shrubs and trees. As expected, from that day onwards, no one rushed to pick up the forbidden fruit nor played around where the tragedy had occurred.

*Cardy and I*

# CHAPTER 16

# Boat Race and Cricket at Juliana

The Berbice river was the setting for many fun days filled with outdoor sports such as boat races, circle tennis (rounders), and cricket. These activities were often accompanied by dancing, drinking, and general merrymaking, usually held in schools and bottom houses.

These recreational activities have been played with enthusiasm for generations. I have enjoyed hearing stories about the famous boat races between old giants such as Abel Smith, Joe (my great maternal grandfather's brother), and his son Thomas Reece of Mariah Henrietta, as well as Jason and Cleophus Nelson of Hollandia/Juliana. They took the races very seriously, devising strategies to outperform each other. Some even consulted with obeah men in New Amsterdam or recruited spies to steal ideas from their rivals, much like in the movie "Stomp the Yard" or the "Junkanoo Ceremony" of The Bahamas.

One of the authentic techniques involved greasing the bottom of the boats with petroleum jelly. These racing boats were sleek vessels skillfully made from tree trunks. They were then dressed and shaped using light boards running along the rims or edges to look like mobile machines. The array of colors and designs added to the excitement and admiration. The race boats could range from four, five, and seven paddles (the number of paddlers), and the participants would usually be uniformly attired. They would sing 'chantos' or funny chants before the race began. Many of the tunes, were quite vulgar and taunting to their rival paddlers.

"Oh, my grandfather's home was da city hotel, oh boy, Billy boy, we roam and go. We roll today and roll in da morning, goodbye, farewell to da city hotel."

"King David moaned for his son, Absalom. Oh...Billy boy."

Thomas Reece's boat, Miracle, had just trounced Jason Nelson's, Take It Easy. It was a close and very exciting contest. At one time, it seemed as though the locals were going to stay ahead and consolidate their earlier advantage, but this was not to be. Miracle kept a steady, firm pace. Their experienced rowers kept up the pressure and didn't panic. Take It Easy came close again on two other occasions but Miracle held on to the slim lead. All this time, the crowd was cheering and spurring on the locals. Occasionally, someone would shout out encouraging words in favor of the outnumbered visitors only to receive a barrage of insults from my fellow home-grown supporters. All of this excitement lasted merely for a few minutes, but it was a tense and nail-biting experience.

*Paddles Racing Boat*

The race was over and done; now it was time to look for faults. The experts weighed in on what strategies should have been used. There was talk about a rematch and whose paddlers didn't pull their weight. Those who betted collected their winnings, or paid their losses from the trustworthy Menzo Bender, into whose safekeeping

were the bets placed. The little ones, me included, paid rapt attention to all of the arguments and heated discussions. We always had fun on these occasions but were always under the watchful eyes of our elders - not necessarily those of Mom and Papa, but of concerned grown-ups of the community. We dared not misbehave in their presence. Sweet reggae music of Eric Donaldson, Jimmy Cliff, Bob Marley, and Gregory Isaacs blared from Uncle Brindley's jukebox. There was so much fun in the air! We were having an awesome and fabulous time!

There were many other side attractions and games, including the greasy pole and sticky pig, two other exciting features at this and similar events. A twenty feet pole was coated with grease and oil and a prize (usually money) was placed at the very top. Whoever was skillful enough to get to the top claimed the coveted treasure. Some youngsters, including Roger Peters, one of the 'rough necks' attempted once and failed. Roger then soaked himself in the river, rolled up in loose sand and before we knew it, he was at the top of the pole.

He also caught the frightened greasy pig as it tried in vain to escape Roger's sandy hands. All these events added to the day's excitement. Sadly, this sport of boat racing is dying a slow death. It was thought to have existed since the days of slavery or there about. The art of building canoes is also slowly becoming extinct.

The river boys and girls are also champions at cricket. This game formed part of our beings from when we were very young. I remember marveling at how the announcers, Henry Blofeld, Tony Cozier, and Reds Pereira described on the radio, the bright cricket atmosphere before the beginning of international cricket matches. The feeling was one of anticipation and excitement. This was quite similar to the sentiments experienced before and during our great cricket games. Oh, what an immense joy it gave me to see Ken running up to deliver lightning-fast deliveries and to see the opponent's stumps falling. To see Collin, strike a pitched-up ball through the off side, bisecting the fielders on its way to the boundary board. I marveled at how the bowlers struggled to get Joshua out; he would stubbornly bat on for hours. Personally, to cunningly stump a batsman as he danced down the crease, and to yell "Ahhhh!" With my right hand raised, at the square leg umpire to send him packing. I was an ardent cricketer to the bone and was totally fulfilled by my cricketing experiences in the river. I vividly recall one cricket match in particular.

It was one awesome day for sports and fun at the picturesque Juliana cricket ground. This area, by the way, was in the backyard of the D'Anrades, a large and powerful Berbice River family. There were similar cricket grounds in other riverain villages. These included the Agards, Boyles, the schools, and churches.

The rivaling cricket teams were now about to commence another contest. Sand Hills vs Juliana "All Stars." The Sand Hills team included persons from Fort Nassau, De'Veldt, and Gaietroy, while Juliana included players from Ebini, Kimbia, Haraculi, Hollandia, and a few from Mariah Henrietta. So, in essence, the teams were from up river and down river. Stanley and Dennis Fredericks had opened the batting for Sand Hills. They were smartly attired in their white cricketing gear. Both batsmen wore two slightly discolored pads and their bats had visible marks where balls had repeatedly struck. Dennis had a few of his shirt buttons loose, which seemingly gave him an air of confidence. These two were feared batsmen who dominated any bowling attack. They were left and right-handed batters and offered a great opening combination for their team.

The "All Stars" had a formidable team with the Hartman brothers, Glen and John, two of the best batsmen in the river. Lance Boyle, my uncle, was a left-handed batsman often compared to the late Roy Fredericks for his elegant stroke play. Ralph Osborne bowled mystery deliveries that turned unexpectedly, confusing opponents. Kenrick Nelson held the shiny red ball and began his run-up from almost the boundary line due to his height. He was known for delivering a good bouncer, but sometimes struggled with his direction and line. Captain Cleophus Nelson, who had just finished paddling, urged his players on, "Come on boys, Kenrick, take your time."

Kenrick began his rapid approach with a determined look on his face. He jumped and delivered a lightning-fast ball that flew past the edge of Stanley's bat, and Glen Hartman skillfully gathered the ball behind the stumps. *This is going to be a good match*, I thought to myself. Clapping his hands from the first slip position, Captain Cleophus encouraged his players, "Good one Kenrick, keep it just so!"

Kenrick, who now seemed to brim with enthusiasm and confidence, strode back to restart his run-up. It was evident that the appreciation shown by his teammates gave him that extra boost. I've found that even in the regular work environment, it helps to boost one's morale by simply offering words of encouragement. "Good job stalwart, well done, keep it up."

Bob Nelson, who was fielding at long-on, rubbed the red cherry ball vigorously on his flannels. Shining one side of the ball helps to cause it to swing in the air before landing on the pitch; quite an effective strategy. The confident bowler was about to deliver the next ball when there were screams and shouts coming from the riverside. An aluminum speed boat coming from Ebini had capsized.

This small craft approached with great speed and made a rash turn as they approached the landing. Ordinarily, one would have slowed down before making such a sharp turn. The boat had turned over, throwing the four occupants out. There were screams and pandemonium broke loose. The confused cricketers, and the frantic crowd, all scampered towards the riverside. Quick-thinking men jumped into boats and rushed, some paddled, while a few drove their outboard engine boats, to reach towards the middle of the river where the tragedy occurred. Women wailed and urged the men to urgently do something, "For God's sake, hurry!" They prayed and begged loudly. At this point, the four people who had been on the capsized boat had already started swimming to safety. It was a chaotic scene, with screams and shouts filling the air. People were making all sorts of suggestions, even though no one seemed to be listening or taking any action. The blaring music had stopped, leaving only the sound of frantic voices.

From my vantage point, I saw people swimming frantically. All I could see were arms desperately splashing water in an attempt to save themselves. The rescue boats and canoes arrived where the swimmers were and it was difficult to tell what was happening, I saw someone being hauled out of the welcoming grasps of the murky black water. Then another and yet another, into two other boats. Sadly, within seconds after the accident, Jack Fox, one of the passengers of the ill-fated craft, apparently couldn't swim and was swallowed up by the silent water. With desperate attempts to clutch at anything, and outstretched hands, he disappeared quickly into the murky blackness.

Later, I learned that Cousin Winston Thomas and two others were the ones who managed to swim to safety and were rescued by the frantic lifesavers who were able to reach them. It was subsequently found out that these four travelers had imbibed heavily and were deeply under the influence of alcohol. To add insult to injury, it was said that they were all wearing long boots but absolutely no life jackets. This tragic accident brought this fun exercise to an abrupt and premature end. Oh, what a disaster! As a result of this unfortunate incident, we stopped drinking water from the river. This was simply because of fear of consuming contaminated 'drowned man' water.

There are two valuable lessons learned from this sad tragedy. One, safety gear should always be worn when stipulated. Secondly, no one should imbibe so much alcohol. "If one oversteps the bounds of moderation, the greatest pleasures cease to please." (Ancient Greek philosopher.) Thirdly, one should not wear long boots or any other debilitating garment while traveling in boats.

*Loaded passenger boat*

# CHAPTER 17

# Burning of Feathers

Berbicians are very much *au fait* with the reason for burning of feathers. It is said that when you burn feathers near to someone who has a scrotal hernia, commonly called 'goody,' 'sungu' or sometimes referred to as he is carrying a 'son,' it causes the affected anatomy to roll uncomfortably.

During our childhood days, there were quite a few affected older men with this striking and often shameful pathology. Cousin Benny, Chummy, Mr. Baker (the carpenter), and Jimmy (the cow buyer), to name a few. One day, when I was around eight years old, Mr. Baker was doing some minor repairs to our house. Collin, Glenny, and I were playing in the vicinity where he worked. Collin took one glance at me; it was as if we were thinking the same thing. "Glenny, go get the matches," he urged quietly with that silly smirk of his.

"Ok Bro. Col," he answered with obedience and ran to collect the matches. Collin and I searched to find fowl feathers from around the yard. We then made a little fire upwind (so the wind could blow the smoke from the blaze to where the innocent, unsuspecting carpenter was) with the dried feather. We sat quietly, watched, giggled, and waited for the effects of the burning feathers. Strangely, nothing immediately happened, but we anxiously waited while Collin added a few more feathers.

Suddenly, our ever-vigilant Mom noticed our movements and immediately called us aside and gave us a stern tongue-lashing. This was clearly not our first time trying out this stunt. After Mom had rebuked us, Mr. Baker called out from downstairs to say he was not feeling well and wanted to take the day off. *Did our scheme work?* We all had a good giggle. Oh, the things that little boys do! Who knows, maybe it really did work, or perhaps he simply played along with our game.

They say that belief both kills and cures. In addition to the silly myth about burning feathers, there are many strange beliefs in the Berbice River. As children, we were extremely afraid of some of these local mythical creatures, such as Ole Haigue, Water People (Mermaids), Massacooramaan (a huge, hairy man-like creature that lives in rivers in the interior), and Spirits (jumbie or ghosts). Tales of these weird creatures are now seldom told, perhaps because river people are becoming more modernized or exposed to urban cultures.

# CHAPTER 18

# The Time When Papa Turned Against Me

The school exams, now called the National Grade Six Assessment, were known as Common Entrance in my days. Preparation for these exams was done more on a personal basis by the teachers responsible. If they felt that there was a slim chance that the students would perform well, then they spent additional time going through the concepts a few days prior to those exams. It's so different with the urban children, where they have 6:00 am lessons and late in the evenings too. Kids, in my opinion, need to be treated as such and allowed the freedom to learn and play. The lessons phenomenon is taking the lives away from these little souls. My children were also subjected to the rigors of lessons too because it's a way of life in Georgetown. Joining the bandwagon meant giving them the tools to compete with others.

Sir. Victor Kersting, the master, was my common entrance teacher. He was particularly meticulous with his tutoring and invited a few of us, Brian Boyle (my cousin), Vin Gordon and myself, to spend the weekend prior to exams, at his home. He lived about fifty miles from

Kimbia, further up the river, in a village called Ituni district, located similarly along the river but in the upper Berbice River area.

Even though Math, English, and Reasoning dominated the discussions during that fun-filled weekend, we also looked at the guiding principles of being positive and having an optimistic view of life. That weekend with Sir Victor taught me self-belief and gave me a better perspective on my imminent future. It also reinforced the idea that no matter what the outcome of the exams, we are proud and happy people. He reminded us of the amazing quote by Napoleon Hill, "Whatever the mind of a man can conceive and believe, it can achieve." During one of the sessions, he actually asked us to close our eyes and imagine being in the future. This sense of optimism was further invigorated during my first form years when I read "The Power of Positive Thinking" by Norman Vincent Peale, a book given to me by my brother, Collin. That weekend was the first time I saw cocoa trees and ate the fruit. The very accommodating and amiable Kersting family members were simple and without frills.

As I reminisced on this rendezvous, the cool breeze that gushed beneath the thatched roof made a lasting memory. The light glow of the fireside, coupled with that of the flickering flambeau, added a homely flavor to the simple and humble environment. They lived a very contented and peaceful life and seemed to be generally happy. It was not easy being away from home, but the fact that I had no chores and spent practically the entire time going through past exam papers made it feel like a vacation. The change in the environment also had a relaxing impact on me. There was where we experienced bonding amongst the few students and our kind and generous tutor.

The weekend flew by so quickly and before we knew it, it was time to return to our respective homes. We bid farewell to our generous hosts and caught a ride with a passing Guymine tug. It was really worth the while and we all rated our amazing few days very highly. My life has been tremendously influenced by the positive exposures of that telltale weekend.

The examination day had arrived and we were well prepared and overflowing with confidence. The Common Entrance exams were conducted over two days at Sand Hills, which was situated some 18 miles down the river from Haraculi. Daddy transported all of the children from the villages between Haraculi/Kimbia and Sand Hills. That journey took about an hour, but he, for safety and surety, left home some three hours before the time. So, we were on our way at 6 a.m. for a 9 a.m. exam. If you were not ready at six o'clock sharp, then you were on your own. Daddy was extremely strict about time and would leave anyone stranded if you were late. Whenever he had to reach somewhere for any specific time, he'd be there sometimes half of an hour earlier. Daddy used to say that it was disrespectful to have someone wait on you. It and it also shows that you are disorganized when you are habitually late.

I was not nervous as most of my colleagues were. I was ready and, as was advised, took my time and read the questions very carefully. Similarly, on the second day, I paced myself and gave it my all. I thought it was relatively simple and that I had done well. Deep down, I really thought I had nailed it but didn't want to sound too cocky and 'upstartish,' I told everyone that it was okay, and I thought I passed.

Papa, oh, what a lovely soul he was, used to tell all his friends that I was the smartest of his children and that I would go far in life. While I'm grateful for the fact that he spoke and may have prophesied positivity into my life, I don't agree with the comparison of siblings. Even if you do, it should be in your thoughts and never openly divulged or demonstrated.

The ensuing three months were arduous and very difficult for me. *What if I didn't pass?* That was my only opportunity to write the examination, I didn't have another chance to redeem myself. I was already eleven and considered to be too old to have a re-sit the following year. *What if my grades were not sufficient to catapult me into one of the top schools?* Ken and Collin had already commenced High Schools in New Amsterdam, having secured passes in CP and Prelim, respectively. These were London Exams, as they were not privileged to write the Common Entrance Exams. Ken was one of the first students of The New Amsterdam Government Secondary School (later renamed the New Amsterdam Multilateral School). Collin had commenced attending Berbice High School.

That early Tuesday morning, when the Steamer arrived, I was still plagued with mixed feelings. The late Aunty Agnes Boyle came with the news, her son, my first cousin, Brian Boyle, and my pal, Vin Gordon, had both secured places in the Berbice Educational Institute. Papa was with her when the envelopes were opened. I took one look at his face and immediately knew that something had gone terribly amiss. *No, this can't be! I was supposed to be the strongest student; surely, there must have been a horrible mistake.* My results read, "This student has passed for the secondary department of the Kimbia Primary school." I felt as if my world had literally crumbled. Was this the end? How could this have happened? I began to cry as if there would have been no tomorrow. Mom, oh my dear precious, ever-present and consoling mother, hugged me, and told me that God knows best and that it will be alright.

Papa, on the other hand, just sucked his teeth and fretted about me playing too much. He was extremely upset and disappointed in me. I clearly knew it; Papa had turned against me. Ken and Collin rubbed my face into the mess and taunted me by saying the most hurtful things. They suggested that I take my fancy brains and build a camp deep in the Haraculi creek and that I was not smart enough to attend high school. I was called a practice star, who was good enough just for the local matches and couldn't stand up when the goings got tough. Children can be the cruelest beings and say and do the most horrendous things to each other. I have never been nor have I ever considered being suicidal but the pain I received that day and the days that followed was inexplicable. Holy Jesus, my castle in the sky had crumbled.

Silently, I thought about my next move. I will be a farmer; you know what, I was going to be the best one. That would mean me having to learn the ins and outs from my Papa, but I'm sure he would not allow that. During those difficult days, he practically didn't say a word to me. He was not the easiest person to work with, though, we would cross that bridge later. If ever you find yourself in such a dilemma, I strongly advise you to move on to plan B. In life, there will always be other options, perhaps many more.

My sadness was short-lived. A few days later, I got the good news. Papa was livid and extremely furious. Even though he had been upset and disappointed, deep down, he had believed in his little William and therefore decided to go to the Ministry of Education to query my shameful results. It was not very surprising but surely amazing when the truth came out; strangely, it was discovered that a ridiculous mistake had been made. I, William Andrew Boyle, had topped all of the students of the Berbice River and was awarded a place in the New Amsterdam Multilateral School, one of the highest schools in the country. High school placements are usually made based on the proximity of their homes and the awarded secondary schools. For example, Berbice students are offered places in New Amsterdam high schools and those of Demerara given places in Georgetown. This was no ordinary feat! Finally, I had made my parents and family proud. This gave Papa even more fuel for his already inflated ego and praises came from all over, near and far. Now, this was what I had envisaged and rehearsed in my mind over and over; it was a part of my vision. After all, my castles were not demolished, they were still standing quite firmly. Glory to God, I had done it!

Youngsters, create visions, work diligently and always believe in your potential to excel.

# CHAPTER 19

# New Amsterdam Multilateral School

Papa was an extremely hard worker. He was originally a logger and then later became a farmer. As a logger with his father and brothers, he spent extended periods away from home. Their timber grant was located at Kaboyari (commonly called Caboyarro) landing, about sixty miles upriver from Good Hope/ Haraculi. During his early days of marriage, it was very difficult for Mom being alone while he worked away from home. He then decided to become a farmer and did the cultivating in close proximity to our home. Both him and Mom concluded that their children would be embracing the clutches of education. Neither of them was privileged to have gone to high school. Mom, being a female and an only child, was easily excused because, in her younger days, it was not customary that girls be sent to receive an education. Papa, on the other hand, came from a large family of seventeen siblings and only one of his brothers was given the golden opportunity of going to secondary school. Papa's brother squandered it and didn't manage to finish high school. He had followed bad company and ended up wasting the chance.

My parents probably thought that the work of a farmer was too laborious and that they would much prefer to have us become engineers, lawyers, and doctors instead. They decided to put their all into the development of their offspring. It meant making huge sacrifices to find suitable places to stay in New Amsterdam, the closest town. Papa Dee, initially from Baracara, Canje creek, managed a rundown, five-and-a-half-bedroom guest house in Shoe Lane, New Amsterdam. Travelers from the Berbice river and Canje creek, who visited the town to do business, stayed at that guest house. This was where our first boarding and lodging experience began.

Collin and I shared a little room with a double bunk bed. The two walls of this makeshift room commenced from about six inches above the floor. These two walls only reached halfway up the ceiling, while the other two formed one of the sides of the building and kitchen, respectively. This meant that we were not totally private, but we were indeed thankful for small mercies. The surroundings were not exactly conducive to studying because of the constant noises and in and out traffic of visitors. The boarding facilities were relatively untidy as they reared chicken in the kitchen, where soot from the smoky coal pots added to the deplorable ambiance. It was not uncommon to encounter chicken droppings on the rickety dining table that rested against one of the kitchen walls.

"Water downstairs!" Someone would shout if they were taking a bath in the bathroom upstairs and the water went off. This would happen when one of the taps downstairs was turned on. We tried to use the one and only bathroom, which always had a slimy floor, that served those five bedrooms before the crowd got up. This was indeed a real sacrifice;

we realized the importance of getting an early start. Successful parents always try to instill the cultivation of good qualities and they are usually noticed later on in their life.

A jute bag filled with ground provisions, green plantains, fruits, and vegetables was provided to our guardian by my parents on a monthly basis. An occasional container of fresh cow's milk, eggs, and other vital supplies were also sent to assist with our upkeep, coupled with a mutually agreed monthly financial boarding and lodging fee. Our monthly allowances (locally called pocket pieces) barely took care of our routine needs. Perhaps, Papa thought he was dealing with one of his farm hands. He used to say that we needed to make sacrifices and that eventually would reap the fruits of our extended labor. Mom, on the other hand, would sneak in an occasional, additional few dollars, of course, unknown to Papa.

Our first week was the most difficult one; this was the longest time we had ever spent away from home. The filthy environment and even the aroma and taste of the dishes led to extreme resentment. I cried for the first couple of days and wanted to go back home to our sanctuary. Collin and I bonded during those trying moments and encouraged each other when the 'goings got tough.' We consoled and reminded one another that this was going to be a temporary stay and that we were there for a purpose, a much bigger one, i.e., to get an education. Come what may, we were destined and determined to excel.

Living away from home was extremely challenging and difficult at times, but along with these negative aspects came positive ones too. We, for the most part, controlled our lives but needed to be cautious not to allow our relative freedom to be a distraction from our goals.

The DeSouza's house was situated obliquely across from where we stayed. Herman, Michael and Donna were the DeSousa siblings. Both Collin and I had a crush on Donna but were both afraid and too shy to let her know how we felt. She used to sit at her windows and play the Jim Reeves tune, "Stand at your windows some night." After completing our various school assignments, or sometimes even before, we used to race to get our seats to stare over at where Donna sat. The ingenuity of Collin led him to play the song "Oh Donna" by Dobby Dobson on our poorly functioning turntable. Sadly, the volume was not enough to project to the intended target and on a few occasions, it actually resulted in the house guests shouting for us to turn down the 'blasted' volume of the music. Oh, how silly growing up was! We might have done similar ridiculous feats for an eternity.

Monday, September 6th, 1976 was my first day of school. Mom had been the one tasked with taking me to commence my high school journey. Though outgoing, Papa was not the patient and gentle type. This new student was smartly dressed in a pair of well-ironed, short khaki pants and a light blue shirt. I donned my brand-new black boots, and white socks and slung a sleek haversack over my little shoulders. The shoes fit fine, but my toes felt weird especially the big ones. They were burning and it was a bit uncomfortable but manageable. Dressing in footwear now for school proved to be quite uncomfortable initially, but I got used to them. In fact, it later became a regular member of my external attire and it was difficult to go without. My hair was nicely trimmed and groomed and I was sharp and ready for this new scholastic voyage.

"William Boyle!" Silence.

"William Boyle!" Still, silence.

"Who Is William?"

*Was that me to whom Ms. Mignon Blake, my form teacher, was referring? Oops, that was the first one!* I feebly raised my hands and said with a nervous, squeaky voice, "Present Miss." All my twelve years, I had become used to being called Andy or Andrew, but never William. It was an honor to be called by my father's name, but it felt strange and different. So, throughout my high school tenure, I was called William. Patrick Narayan, one of my big brothers' colleagues, used to press even further and referred to me as Bill or, sometimes, Billy. If someone now calls me William, several decades after my secondary experience, it would be because they would have attended high school with me.

The late Ms. Joyce Thomas was the head mistress, oh what a terror she was. She made it her duty to know every child by name, well, so it seemed. She knew mine, and very well too. Thomo, as we used to call her, was a stickler for discipline. We all thought that she was mad and always seemed upset, fretting and making a fuss over little things. During recess, she would come out of her office and insist that we walk in an orderly and single file manner along the corridors, speaking softly and carrying ourselves with decorum. I had several encounters with her, and on one occasion, she pulled me into a corner and gave me a tongue lashing. I had been caught running along the corridors, with my shirt out of my trousers and my shoe laces untied. On another occasion, I was speaking loudly with my peers and being a "ring leader" for trouble, as she termed it. I'm sure every student had some sort of unpleasant interaction with her. I was told that she even reprimanded a school boy on the road on a Saturday morning for carrying himself in an "unmulti-like" manner.

She encouraged us to be the best and to strive for excellence, that we should carry ourselves well and with class, both in and out of school. This is the same sort of discipline and deportment that characterizes those successful schools like St. Stanislaus College, the Bishops High School and Queens' College. In retrospect, though, we really needed a drill sergeant to properly run our school. It was after several years that we came to the realization that she was a great leader, and it was because of her discipline and no-nonsense approach that most of us became respected members of society.

I had never, ever seen so many persons congregate in one area. During school assemblies, there were more than one thousand children. The girls were pretty but seemed much bigger and appeared more mature than we were. It was later I understood that girls mature faster than their male counterparts. Tammy, Mary, Maxine, Ansi, Vanessa, Denise, Debra, Camille, Carol, Ann, Maxine, Simone, Sharon, Juanita, Jackie, Kim, Maxine, Joan, Sabita, the late Gillian, etc., were all exceedingly gorgeous school girls. Extremely attractive individuals of the opposite sex, now this was a good start, I told myself that this was life and that I was going to enjoy every minute of it.

I later developed a deep bond of friendship with Warren LaFleur, who was also known as Oats. He, like me, came from out of town - specifically, Kwakwani - and had several siblings (Denise, Ian, Curtis, Bertram, Collin, and Areta) attending the same grand and awesome school as us. His dad was a dispenser (a medic who worked like a doctor) and his mother, Stella, was a very nice person. Warren earned the nickname Oats because he loved to consume Quaker Oats. We often had lunch together, which typically consisted of tennis rolls (a kind of bread-roll) and cheese, a cassava ball, and a glass of mauby. Our friendship was immediate and sincere; we became buddies for life and kept each other grounded and focused. After completing his education, Warren studied computer science in the Soviet Union and eventually moved to South Africa. Nevertheless, our bond remains as strong as ever.

Brian Payne, who later also studied computer science in The Soviet Union and moved to Canada, he too was one of my pals. He was not a youngster of many words but was a solid and genuine buddy. We used to tease each other, in a nice way, about our mothers. Brenda was Brian's mother and we actually ended up calling him "Brenda." Funny and difficult to understand, but that's how we operated as 11-14 year-old boys. Paul Arthur, another of my dear school buddies, was the fastest sprinter in school. I remember how he used to run away from the other participants during the school's track and field sports. One day, we had some sort of engagement at the local town hall and Paul was downstairs hanging out while some of us were upstairs. The next thing we knew was that Paul came bursting through the door of the office where we were, closely pursued by a half-naked 'push cart' man. It was generally thought that 'Gold Finger' was of unsound mind who did odds and ends for the market vendors. He had apparently called the man by his known nickname "Gold finger." Paul was very apologetic and expressed deep regrets for calling him so, while the town officers in attendance asked for him to be forgiven. Thankfully, it ended quite amicably and Paul swore never to tease anyone ever again.

Paul and I had a crush on Deborah Deoram (not her real name) and I think he won in the end. Young Arthur later excelled in the Guyana Defense Force, where he was highly respected and ascended to the rank of lieutenant colonel. He was one of the guys who "showed us the ropes" and helped us to learn the town life, so to speak. We also protected each other. We were truly like brothers in every way. Those were my three best friends during the entire period of high school. The late Michael Desouza later joined our group but not until our A' Level's class. I did develop other friendships along the way, Nigel Boatswain, Emsley, Ronald Bahadur, Bheer Rampersaud (aka Pixie), Vanessa Ramjeet, Michael Noel, Bobby Alphonso, Patrick and the Late Peter Naraine, Carol Humphrey, and Moore, to name a few.

We used to ride our bikes after school, sometimes up to and over the Canje bridge. The riders, as we called ourselves, did have fun while we exercised and bonded. That must have been during and probably around second and third form. Paul and I rode similar blue Raleigh bicycles, but I can't remember what the others rode. I only learned to ride a bicycle when I started secondary school. Oh, the number of bruises and cuts I received during my desperate attempts to learn how to ride bicycles. All of my friends knew how to ride; it was as if they knew to ride from birth. Their fathers taught them how to ride very early in their lives. Collin and I, on the other hand, didn't even know that those means of transportation and fun ever existed.

I meant to succeed and made stringent efforts to do so. In my first report card, I was awarded third place in class. Terence Chand and Sabeeta Taharally received first and second places, respectively. These were serious times and required discipline and control. It was a very different life, one that needed readjustments and adaptations for a little rural boy. My cruel peers, at times, used to make fun of my siblings and I. Little did they know that the taunts and ridicule were used to motivate us. Collin and I discussed those trying moments and vowed to use them to influence the construction of the firm foundation that we now have. "Country come to town!" "Country come see," "Bushman!" "Buckman!" "Riverman!" were some of those degrading and belittling names that we were called. Sometimes we were even ashamed to say where we had come from.

Now I can say with pride and maybe shout from the rooftop that I am from the Berbice River. Strange enough, this similarly happens sometimes in the US. Guyanese often disown their roots and say that they are from Jamaica when asked where they are from. It's so exotic, so rewarding and honorous to recognize from whence you came. When we speak highly of our roots, it's, in essence, paying glowing tributes to our ancestors who worked tirelessly to assist with our molding.

I've noticed that some of my nieces, little cousins, and nephews would say that they are from Kwakwani when asked about their homeland. I really understand why they do so. I did the same but now I strongly disagree. Let the world know where you are from, they will respect you much more. You will also make those who continue to live there proud and happy to know that you associate and relate with them.

My first experience watching a movie was during my first year in high school. I clearly remembered watching, as James Bond, with full diving gear, emerged from the water and aimed his pistol directly toward where I was sitting. In my mind, I thought, this is it - Andy, it's over; he was going to shoot me now. Without warning, I dove to the bottom of the theater, shouting, "Oh God, Ah Dead!" much to the amusement of those sitting around me. I was so embarrassed, but I honestly didn't know any better. I became the laughingstock of the entire school and this went on for several months. "The chap who dodged James Bond's bullet."

We might have boarded and lodged at Papa Dee for a couple of terms. We also stayed at five other homes during our secondary school journey. Our three paternal aunts, Claudette, called Girlie, Violet, called Baba and Norma, called Fan, provided us with invaluable assistance. It was very kind and caring of them to have offered to assist. We had wonderful and bad times but, in my opinion, the good times clearly outweighed the horrible ones. Aunt Norma probably served as the longest host towards the end of my high school days. I practically grew up with my young cousin Nigel, and Wendell, to some extent, who eventually went off to become a cadet officer in the Guyana Defense Force.

I have one vivid recollection of Wendell as a cadet officer. I had taken my watch to be repaired at a stall in the New Amsterdam market. It was a regular clock repair service, a simple glass case placed on top of upturned cardboard boxes. He told me to return within a few days to uplift my fixed watch. It was a Timex brand, one that was given to me by my grandfather Menzo. It had lasted me for about four years but was now dropping time, a few minutes each and every day. I handed over the watch to the watch repairman, who looked at it and seemed intrigued by its beauty and was told to return it within 36 hours. It so happened that when I returned, the guy asked me what I was talking about, that he had never ever collected my watch. This was very upsetting indeed; how could he do this to me? I tried to point out to him, in a respectful and firm but quiet voice, that a few days ago, I had taken the device to him. My grandfather instilled into us that we should speak quietly, that quiet speech was a mark of refinement. I was fuming and was very angry and upset by now and both of our voices were raised as we accused each other of lying.

While arguing with the dishonest repairman, I noticed at the corner of my eye my cousin Wendell in his army uniform. He seemed to exude sheer confidence as he wore his shiny new lieutenant pips on his shoulder. Wendell's face was adorned with a half-smile, almost as if he knew that all eyes were trained upon this proud son of the soil. He hailed out to me as he approached," What's up Cuz?" I quickly explained what had transpired and wiping away that pseudo smile, he angrily shouted at the shaking repairman who held on to his initial story. With the swiftness of a huge jaguar, my cousin snatched up the glass case of various watches, and threatened to take it to the police. By then, the confused repairman had changed his story and now offered to have the lost watch replaced.

W.F.A. King then asked me to choose my watch or one that was similar to my Timex. I collected a nice Seiko brand as there were no other watches that were similar to mine. It was a rude awakening for the dishonest watch repairman. What a lesson he would have learned! After I had collected my Seiko watch, he hurriedly closed up shop and scurried away. Curious onlookers had begun to hurl accusations to the cunning repairman.

We never missed the opportunity to go home during the long weekends and most certainly on holidays. It was always an immense pleasure to head home to enjoy Mommy's cooking and to bask in the ambiance of my lovely homeland, even if it meant it was just for a few days. The sentiments experienced, especially when the boat is on the verge of arriving at my home, just around the turn or, as the locals say, 'around the point head,' is hard to describe. It is similar to those felt on your return from a long stay overseas. The feelings grip you and you scream out inside, "Wow! It's great to be home." I experience those same feelings on every occasion I travel back home.

Getting to our destination typically involved hitching a ride on one of the Guymine tugs or the government steamer. However, the journey back home was always long and arduous. "Geeze!" It would take approximately 12 hours each way, and traveling in this manner felt like pure punishment. I promised myself that I would buy a fast boat once I grew up because it pained me to see the deplorable conditions and the wastefulness of time involved in traveling to and from home. Inhumane is one word to describe conditions on that river boat. I clearly remembered one such journey on the river boat. It was 8:30 p.m. and I had managed to secure a deck chair (a sort of folding chair), a luxury in those days, on the MV Lukanani. The river steamer would normally leave New Amsterdam at 9:00 p.m. on Mondays and return on Wednesday evenings. It was a moving shop where hucksters sold items to the natives and bought their agricultural produce in return.

That evening I was so happy to have collected a comfortable resting chair to spend the night; this was one of the benefits of boarding early. It was very comforting to hear the lovely sound of the horns being blared to announce the departure of the steamer from the New Amsterdam wharf. I thought to myself that I was going to get some much-needed rest during the all-night trip. My sentiments were short-lived when not far away from where I rested was my cousin Crystal Lindie-Lewis. She was probably about eight months pregnant. I immediately called my cousin over and handed her my chair. It would have been very difficult and distasteful of me to be relaxing in comfort while she suffered during that endless journey. Surely, I would be able to find myself a reasonable corner, I thought.

The boat was packed to capacity and there was no comfortable place to sit and relax. It was a huge task to maneuver around without threading on one of the many sleeping passengers who lay all over the floor of this vessel. I managed to squeeze into an area where I thought was secure and relatively comfy. It might have been an hour or two in the journey when it started to rain and rained it really did. There was water everywhere. It was dark, damp, and uncomfortable. I stood up and braced myself against one of the inner walls. That was one hell of a trip, one that was horribly uncomfortable. This was an example of the sad reality of the rigors of traveling up the Berbice river. Would you want that for your family? Despite the roughness of the journey, going home was such an immense joy, one to look forward to, even if it was just for one day.

I was on one of those short trips back home and there was a massive house party at the Lindie's home. It was not uncommon for them to have regular sports (parties) which attracted lots of girls. The mere thought of me missing that social event was inconceivable. Glendon (my younger brother) and I badly wanted to go to one of those parties but were refused permission by Papa. He said that I had exams coming up and that I should be studying instead. Papa really meant well but his attitude was sometimes too rigid. He had really wanted me to excel in my studies and, according to him, "to make his efforts worthwhile." He was obviously banking on my success and this was openly said. On several occasions, sometimes before tough exams, I would mutter, "this one's for you, Papa."

The sweet and saucy reggae sounds of Bob Marley and Gregory Isaacs lit up the atmosphere of the usually quiet and serene neighborhood. Papa had said no and there was simply no way of getting over that hurdle. Any attempts at asking again would have been met with a barrage of insults and probably even sanctions. Mom, who had gone to New Amsterdam to do shopping, was not there to throw in a word on our behalf either, not that it would have mattered. She might have also come under fire for encouraging us to be reckless and wayward.

Glenny and I watched each other and we both knew what was to follow, it was as though we had rehearsed our next move. We made up fake bodies in our respective beds that would appear as if we were both sleeping peacefully. We expected Papa to check on us during the course of the evening, particularly at around 1 or 2 a.m. With a couple of bed sheets strongly attached to the window post to form a roughly made ladder, we gently let ourselves down to the ground, just about 15 feet below. The sheets were tied together and knots were placed at two feet intervals for easy climbing. We were now happy with our innovation and off to the party we went.

Oh, it was a fantastic evening; we danced and had a whale of a time. How in Heaven's name could we have missed that rocking party? We both had some serious fun, but not before stupidly bragging about our escapade to all and sundry. It should be noted that, that's exactly how perpetrators of crimes are caught by the police. They brag about their delinquencies to their supposed friends, who in turn help to spread the word of their feat.

It was probably around 3:30 a.m. when we climbed up the rope ladder and went to sleep, very pleased with ourselves. We were careful to ensure that we got up early and proceeded to complete our chores as if we had received a whole night's rest. I remember seeing Papa early as he made a snide remark:

"You see how bright you are now? If you had gone to the dance, you would have been like a dead dog now."

Little did he know that we had defied his orders and had our own way. It was much later, probably about a few days afterwards, when some troublesome person told Papa what had happened, yes, as you suspected, he was not very pleased. He gave us some strong talks and said that we would understand later why he had insisted on being firm.

Children, listen to your parents, they most times mean well. They would have been youngsters at some time during their lives and would have experienced it all. Your time will come, and then you can make informed and responsible decisions.

# CHAPTER 20

# Multi's Day of Sports

I used to relish attending school sports. I loved the music, the sporty atmosphere, the snow cones with condensed milk on top, the icicles, custard blocks and simply the air of competitiveness. I was a proud member of the Spurwing house. The entire school was divided into 'houses' and named after local birds: Toucans, Macaws, Canje pheasants, Eagles and Spurwings. My specialty was distance running and I would usually outrun my peers. Maybe it was probably the practice sessions we had as kids in the Berbice River when we chased after calves. I was generally quite athletic but not a fast runner. I ran relatively well at 400- and 800-meters races.

It was a magical day for me! I ran both the 400m and 800m races and later, towards the end of the day, the slow bicycle race. During those two long-distance races, I kept the pace with my fellow runners and had enough 'fuel' to maintain in the last lap and to significantly extend the lead. They were tiring, but the fruits of my labor felt extremely rewarding. Strangely, I also mastered the slow bicycle race. We were given a stretch of 50 meters to ride and the winner was the one who took the longest to get to the finish line. It might have been during my fifth year in school when Jerry John and I were the only two slow race riders left in the race. The others had fallen and I was closer to the finish line than he was. Obviously, he was the better slow rider. The crowd cheered and my supporters wished that he, Jerry, would fall.

I concentrated and tried all of my skills but Jerry was probably two bicycle lengths behind me. If I had reached the end of the race, he would have been declared as the winner. By this time, the cheering crowd had practically converged on us. Mr. Dundas (Dundie), Ms. Elgin and other members of the teaching staff tried to keep the cheering and unruly students at bay. I might have been just one bicycle length from the finish line and was desperately trying to stall and 'stickle' without falling when someone shouted, "Winner!" Yay, I had won! Jerry had fallen! Later, I was told that Shellon Hunte, one of my pals, had unfortunately pushed him down. I was awarded the winning trophy because the officials didn't actually see when the tragedy had occurred.

I was no match for the inter-schools runners and it was not a 'bed of roses' competing with the best long-distance runners from the other schools. I remember racing against 'Brown Boy' who was considered to be the best of the distance runners in Berbice at that particular time. I had kept the lead for most of the race but when he began to advance, I dug deeply for 'fuel.' I just couldn't come up with an answer but kept going and ended up ahead of the rest but second to Brown Boy, who clearly won and was definitely a superior runner. I dabbled with other forms of sports and board games; I was quite good at playing chess, a game I truly love.

I did enjoy playing cricket and was quite good at it. My preferences were batting at number three and wicketkeeping. I might have benefited from the name that my big brother, Ken, had carefully carved for himself as a great cricketer. He was a feared and fierce fast bowler. He played at many regional levels and might have even been lucky to have been picked for our national team or the West Indies. Repeated injuries which he constantly sustained along with pressing school duties, might have hindered his development as a player.

It's pertinent to balance schoolwork with extracurricular activities. Nothing beats an educated, well-rounded individual or an accomplished sportsperson who is educated. That world-renowned football (soccer) giant, Dr. Socrates, comes to mind.

"Young people, having an education is of paramount importance." It was Nelson Mandela who rightfully said, "Education is the most powerful weapon which you can use to change the world."

# CHAPTER 21

# Gamma (Grandmother)

Eloise Bender née Gladstone, was one of the gentlest and nicest persons I've ever known. She was my maternal grandmother, and wife of my grandfather, Menzo Phillip Bender. I have very fond and loving memories of her.

I'm told that as a child, I used a pointed stick to pick up the fallen leaves from a long-john tree that was situated several yards behind her house. These were collected under the pretext of shooting the moon and stars for her to cook. Who knows, maybe since those early days, I was aiming for the skies. Yes! "The sky is indeed the limit." Cervantes in Don Quixote.

Cooking was a true passion for my grandmother, and she poured all her energy into it. Her repertoire included cornbread, cakes, regular homemade bread, and "conkie" - an African cake made from cornmeal, raisins, ripe plantains, and various other condiments, wrapped in "achibanna" leaves. This cake is quite similar to plantain and banana. Like every grandmother, she enjoyed seeing us eat well and took great pleasure in it. I looked forward to those harvest sales at the Sand Hills Anglican Church. She and her cousin, Emily Patoir, would make homemade juices, drinks and 'flys' (local fermented juice drink). They would showcase their exotic drinks which would all be sold out or finished in a jiffy. I particularly loved the 'cashirrie' drink which is made of a special variety of purple sweet potatoes. She cooked, using a fireside system and bluntly refused to upgrade to using a gas stove. Apparently, she was afraid of the improved technology and preferred to hold on to cooking with her fireside. Yes indeed, she thought that gas stoves were dangerous.

Her love for the simple, humble life was quite evident in the way she carried her lovely self. It was sometime in 1972, her brother, Leslie, had returned from England, the first time after sixteen years. Uncle Leslie and Papa were all over the place, painting the villages red. Gamma kept advising her brother to be careful as Papa was 'tough as nails' while the two old friends were on the rampage. I clearly remember hearing them sing other popular songs in their state of merriness, like, 'Oh Madeline, Sweet, Sweet Madeline,' and 'While Shepherds Watched Their Flocks by Night.'

Uncle Leslie, by the way, had brought toys and gifts for me, all of my siblings, cousins and other relatives. This was truly remarkable and extremely generous of him. Though Gamma was usually a mediator, she often sided with her grands. Saying that she spoiled us would not be far from the truth. She sewed our pajamas and our school clothing and relished the opportunity to 'dress us up.' Ken grew up under her care and experienced her love and attention in a very direct and special way.

Sometime during my secondary school tenure, we received letters saying that Gamma was very sick and was in a pretty bad shape physically. I don't remember the details, but the sight of her lying with an extremely distended abdomen remained with me. She had colon cancer and had tried every possible treatment. I'm told that Dr. Vanwest Charles was a medical intern doing his rotations at Kimbia National Service. This paramilitary center was among several similar entities that served to train and mold young Guyanese. Through his kind intervention, she was flown to Georgetown for further medical assistance. Her condition was too advanced and there was nothing that could have been done to alleviate the suffering she was experiencing. Daddy later confessed that he went so far as to ask his Bishop to pray for Gamma's death. Such was the severity of her condition. It was later told to me that she had secretly sewed her burial dress. Obviously, she didn't want to upset her family members and had given it to Daddy's sister, Aunt Theresa. Her burial attire was given with special instructions that 'on her death, she should be dressed with it.' Despite her dying at the young age of 54 years, she left an amazing legacy, one that we will always hold dearly.

# CHAPTER 22

# Natalia

High school was truly an amazing experience for me personally. It transformed me, not completely, but it afforded me the opportunity to be more self-confident and outgoing. This exposure might also have caused me to have strengthened my management qualities. It seemed that I was always in the thick of things in and out of class and frequently called upon to provide leadership. It wouldn't be incorrect to point out that I did have an affinity for the opposite sex. Come on, I didn't mean to sound like that but nevertheless, I'll leave it at that.

I may have been about thirteen years old when Natalia (not her real name for privacy), my first girlfriend, allowed me my first real smooch. She was related to the wife of one of my great uncles, so I used to arrange regular trips to Philadelphia Street, where my cousins lived. On one of those occasions, over at the Benders' I met Natalia. I mustered the courage to talk to her and was very surprised at her boldness. We chatted a bit about all kinds of frivolous issues, including whether or not she was involved in a close relationship with another boy.

"I would like to be your intimate friend, would you mind being my girlfriend?" Those words were learned from my big brother Ken and later memorized for possible execution. He had advised that I look deeply into her eyes and to also ensure that I had her undivided attention. Having bigger brothers to advise and counsel you, especially in those new experiences is priceless. To my complete amazement and surprise, Natalia simply looked at me and said:

"Yes, no problem."

This marked the commencement of my first real relationship. This arrangement did not last very long; might have been a few terms. I was quite satisfied with the few and far visits to her home but one day we planned to 'check-out' a good movie.

It happened one afternoon during a visit to the cinema, we had agreed to meet there for a 4:30 p.m. movie. For fear of being late, I decided to get there just after 4:00 p.m. It was then probably the longest 25 minutes I'd ever waited. What if she didn't show up? I had already bragged to Collin that I had this fancy date; surely, he was looking forward to hearing the explicit details afterward. What would I tell him now?

Then just about 4:25 p.m., I noticed a dilapidated brown Morris Oxford with black stripes pull up. Natalia's uncle had dropped her off just in time to catch the movie. By that time, I had already organized two tickets for "balcony" from my savings. This special area afforded some privacy and felt good but the cost was more than three times for regular areas of house and pit. Normally, I would watch movies from the "pit" which was the cheapest and all of my buddies and peers also felt comfortable being there. It was often said that the pit was infested by bed bugs but that really didn't matter to me, all I was interested in was seeing the films. I would seldom go to the section called "house," but of course only on special occasions.

I was unaware of how to kiss a girl and was taken completely by surprise when it happened. We sat there together as the movie commenced. All I could think of was how lucky I was; my mind was certainly elsewhere. She placed her fingers gently onto my cold sweaty hands. My pulse rate had jumped up and a sneaky and hidden smile came to my lips.

"This is the life!" Boy, Collin would love to hear this one!

I was confused and honestly had no clue on whether to say something or not. I felt a ball in my throat and was speechless as I glanced sheepishly towards her as she looked directly at me with her lips slightly apart. Her face seemed to be coming closer to mine but it was too dark for me to be sure. I mustered the courage and turned around to face her squarely and before I knew what was happening, our lips locked. I couldn't think coherently. The indescribable sentiments felt were overwhelming, especially for a rookie thirteen-year-old. My entire body was affected. It was as though that elusive experience had pressed a button to heighten all of my physical being. That was my first kiss and it knocked me off of my feet and caused my little heart to throb incessantly. The feelings were inexplicable but really felt awesome.

She was a dark and lovely girl, a very smart one too. We became good friends but later I found her to be a bit of a distraction. She wanted to be in my presence around the clock and I felt somewhat stifled. Maybe because of my yearning desire to succeed, I didn't allow myself to be too distracted. We dated for a few years but somehow, drifted apart. Maybe we had lost interest in each other.

During my high school tenure, I had many relationships with very pretty girls. I was given the impression that I was a dashing young man with a curly afro and a drop-dead smile. I remained focused though and managed to balance my social and school lives.

Mom and other elderly folks warned of girls doing all sorts of tricks to trap men or young boys. It is a common belief in Guyana that they could give you something to drink that would cause you to become hooked on them. In Amerindian villages, it's called Beena and lots of people do believe that they are effective. I've heard that it's a plant or herb that the indigenous people grow which is used to create the bonding effect. Regardless of its potency, I have never had the pleasure of being able to dispute its efficacy.

# CHAPTER 23

# Rosebud

Rosebud (not her real name for privacy) was a very quiet and easy-going girl. She was not the regular, fancy and popular chick. Rosebud was strikingly gorgeous, but it was a different kind of beauty she had. It was as though she did not know how attractive she was. On several instances I attempted to get her attention to no avail; she would simply brush me aside and not respond. It was as if she was shy and didn't want any involvement whatsoever. One day, I noticed her; she seemed sad and stood there alone in the corridor near the cafeteria. I approached and mustered the courage to ask, "Hello Rosebud, how are you doing?"

She looked at me and gave me an awesome smile, one that caused me to forget all the nice things I was planning on telling her. Ideally, it would have been nice to talk and get to know more about each other but that was not how it happened. My strategies were thwarted and I rudely asked her if she would be my girlfriend. Yes, I did that and surprisingly she said that she was going to think about it. Later she actually confessed that she had wanted to say 'yes,' immediately but was too shy to say so.

The following day I made sure that I was in the vicinity of her classroom during the morning break. As I stood there, waiting to receive my answer, several friends passed by and wanted to form conversations with me. Those would have been counterproductive and slowed down the process. As they came by and stood around, I told them that I was working on something and that I was not available to chat. My acquaintances tell me that I'm easy to talk to and that I exude an inviting air. It's therefore easy for people to chat with me and to seek my guidance wherever needed. To add insult to injury, I'm always expected to have the contact details of others. "Do you have the telephone number for Dr. Jack Spratt?" This, I find to be quite strange but it doesn't bother me.

She appeared more radiant and lovelier than ever and was the last one to leave the classroom. Apparently, my friend had gone to the salon and had herself spruced up shortly after we had spoken the previous day. Oh, the lengths to which men and women go to attract the opposite sex. In the animal kingdom, the male species are also known to do all kinds of acrobatics and sexual gestures to gain the favor of their mates.

She bravely came up to me and before I could utter a word, whispered relatively close to my ears,

"Yes."

I muttered in a muffled, timid voice, "Thank you."

I wanted to jump and scream out loud but that would not have been the gentlemanly thing to do. Maybe you can imagine the shouts / screams of approval I blurted out when I was locked away in the confines and privacy, behind closed doors when I went home. She afterward confessed that she thought it was so mannerly of me when I had said "thank you."

This commenced a beautiful relationship between us.

# CHAPTER 24

# My Awesome Siblings

Six sons and four daughters made up the brigade of the Boyle's clan.

Ken (Sheik/Balgo),

Collin (Balram/Pado/Pilate/Governor),

Andy (Bal/Ram, Amerindian Wakwai Buck Bitch (AWB) Glendon (Cullit/Milk/Ganny),

Valerie (Dath),

Joshua (Fada/Dank/Joshie),

Ashton (Baroone/Spirit/Panther/Ashie/Capo),

Ellenore (Ellie/Wiggers),

Camille (Gramp/ Kyat),

and Felecia (Fee/ Flip/ Lydia/Boney).

In that order are my dear and awesome siblings. Everyone had their false names (nicknames) and that was one of the many customs of our river people. It was also not uncommon to refer to the elders as cousin, aunty or uncle, even though there were no obvious family connections. Further, in my family, the older brothers were referred to as (brother) bro. Ken, bro. Col and very rarely bro. Andy. It was as if I was sometimes not considered to be in the league of the older siblings. We all are very distinct persons but a bit similar in some respects. We have very strong genes and resemble each other, quite strikingly. Glendon, Valerie and Camille cannot drink a drop of alcohol because it causes them to be badly affected. Their tolerance level is extremely low. It means therefore that they would be very tipsy after imbibing only one glass of wine. This trait must have been inherited from our father. While Ellenore and Felecia could withstand the tests of time as their tolerance levels are amazingly high, not dissimilar to their other male siblings.

Sadly, our parents took up a stance not to send our sisters out of Haraculi to further their studies. This phenomenon is not uncommon in the rural or country areas of Guyana. This silly custom puts women and girls at a disadvantage in their lives and it's totally unfair. This was a way of protecting their naive girl babies from roaming predators. I do understand the rationale behind this custom but I totally disagree with it in equal measure. Some of my sisters did suffer the consequence of not being allowed to go out of the river to study at an early age, not until about the age of sixteen; the younger ones managed to get sent out at around the age of eleven. This was simply because some of us, the bigger siblings, were able to provide suitable accommodation later in their lives.

Felecia lived with Valerie in New Amsterdam and then later in St Vincent with Collin. Camille lived with me also for a few years. Ken, a mechanical engineer lives in England and has three awesome children in Ken Jnr, Juanna and Bheje; and Collin, a veterinarian, is married to Dr. Rosemary Shallow-Boyle, they live in St. Vincent, W. I and have two wonderful children in Dr. Annique, also a veterinarian and Ayeisha. Valerie who now lives in Orlando is married to Kurt Alphonso and they have four wonderful children, Rocky, Jeremey, Zack and Keyon. Val was proficient at her hairdressing skills before the children came along. In fact, long before them, she gave Joshie a very nice and attractive haircut, well, she actually thought it was, using a meat chopper. We all thought it was ridiculous and terrible but she clearly thought otherwise.

Her four bigger brothers taught her to climb most trees, including coconut trees . I'm reminded that she, on her own, had climbed and picked water coconuts for one of Daddy's birthdays. Yes, in essence, Val grew up as a tomboy because of our influence. Ellenore aka Wiggers or Elly is one of those extremely strong-headed individuals. If she decides to do X, she will do it, despite the persuasions and negative opinions of others. One day when she was probably around three or four years old, the bigger siblings were going into the backdam to bail ponds in order to catch fingerlings to be used as bait

In the backdam, during the dry weather, there were several partially dried out creeks filled with these little fishes that served as bait to catch larger fishes. This bailing exercise was an operation to remove the excess water so that these baits (fingerlings) can be easily caught. It meant using buckets, pans and walking in thick, soft mud. Invariably, at the end of these exercises, we would all be covered in mud. Elly had insisted on coming with us but because of her age, we refused to take her along with us. We went our merry way and thought she had obediently stayed home.

After a few hours, we returned with our catch, all nicely colored in mud except for our little eyes. Mom asked for the whereabouts of our sister Elly, as she did not return with us. That afternoon pandemonium had broken loose and we began searching wildly for our sister. By this time Mom was hysterical and in tears and insisted that we check in the water to see if she had drowned. We dived and looked in the mud flat or shallow waters all to no avail. By that time Daddy had heard our screams and cries. He came over and suggested that we retraced our steps, perhaps she had followed us into the jungle. The dogs were released from their kennels and we all headed into the backdam in search of the little one. As we entered the low bushes prior to going into the actual jungle we heard what sounded like the bleating of a sheep. This area was an overgrown field with little shrubs and tree stumps that were previously cut down for farming. There we found little Elly, standing on a tree stump, all covered in red ants. The bleating sound was her cries, she had been crying for a while and had no more energy to cry any louder. Yes, she had insisted on following us and got lost in the process. We all received a trashing for not taking care of our little sister.

Elly who lives in Orlando, is married to Anthony Beaton, a fellow River man and they have three lovely children, Shannon, Elion and Shenell. Glendon, Joshua and Ashton, the smaller of the male siblings, made their mark as young members of the Boyle's clan. Glendon is married to Cinnetta and they have four gorgeous girls, Mandy, Tamasha who lived with us during her high school years, Shanna and Shanniah. He continues to shoulder the heavy responsibilities of carrying on the family farm and shop at Haraculi. Joshua became an entrepreneur and works out of Georgetown. Joshie had started attending Kwakwani High School just after grade six exams. I was given the task of having him transferred to my school, The New Amsterdam Multilateral School. During my visit to Kwakwani, I was fortunate to meet a youngster named Felecia Ross who was a friend of two of my first cousins, Verlene and Kim. Later I would name our last sister after her (Felecia). Joshie is happily married to Lisa and they have three lovely children in Javier, Javid and Sofie. He also had others from a previous marriage.

Ashton became a thoshoa (Amerindian Captain) for Kimbia but later immigrated to seek better opportunities in Bolivia. In this Latin American society, he is married to Zoey and they have two pretty daughters, little Valerie and Ellenore.

Camille, who is our ninth sibling, lived with my family for a few years and it was indeed an immense pleasure having her as part of my home circle. She completed high school and then went on to the University of Guyana and pursued higher education. Among other countries, she also had a stint in Cuba, where she also became fluent in Spanish. Kyat, as Andrew, my youngest son called her when he was a toddler, is quite a phenomenal business consultant and entrepreneur. She is an avid reader and writer and is extremely positive about life. In fact, her favorite thing to do is to listen to motivational tapes. Camille has three wonderful children: Eron, Tati, and Le Bronne.

That name, Felecia, was given to my little sister. Strange enough, this youngest of our siblings, though very sweet, knowledgeable, and qualified, thinks that she is large and in charge. Felecia Mariam Candacy Boyle, a very smart and charismatic young leader is our proud baby sister. This young and effervescent leader, an established accountant/entrepreneur, thinks she can rule her much older siblings. Little Fee is married to Dr. Kent Bazard and they have two lovely children, Kia Lynn and Kalen (aka Puppy or soccer Kalen). Kyat and Flip, two 'go-getters' have teamed up to set up Executive Business Solutions (EBS) both in the Bahamas and Guyana and are instrumental in bringing Kanoo Inc., a money transfer company to Guyana and the Caribbean at large.

I'm truly proud of my fabulous siblings and we are an extremely close-knit family.

*Part of my family*

*Andy, Collin & Fee*

*Valerie, Ellenore, Camille and Andy*

# CHAPTER 25

# After High School

After A' Level exams, I had spent quite a few months at home, on the farm, where I practically operated my parents' groceries and beverages shop. It was my task to frequently visit New Amsterdam to purchase supplies and to ensure that our shop was properly stocked. It was quite rewarding as it afforded me the opportunity to travel back and forth on a fairly regular basis. The frequent shoppers would buy rice, salt, sugar, flour, and cooking oil. Any other items would be luxury.

The residents in my community were quite a happy and satisfied bunch. Apart from groceries and dry goods, they consumed lots of liquor. I stayed up very late on weekends while regular patrons imbibed, played dominoes, listened to music, and sometimes danced. Wilton Lindie (Uncle Willo), Lance Boyle (Uncle Lance), Sir James, H. E (Herbert English), and Cousin John Lindie were regular visitors. Wilton once told me he had stopped drinking and only drank beers. Most drinkers drank rum, vodka, or high wine (a very strong grade of alcohol, with about 69%). Sometimes they would stay until 2:00 a.m. By then, we had a two-cylinder Lister generator that provided electrical

ASPIRE: DARE TO DREAM

energy for lights and cold drinks. It was not a bad business. I was happy that I could take the load off of my hard-working parents' shoulders.

On Saturday nights, we couldn't go past midnight, especially if we were playing loud music. Daddy would come over and give us some tongue lashing,

"Come on, it's the Sabbath, you need to keep it holy."

When we had a social session on Saturday evening, we had to make sure that the music was turned down enough not to disturb Daddy. Fridays, therefore, were better evenings to have a sport.

This life was relatively good for me but I felt somewhat unfulfilled and was not challenged enough. I enjoyed being at home but I felt as though something was missing. Was this my destiny?

It so happened that there was a vacancy for "Pilot trainees" in the newspapers. I decided to apply and was successful. This meant moving into another direction in life. Was this going to be the new road to my future? Marine pilots are skilled individuals who steer large ships into and through the channels of two of our main rivers, Demerara and rarely Berbice. It meant that those individuals had to have great knowledge of the underwater geography of the channels and the water currents and tides.

The period of training required four years of theory and practice. Papa was not too keen on the idea because he couldn't separate captains of the steamers (the huge ships that traversed the rivers) from the marine pilots. In his opinion, they all liked to drink alcohol and didn't command the sort of respect deserving of his son. He said that God's plan for my life was much bigger and that I should look into other avenues. *Was this going to be my new destiny?*

I decided to pursue my dreams despite Papa's reluctance . I believe parents should guide and not necessarily force their children to fulfill their dreams. Most parents want their offspring to live and experience a better quality of life than they ever had. However, despite Papa's thoughts at that time, I simply couldn't relinquish the idea of being a marine pilot, one smartly attired in my white shirt, shoulder bars, dark blue trousers, and captains' hat.

The idea was simply enticing. The theoretical aspects were very intriguing and exciting as they dealt with various navigational training. That's where I learned about ORION, the Big Dipper and other constellations. The practical aspects, however, commenced by having us chip away the rust from various parked vessels. We chipped, with a pointed hammer, for extended periods, sometimes after or before classes. We used goggles but I experienced tremendous difficulties and frustrations while performing those tasks. Though it is understood why those experiences are necessary, I just never enjoyed them . We were once taken on a trip out to international waters on a pilot launch. It was a strange but exciting journey. The atmosphere was lovely and it was sunny and bright. We couldn't have chosen a better day. I never imagined that it would have been so beautiful out there. International waters commence from about 12 miles from our shoreline. The water out there had a fantastic blue color, one that was clean and sparkling and it was also calm and placid that day. The change is not gradual; there is clearly a line of separation between the murky brown Demerara and the pristine blue international waters. The discoloration in Guyana is due to the large amount of silt and degraded leaves that are brought out from huge rivers of the Amazon rainforest.

We dropped off the on-duty pilot onto the huge bauxite ship. It was the biggest ship I had ever seen. Our pilot launch bobbed and weaved near the large vessel. The pilot, with a safety harness strapped around his waist, quickly and expertly climbed the flexible rope (Jacob's) ladder which I estimated to have a height of about one hundred feet or even more, to the captain's bridge or wheel house. *Was this going to be expected of me as a future pilot?* I thought to myself, *There is no way that they were going to get me to climb that scary-looking ladder." I'm scared of heights and surely this was not meant for me. Wasn't there an easier way to ascend to those heights? Maybe an elevator system through a tube?*

To add insult to injury, I began to feel upset. Was it because of the rocking of our craft as it came closer to the monster ship? Or was it the fear generated when I saw the pilot climb on the rope ladder? I was seasick! Oh, what a horrible feeling! I began to vomit out my soul and it seemed my entire inside was coming out. Oh, was I going to die? The captain of the launch told the guys to give me sea water to drink, that it would help me. I took a gulp of the blue water but that seemed to have made it worse, I became sick like a puppy. My trip back to the wharf was not a pleasant one. Again, I was the laughing stock of my colleagues. The river man got seasick! The Buck man is afraid of water. My ridicule was the subject of my pals over the ensuing days. They said that I would get accustomed to the sea after a few trips. I secretly told myself that this was not my cup of tea. I spent several months on the course and learned a whole lot but I came to realize that this life was not the type I wanted.

My boarding and lodging were provided by cousin Mary (formally Lindie) and Murtland Gibson, Prashad Nagar. I had my own room and they were the perfect family to live with since my student stipend was not enough to sustain my upkeep and living with the family was mandated. I gave Cos. Mary a fraction of my salary, used a portion for social activities, transportation, etc., and saved some. Prudence, Shawndel, Rawle, Harley and later Deyounto, their children were like my siblings, we bonded nicely and partied together. Living with extended families was so seemingly routine for me and I had become accustomed to that kind of life. I lived throughout my high school years with extended families and friends.

Uncle Murtland or uncle big G, as he was usually called, owned and operated, together with his brother, Cleveland, a small vessel that traversed to Caribbean islands. They took rice, sugar and other local products to various islands of the West Indies and brought in cigarettes, foreign liquors, whiskeys, electrical equipment and other "hard to get" items. These supplies fetched attractive prices. They therefore had a very comfortable and lavish lifestyle.

After arriving from one of his trips, Uncle Big G came home and asked me to help him offload some items. He took me and a few others to an area at the back of the Stabroek market wharf, where two small row boats (like lifeboats) had collected items from their vessel which was anchored in the middle of the river. We quickly offloaded the jute bags and suitcases and were instructed to load them into the trunks of a few awaiting taxis. We were about five people in total and all of us had our fair share of heavy luggage. It was probably 2:00 a.m. Out of the blue, in the dark and dim light, two plain clothes policemen appeared and showed us their badges.

"You need to accompany us to the police station; you are under arrest."

I was perplexed. This seemed to be a legitimate exercise. What did we do wrong?

One guy dropped his bags and disappeared into the nearby dark alleyways. Why did he run?

Uncle big G took the two police aside. They spoke for a few minutes and then two of those heavy bags were given to them. I didn't have a clue that we had committed a crime. It was afterward that I realized that we were actually smuggling contraband into the country. We all could have been locked up for sneaking in cooking oil, sardines, Thunderbolt wheat flour, Johnny Walker whiskey, corned beef, champagne and bottles of fine wine. It should be noted that during this era, those items were banned and it was illegal to bring them into the country without a proper license. I was oblivious to this and thought to myself that I had to have more control of my life. Even though we had a good laugh about it, I resolved never to do that again.

I had previously applied to the Public Service Ministry for a scholarship to study science, even before I had commenced the pilot trainee program. I received word that I had been accepted but the wait to make the actual trip was a few months out. I had been having trouble repeatedly with being seasick and made a decision, after deep consideration, to quit the program and return home.

My stay with the Gibsons was truly a nice homely experience. Cousin Mary, like her mother, the gentile little lady who delivered me was hospitable and warm. I owe them all a debt of gratitude for their kindness. Clearly, this was one of my better experiences while living away from my home.

# CHAPTER 26

# Back Home for a Bit

Upon returning home after my attempts at becoming a marine pilot had been voluntarily brought to an abrupt end, it was quickly recognized that the shop was not going as I had hoped and needed much attention. I immediately set about to have it resuscitated.

Having traveled a bit and experienced how other facilities are being run gave me some invaluable inputs. I earnestly began to inject energy and systems into the functioning of my new workplace and recreational facility. Not too long afterward it was back on a firm footing. I dare to say the outcome was better than it had ever been. It was later told to me that my customers had stopped coming because of my absence. People like the extra touch when provided. And why not? Even when a customer may have bought a small item, e.g., one pound of salt, I'm told that my mannerism made them feel wanted and that they were encouraged to come again. The affluent ones were encouraged to try new products. We have a new brand of coffee; would you like to try it? Oh, did you buy our salted fish, it's Trout and not Banga Mary. Though these tactics may have been intrinsic or even instinctive methods, it was much later I learned that that was a form of great customer service.

Here is where the principles learned later in my life during my MBA would have come in handy.

Little Diamond, a 'bottom house' entertainment spot my parents started, began to blossom into a worthwhile venture. The name, Little Diamond, was derived from an idea that was used several years before my time. Skipper John, as he was called, was one of my ancestors, my maternal great-grandmother's brother and the owner of Big Diamond. His facilities were located just about 300 yards away and midway between Granddad Menzo's house and ours. Uncle John Swarving had a rum shop which was famous for his renowned Jamoon wine. Jokingly it was claimed that he strained the Jamoon concoction with his "shorts" or underwear.

Little Diamond provided an area to play indoor games, listen to great music using a cassette player, watch movies via a VCR and of course, drink a good and refreshing, cold beverage. This was indeed a center of relative luxury. Two of the main attractions were electricity and cold drinks since these were not common in those areas. The venue also included a dancing floor which allowed dancers to show off their talents. We, the river people, are known to be fabulous dancers, well, we probably tell that to ourselves.

Things had turned around and visitors would drive their speed boats from as far as DeVeldt down river, some 35 miles away and Mariah Henrrieta in the opposite direction, to spend a few quality hours at the Little Diamond.

Temporarily, I had just carved out my niche which was both profitable and enjoyable even though it sometimes required me to push long hours, especially during weekends. Was this life meant for me? Was this enough and satisfying for me or was my proposed scholarship going to be the pathway to my destiny?

# CHAPTER 27

# Cuba Here I Come

Just as I was about to get comfortable, my destiny was decided. I had been awarded a place to study Microbiology in Cuba but had to wait to receive the appropriate documents. It meant another waiting period, which I didn't mind because it afforded me some more time to weigh the pros and cons. I eventually received the required paperwork and immediately commenced making arrangements to travel. My pros outweighed the cons. My brother, Collin had also been accepted to go to Cuba to do Veterinary medicine and he was in the process of preparing to travel. My existing customers were upset that I was planning on leaving again.

"What is going to happen to Little Diamond?" they asked. Uncle Edward Bender was extremely upset and vociferous when he complained to Papa. He argued that we already had a thriving business and that it provided an avenue for great entertainment for our river folks. He stated that I should have continued to build my enterprise and further opined that after Cuba I was going to be working for a salary and being "hand to mouth."

"William, please don't have your son waste his life," he angrily stressed. Mom chimed in that she thought that it was all up to me, after all, it was my life. Papa wanted more for me; and thought that I should have embraced the opportunity given; that I was destined to do better. He later told me that this is exactly how he had envisaged my future, that he had relished the idea that I was about to go to further my studies. In his opinion, the shop was generally fine but there was no scope for upward mobility. He was surely no ordinary man, a person with wisdom, one surely beyond his years. It was a rather difficult decision for me to make. I was relatively comfortable and thought about something Papa had whispered in my ears: "Son, you'll understand later, afterwards you can also invest in projects up here, but get some further education first." That statement sealed the deal. He must have said similar words maybe a dozen times later.

I had to get my passport ready and secure a fair amount of foreign currency. Twenty-five Guyanese dollars could have bought one US dollar in those days, but the amount allowed per traveler was extremely rationed. I was allowed a few hundred US dollars and mainly in travelers' cheques.

I also managed to see Rosebud before I left and as usual, it was great catching up again. Was this going to be the end of our relationship? I felt sad that we were going to be apart but was also excited about my future prospects. Distant relationships are not very healthy; they don't usually survive. We both assured each other that we were going to stay in touch, no matter what. "Come hell or high water," as the saying goes.

Shortly before my departure, we were greeted with the sad news that our President, Linden Forbes Samson Burnham had died suddenly. It was indeed tragic and very unexpected since he was not ill and no one had anticipated this. This sad news was greeted with mixed reactions. Some people like those "die hard" PNC stalwarts were extremely saddened, while on the other hand, there were a few others who rejoiced at his death.

The overseas students were required to stand at attention at strategic locations at the National Cultural Center, where his body laid in state. It was a strange feeling that came over me while I stood in my white embroidered shirt jack and black trousers. Again, the feeling of doubt hit me. Was I taking a step in the right direction? Maybe the tense and sad atmosphere as I stood near the clothed remains of our fallen leader contributed to my mixed feelings. It was a solemn ceremony but I felt honored to stand with my fellow students. Oh, what a sad but proud moment it was!

The red, white, and blue aircraft of the Cubana Airlines taxied on the tarmac at the Timehri international airport and waited for us to board. That day was truly awesome, one that was very sunny and nice. I felt generally sad but at the same time happy and super excited to burst into this new era. The mere thought of me, 'the river boy,' flying to Cuba was overwhelming. It felt good but the sight of my Mom sobbing sadly did not make it easy for me, she was worried and quite rightly so. There had been a tragic Cubana air disaster less than ten years before when a terrorist had planted a bomb on that ill-fated craft. The lives of several young Guyanese students had been lost when the aircraft that was taking them to Cuba exploded in midair. I felt a tingle of sadness as I hugged and kissed my mama, who was now crying uncontrollably.

Papa was a tough cookie, who generally didn't show much emotions. He shook my hands with his rock-like, hardened right hand, calloused and bruised by the rigors of the extended use of cutlasses and axes in manual labor. His hands were the hardest ones I've ever felt in all my life. He then whispered in my ears as he held me with a firm, bear like hug:

"Make us proud son, do your best."

I smiled sheepishly "sure Papa;" but deep inside I vowed to put my all in 'just for u Papa.' Those words resonated in me over many years, especially when the going got tough, they acted like a catalyst to spur me on. I would never ever forget that deep and encouraging look of approval that he gave me. The lump I felt in my throat was real and a huge teardrop made its way down from the corner of my eyes. My sheepish smile might have prevented other teardrops from following the first few. Those sad sentiments lingered as I kissed them goodbye. What if something happened to them while I was overseas? What if something happened to me? Oh, my poor Mom, she was sobbing by now with her eyes all blood red and there was no shortage of tears.

I smiled again and tried desperately to hide my feelings. The other parents were also freely expressing themselves as their youngsters bid them goodbye. It was later told to me that one of the attending mothers had fainted during the farewell ceremony.

It was my first time on an airplane and the flight path was to Cuba via Barbados. The flight was a relatively smooth one and I was practically too overwhelmed with joy to have noticed the actual duration of the flight. Alva Edison Griffith (my classmate), Dr. Mark Pierre, Dr. Dolly,

Dr. Dexter Alleyne, Dr. Janice Imhoff, Dr. Jennifer Westford, Dr. Joshua DaSilva, Dr. Michelle Collins, Dr. Clement McEwan, and Dr. Maxine Swain were a part of my crew. Some of whom were returning to school after holidaying in Guyana.

The exotic aroma of Cuban cigars was pronounced in the Jose Marti International Airport. The surroundings were modern and the sound of the Spanish tongue was peculiar and sophisticated. I was in another country, and had arrived! All was going as was envisaged, yes, I could live with this. I tried to figure out what they were saying but couldn't understand a thing, not a single word. They spoke so quickly I couldn't grasp what was being said. Mrs. Mignon Blake, my third-form Spanish teacher wouldn't have been proud of me at that moment.

With the assistance of two men in shirt jack, who spoke fluent English, we cleared immigration and Alva and I, the only two freshmen, were taken into quarantine. It was a strict requirement, so really, it certainly didn't matter to me. My mind began to race when we were given hospital gowns to wear and strange-looking pills to drink. It was already around midnight when we settled in and consoled ourselves that this was only going to be a temporary stay.

The hospital's sleeping area where we were placed had about twenty-five beds, all in an open ward. We were both super tired and must have fallen to sleep as soon as we "hit the sack." I'm not sure if an hour had passed when we were awakened by some serious-looking nurses who took our blood samples. No, this couldn't be happening again! Andy, did you make a grave mistake? Should I have stayed and managed Little Diamond? Was Cousin Edward right? These negative thoughts flooded across my mind once more. I remembered Papa's famous phrase, "Man ah man, man nah tobacco stick." This saying meant that man is tough and not made of tobacco sticks. Come on Andy, you are stronger than that, this was probably just a bad beginning of a fabulous journey.

As I lay there trying to suppress the negative thoughts, something further shocked me. Some fellow "inmates/patients" were coughing and spitting. They were "hacking" and spitting on the floor, right there near their beds, just next to where I slept. One of them had a very intense, uncontrollable, and productive cough. What if he had Tuberculosis (TB)? Having suffered from the rigors of travel I eventually dropped to sleep but not before tossing, turning, and worrying a bit.

The next morning, I felt like a zombie; it must have been the effects of the pills and maybe the lack of sleep. We were given chloroquine, which are anti-malaria tablets that made us feel drowsy and listless. This medication was meant to make the detection of latent malaria much easier than normal.

During those few days, I was very careful to select where I placed my feet, and didn't want to slide down on the slimy, 'spitty' floors. My rubber slippers (yes, I had eventually learned how to walk in them) were somewhere at the bottom of my suitcase, so I donned my high-top Nike booths which I had traveled in. This must have been a funny sight, me in the hospital gown and high-top boots. The food tasted terrible and lacked seasoning; and we were offered black, strong coffee in baby teacups. The long, hard bread could have been easily used as a weapon; even the water tasted like medicine.

Alva and I were the only English-speaking patients, the others seemed to be all speaking with strange-sounding tongues. They spoke to each other as though they were arguing and pointed at one another as opinions were emphasized. It was indeed a different world; one I did not envisage. These were persons with distinct cultural norms and strange-sounding dialects. It was later that I came to the realization that it was perfectly normal for some sections of society to spit without remorse into their immediate surroundings, even if it were their bedrooms.

That quarantine experience made me form a terrible first impression that was clearly a misrepresentation of what Cuba was like. Though those few days were extremely harsh and somewhat like a baptism of fire, I later saw the wisdom of the whole idea. Several of my colleagues, I'm told, were discovered to have had filaria, malaria and other parasites in their systems. It was therefore an effective way of detecting diseases and preventing them from entering Cuba and being spread to its population.

After those three days of medication and hospitalization, we were finally set "free," from what was probably one of the most difficult periods of my life. There was no way to call home to say that we had arrived safely. We had no link to the external world whatsoever. I wondered whether my entire stay was going to be this gray and stressful.

I was amazed at how quickly I learned Spanish and before I knew it, I was thinking and conversing in the language with my peers. My professor couldn't speak one word of English but she skillfully cajoled us into speaking without having to translate from our mother tongue.

I'm told that I have an affinity for languages but I would love to credit Mrs. Mignon Blake for that strong foundation she gave me at NA Multilateral, my secondary school. I also learned to speak French by association, which in my opinion is the best way to learn any language.

My peers relied on me to lead the way and to be the "spokesperson" because of my ability to speak Spanish fluently, long before they managed to grasp the language. In fact, jokingly, I have caused them to either receive slaps or curses when I told them to tell members of the opposite sex, very un-nice Spanish slangs in the hope that they were actually saying rosy phrases to them.

During those months of Spanish classes, we also did some sessions on Cuban history and politics. These were also taught in Spanish but soon after we had grasped the language to some extent. I also took the opportunity to learn French in the evenings and it was easier for me as I had a very close friend from Guadeloupe who tutored me. She would only speak to me in French, so I had no choice but to get a proper hold of the language. Similarly, within a few months, I was also conversing in French too.

My brother arrived in Havana a couple of weeks after I did and after quarantine, was sent to Santiago De Cuba, the Caribbean side of the island. I was in Havana, on the opposite end. It was probably not very long after I had arrived in Cuba, maybe about two months afterward, that I decided to pay him a visit, all the way to Santiago De Cuba.

I left Havana very early on one Friday morning with the hope of arriving in Santiago early that evening. The trains normally took as long as twelve hours and stopped in most of the towns in the almost linear path. The train ride was rickety and not classy, but the mere sight of the different "ways of life" in the other towns and villages was extremely fascinating. There were lots of fresh fruits for sale in the countryside as compared to the bustling city life of Havana. It was quite revealing and intriguing indeed.

Somewhere on the way to my destination, the train developed mechanical problems and was stalled for several hours. It meant therefore that my arrival was severely delayed and this could have resulted in me having to sleep in the train station, not a safe place for a student who knew just enough Spanish for basic communication. It must be noted that my Spanish was not fluent at that moment and I was still "finding my way" with the language. The Cubans speak a very different kind of Spanish; they cut their words and do so very rapidly. So, even though you may know what you want to ask them, they confuse you on the other hand, with their barrage and rapid flurry of words; it takes getting used to. Luckily, I sat near a Cuban Christian minister with Barbadian roots whose English was not extensive but we managed to communicate using both languages. I do believe that this was divine intervention.

All my life, when I'm cornered with no way out or during difficult moments, he (the Great Architect of the Universe) comes through for me. It's difficult for you to understand but it's very real, I've experienced it repeatedly. When we eventually arrived some seven hours later than the expected time, this friendly gentleman invited me to spend the evening with his family. This could have been a very dangerous trip for me but somehow, I was not scared. He and his family made me feel super comfortable during those few hours. I slept so peacefully that I was slightly disoriented the following morning. After consuming a sumptuous Caribbean-style breakfast and the saying of prayers both in broken English and fluent Spanish, I was taken to my brother's University.

When we arrived, we exchanged pleasantries and Collin again thanked the pastor for taking care of his little brother, we both said goodbye to the pastor and started talking about how great it was for me to have traveled all the way to Santiago De Cuba. Collin suddenly remembered to invite the Anglican Priest to a BBQ he was hosting later that day but when we turned around, he had completely vanished. *Oh Lord, was he a real guardian angel?* I really do think he was an angel. His appearance was coincidental indeed. I tried to contact him afterwards but there was simply no trace of the very friendly and helpful gentleman.

Collin was surprised to see me being driven to see him, almost 24 hours after my scheduled arrival. That weekend was truly fun-filled. He had prepared the "wicket" well in anticipation of my stay. There I met with Regla, an extremely gorgeous Cuban medical student. I also discovered that the Santiago De Cuba residents, also called the Orientals, were exceedingly warm and outgoing. They spoke a different kind of Spanish which sounded like music to one's ears, with a raised intonation at the end, in a singing way. It was so enjoyable that I had promised to return to that lovely city before the end of my program.

Studying in another language was not as difficult as it may seem. The key is to think in that particular tongue as it increases one's fluency. One of my favorite pastimes while on this gorgeous island was to go and relax on the beach. I relished the idea of floating in the awesome blue waters and would visit these luxurious sea sides on most weekends.

While there, I sometimes reminisced on my childhood days and wondered how I ended up in this awesome paradise. Oh, what a lovely experience that was, I was so glad that I had decided to go there.

Living in Cuba had its advantages and disadvantages. I recollect very vividly going to shop in La Sevilla, a diplomatic shop (diplotienda) which was situated in Old Havana. This section of Havana was particularly kept in its ancient state to preserve its legacy. The archaic Spanish architecture was clearly evident and I felt honored and privileged to walk down those sixteenth-century cobble roads.

I might have purchased jeans and T-Shirts and was walking gingerly along to grab the Wa Wa (bus). I had just exited the store when two gentlemen who were dressed in civilian clothing approached me. It was as if they were waiting around the corner of the building, I didn't see when they stepped out of the shadows. One held out what looked like a police badge and said under his breath:

"Policia, ensename su carne de indentidad!" (Police, show me your identification card!)

I was taken by surprise and was nervous and somewhat confused. My passport was at hand and I quickly showed it to one of the supposed plain clothes policemen by which time one of them had held on to my arm, in a relatively gentle but firm way.

"I'm a foreigner! I'm not a Cuban! Loose me!" I protested bitterly in Spanish. One of the policemen told me to stop pretending with that fake accent, that he knew I was Cuban. It was very upsetting and embarrassing because various onlookers were beginning to gather around and I was being regarded as a criminal. Within a matter of seconds, several other policemen dressed in their uniforms appeared. I was bundled into a military car and whisked away to the nearby police station. All along they kept lecturing me about how I needed to get a proper job and that I should stop pretending to be a foreigner. They obviously thought that I had forged my passport and had committed a grave crime.

Our journey to the station was brief and swift. By this time, I had become very angry and began to tell them some not so nice words. Why did I have to be treated like a common criminal? How in heaven's name could this be fair? This crime was a very punishable one and Cubans spend as long as several years in prison. I was not really worried or thought that I was going to be jailed; it was simply because I felt ridiculed and embarrassed. It was a perfect waste of my time; I had an exam coming up and wanted to put in some work. It took me about thirty minutes before I was finally released. They eventually realized that they had falsely arrested me for "looking like a Cuban."

Apparently, Cubans were not allowed to purchase in those diplomatic shops. It meant that many foreigners were privileged to buy those exotic items and easily resell them. Some foreign students became shrewd businessmen doing those illegal trades. That incident put aside, my tenure in Cuba was generally a good one. It was filled with awesome and unforgettable experiences.

One day, the foreign students of my university were lucky to have been taken on a day trip to a place called Guam. This luxurious tourist area was exclusive for foreigners and seemed like another world. Most of the buildings had thatched roofs to simulate an indigenous village but these huts were truly elegant on the inside. The transportation to and from Guam was free but we were required to purchase food and drinks. Most of my buddies and I indulged in the local beer called Hatuey which was named after a local indigenous tribe. The Crystal and Buccanero beers became popular after I had already left Cuba.

It turned out to be an awesome day as we danced, ate delicious fried frog legs and drank on the edge of a fancy-looking swimming pool. Some of the girls swam as most of my pals and I ate and drank at the poolside bar. Ben Alli, from Yemen who kept arguing and saying silly things was a Muslim and was not used to drinking and might have secretly over indulged. Thoughtlessly I pushed him into the pool, thinking that this would silence him for a bit and probably deter him from talking more nonsense. He was pushed in at the deep end of the pool and no one was in his vicinity. "Oscurro, oscurro!" we heard this gurgling sound. "He can't swim!" "Oh Lord!" "Somebody help!"

Ben Alli was fighting for his life and screamed for help as he bobbed up and down in the pristine blue water, frantically thrashing around. Without thinking, I jumped into the deep waters of the pool, after all, I was the one who had pushed him in. I grabbed the desperately drowning chap from behind. Had I held him from in front it would have endangered both of our lives. Ben Alli's eyes were wild as he attempted to sink his fingernails into my arms. He uttered insults in Arabic when he realized he was being saved. I was a powerful swimmer and swimming with him was not at all strenuous.

The eager and waiting hands of my friends easily pulled us out of the deep pool. Even though it was very stupid and thoughtless of me to have thrown him into the waters, I received cheers of approval. I was the hero that day for saving Ben Alli's life. He on the other hand continued brandishing me with colorful Arabic words like "Aswad Chermuta," which I later learned, meant 'black whore'. Aswad really meant black man but in a derogatory way, very much like nigger. On our journey back to school, all people talked about was how selfless it was of me to have risked my life to save the Yemenita but little did they know that it was all my fault. I tried to explain what had happened but nobody listened or believed me. I vowed never ever to throw anyone into the water again.

Despite those few minor incidents and hitches, my tenure in Cuba was truly remarkable. It was an extraordinary and a totally unforgettable experience. I developed deep friendships with several people, both Guyanese and Foreigners. Mousa Aboud Jumbe of Zanzibar Tanzania is one such friend. His dad was one of the Vice Presidents in the Julius Nyerere government and he lived a good life while in Cuba. Mousa now heads the department of fisheries and is a well-respected Marine Biologist in Zanzibar. I remember us arguing about where the famous Guyanese singer, Eddy Grant was born; he thought that Grant was South African.

George Amoo, Evelyn, and Yaw Boateng are also three dear Ghanaian friends of mine, just to name a few. Student life allows one to develop deep and meaningful friendships with colleagues. This is a good thing as it helps amazingly with networking and getting to know the various countries with their respective cultures.

# CHAPTER 28

# Hola Miami!

It was approaching July of the year 1987; the summer holidays were beckoning. Extended summer holidays were the order of the day. Most students would either go to their respective countries, remain in Cuba or journey to exotic locations. Joshua DaSilva (Josh), my brother Collin and I decided to seek US visas in Havana, Cuba. Josh had several brothers living in the US while Collin and I have a few relatives but we didn't have concrete information on their exact whereabouts. Strangely, we got the visas without any hassles whatsoever. We armed ourselves with some telephone numbers of a few family members who lived overseas and boarded our American Airlines flight to Miami, USA.

Cuba is a mere 90 miles away from Miami, USA. I don't remember clearly but our financial statuses were not to be proud of. If my memory serves me correctly, we probably had not more than $200 US each. This was a lot of money at that time but clearly, it was really a trip that was not properly planned and coordinated. Ideally, prior arrangements with our relatives should have been made. Sadly, this was not done but we persisted with our crazy journey all the way to Miami. When we arrived, after a relatively short journey it felt as though we were still in Cuba. We actually felt at home when we heard the lovely voices of the Miami Cubans. There were Spanish speakers all over, in and around the airport. It was as though we had arrived in a modern Cuba.

Now, what next? We had a few addresses of our relatives but most were located in New York and New Jersey. Collin and I were definitely in an adventurous mood. We managed to get two dollars changed into quarters in order to make calls from the pay phone that was situated just after the luggage collection area. It now meant that we had to make contact with one of our relatives. Oh, how ludicrous that was. There is no way that we could have coordinated our travels from Cuba. Communication from Cuba to the external world was practically impossible. What if we couldn't locate our relatives? It was indeed a crazy and adventurous trip. We tried calling Aunt Girlie (Claudette Carter), one of Papa's sisters to no avail. She was the nurse who had stitched my wound after the savannah walk. Aunty G was probably sleeping after having worked the night shift. Perhaps, on the other hand, she had gone to work. After all, it was around 9:00 a.m. The pay phone gobbled up the quarters. We barely managed to call two of our relatives before our twenty- five cent pieces were used up.

Somehow, it seems as though the pay telephone system was gobbling up those quarters. We had no more quarters and the shops in the vicinity didn't have either. We had another relative to try... cousin Esther Lindie, Mom's first cousin. My grandfather, Menzo, was her mother Joyce's brother. "Let's call her collect, she wouldn't mind," Collin suggested. That's exactly what we did. When cousin Esther's husband, Merlin answered, the telephone operator sounded like this...

"Good morning, Sir, would you kindly accept a collect call from Collin and Andy Boyle?"

There was a moment of silence then he said, "Oh sure."

I'm not sure if we had a plan B, just in case. The exuberance of youth or some would say, the stupidity as in this case. We didn't plan properly but in retrospect, it really did turn out to be an amazing trip.

Cousin Merlin, though very polite and friendly, remarked in a joking way:

"…but how did you youngsters travel without a blind cent?"

This was not actually true but he obviously presumed that we were 'broke.' Technically we were, even though that thought never crossed our minds. We were told to get a flight that landed in Newark Airport in New Jersey. That was the first time I had ever heard that name. It meant us having to make another collect call to our relatives after we had procured our next flight to New Jersey.

I really don't remember how long the flight took. Brimming with enthusiasm and excitement we exited the airline with our carry-on luggage. We intended to spend in excess of two months with barely enough clothes to last for one week. Was that efficient planning or faith that the good Lord would have provided for us? Perhaps we were thinking that we would shop for enough clothes to last for the duration of our stay in 'Uncle Sam.' I often preach to my friends, family members, and associates to be positive and to have faith. This exercise was clearly a bit far-fetched though because we didn't have the financial resources to replenish our supplies, much less to sustain ourselves throughout the supposedly exciting vacation.

I clearly remember Collin sneaking me a glance, one that said a thousand words. I interpreted it to mean, "Bro, we did it." Readers, it would be difficult for you to come even close to understanding what this felt like. Just picture in your minds two Berbice River scallywags, exiting the airline in the US, with a mere $200 US each and baby / carry-on suitcases to spend in excess of one month's vacation. It was like when Jesus fed the multitude with five loaves of bread and two fish; Matthew 14:13-21 NIV. Our destination was still not certain nor clear but we were assured in our minds that our family ties were solid. Lesson number 'umpteen,'

"Be helpful whenever you can, you never know, maybe your offspring will be repaid for your kindness. Please understand that you should always be kind but never because you wish to reap the rewards in return. Giving should be selfless and genuine."

It was a beautiful day and our exit from the aircraft was not on the actual tarmac as it was, in those days, in Guyana and Cuba. In Guyana, you exited the plane and then had to walk for about 300-400 meters to the terminal (that is different now). In Cuba, bus shuttles were provided to take passengers from the airplane to the terminal. As we disembarked, all happy with ourselves, we scanned the greeters to see if we would recognize our chaperone. Cousin Merlin AKA German had said that his daughter, Erica was going to be there when we arrived. We had no cell phones to make contact with; it was expected that she was going to be there waiting. As we walked, watching as people exclaimed and beckoned to their arriving parties, I thought, *suppose she didn't turn up? What next? Oh yes, we still had the collect call option as a backup plan.*

Towards the end of the crowd, we both saw her at the same moment. There she was, holding up a white cardboard, with Collin & Andy, written in bold blue letters. We both had never seen her before but her face was a carbon copy of the fair-skinned and freckled-faced Cousin Merlin. There was really no need for placards nor IDs, she was our family. Oh, the hugs and kisses, perhaps a tear or two, were quite appropriate and expected. Holy Jesus, thanks for leading us through the darkness! We had arrived! "Behind every dark cloud, there is a silver lining."

"This is all your luggage?" Our second cousin exclaimed. The mere fact that we had one carry-on case each led her to speculate. Clearly, she didn't realize that our plan was falling into place, little by little.

The journey to Patterson, New Jersey, was not very long. We spoke so much that the 30-minute journey felt like 10 minutes. The point of how we are related was clearly explained. Our grandfather, Menzo Phillip Bender was the brother of Erica's grandmother, Joyce Grimmond nee Bender. We were obviously second cousins and they, she and her siblings, were born and grew up in Kwakwani, Berbice River. She was more familiar with her mother's siblings, Adolphus (Dalphus), Durry, Leslie, and Joycee. All who lived in Kwakwani.

Collin, as the elder brother, sat in the front seat and basically led the discussion while I chimed in, from the back seat, from time to time. We didn't have a welcoming party but our cousins were all awaiting our arrival. Young Mortimer (Morty) had not too long arrived from school.

"How is your Mommy Claudia? Your daddy, Papa? Uncle Menzo, how is he?"

All the questions and inquiries were asked, almost simultaneously. Really, we were just as misinformed as they were. I suppose that they were all doing very well. The communication to and from Cuba was most ridiculous. So, in reality, we really didn't know how they were doing.

Amongst the further questions that we faced were...what was it like in Cuba, were we suffering, did we have to line up for food, do we plan on returning, would we consider staying in the US, what's Fidel Castro like, is it really beautiful there, can we speak Spanish? We were properly interrogated but not in a hostile manner. The grilling came from all of the family members present. Cousin Merlin was married to cousin Esther nee Bender and their children... Erica, Morty, Marcy, Jackie, Hutson, and Junie were all present and chimed in to carefully examine their visiting cousins. Coren, the biggest sibling, was not present. She lived elsewhere in the US. They all marveled at how we managed to travel without a sound plan and practically penniless. We were given access to the guest room but Morty insisted that we share his room in the attic. The attic was quite a secluded area, one that was very private and cozy. We could have easily entered or left without being noticed. It surely served its purpose very well.

*Andy, Dr. Joshua Da Silva and Morty*

# CHAPTER 29

# Tree Pruning Time

Cousin Merlin insisted that we checked the local Classified Ads in the daily newspapers for odds and ends jobs. After all, we needed to make money to sustain our new traveling lifestyle. The morning after our arrival there was an Ad in the local newspaper requesting that a tree be pruned for US$300. This sum was equivalent to more than three months' stipends that we received in Cuba. Immediately we sprang into action, got the address and proceeded to Home Depot to procure the necessary tools; two sharpened, 22" cutlasses and Nicholson branded files.

Morty took us over to the house using a printed map which we found to be intriguing. There was no GPS at that time. It meant going on the computer to access the pin point location using Google maps. In his burgundy Oldsmobile we headed to accomplish our first job. After driving for about 30 minutes, we arrived at our destination. There it was! The prominent un-pruned tree stood out like a sore thumb. It was just about 12 to 15 ft. from end to end, measuring horizontally. Vertically it was about thirty feet tall. We knocked at the gate and inquired whether we were at the correct location. Morty, using his

American accent, asked politely about the task at hand. The frail elderly lady asked us where our tools were. Very excitedly we indicated that our machetes (or cutlasses) were good enough to have the job expertly done. She said, "Okay, carry on smartly."

Morty arranged to pick us up in three hours, quite a reasonable enough time to get the job successfully completed. Our plan was to remove the large, overhanging branches first then skillfully cut the smaller ones. We then climbed the proverbial tree and started the careful demolition. Shortly after we commenced the operation, our temporary employer stated that she was heading to the supermarket for a few minutes.

Our task was not as easy as we had initially assumed. The tree was very thick and it was difficult to properly swing our cutlasses. So, it meant trimming the clustering twigs so that proper cutting could have been done. On and on we pushed forward to prune the bushy tree. It really seemed like an endless exercise. One hour afterwards it finally seemed as though we were getting somewhere. By then the landlady had returned. "Wow!" She exclaimed, "This really looks nice and you are not yet finished."

She took out what appeared to me as an Instamatic camera. Before she took snapshots of us, she shouted out but we didn't understand what she was saying.

"Do you mind me taking a picture of you two hard-working young men?" I didn't see anything wrong with her taking our picture, after all, we were not yet celebrities.

It took us just over an hour of chopping and eventually tidying up. This was our first job and I constantly tell my team members that everything that's done, whether it's the first or 100th time, should be done to the best of your abilities.

She offered us pink lemonade and crackers while we waited on Morty. Obviously, she was quite pleased with the results of our efforts. On that glorious day, we were awarded $600 for our labor. She was a very nice and generous person.

A few minutes later, Morty returned and he too was also amazed and pleasantly surprised at the outcome of our efforts.

Lesson learned - always do your best in your endeavors!

# CHAPTER 30

# At The Boardwalk - Atlantic City

New Jersey is one of those large, green states of the USA. Where we stayed, Paterson NJ was situated not very far from NY. In a matter of minutes, with light traffic, one could have easily driven to Brooklyn. On the other hand, places like Atlantic City and NJ, were located several miles away from where we stayed. As the name suggests, it was situated on the Atlantic coast. It was suggested that we take a trip to visit the casinos on the Atlantic coast.

Collin, Morty, and I got dressed very early that morning and prepared to make the journey to that beautiful coastal city. Cousin Merlin gave us $50 each and wished us luck. Cousin Esther, God bless her soul, packed smoked turkey sandwiches and homemade lemonade. We were ready to spend a beautiful Sunday on the move. Our willing chaperone for holidays was most eager to show us an amazing time. The voyage took almost three hours. I didn't manage to properly absorb the various sceneries as we traveled along because most of us slept through the entire trip. It should be clearly understood that Morty, our chaperone, had us out also at nights. Obviously, this would have added to our being so tired and drained on that early Sunday morning.

We finally got to lovely Atlantic City. It was truly amazing. There were lots of high risers, a gorgeous Boardwalk along the seaside. People were hustling and bustling along. It was midmorning on Sunday, but it seemed like a busy weekday. Before we entered the casino, two exercises caught our eyes-the shoe shiners and the human 'pull carts'. I was wearing my Nike high-top boots and those didn't require the services of the shoes shining people. Collin, on the other hand, had on leather shoes and he insisted on having them cleaned. It's a pity we didn't capture those moments on camera. Cell phones were not in existence in those days. We shared a 'pull cart' ride, all three of us nicely snuggled in the well decorated device. The 'pull carts' were simple well decorated carts on two wheels and two protruding arms that are controlled by the operator. I'm told that these carts, now called sitting chairs, are even more colorful and grand.

Collin jokingly heckled, "Giddyup, giddyup," (words used locally by real donkey and horse cart operators to spur on their harnessed animals to move faster, sometimes also used by jockeys to communicate with their horses) and pretended to lash the 'puller' with a figurative whip. We felt like real tourists, Collin took one glance at me with a wicked smirk on his face. I knew exactly what he was thinking. He was probably saying, *Bro, look at where we are now, eh!*

We did a few rides along the boardwalk. It really felt good being out there, to not only enjoy the scenery but to have the fresh, cool breeze gently caressing our faces. Simply being there was incredibly pleasurable. There was no need to enter the welcoming casinos, this was enough. After traversing parts of the huge boardwalks, we finally decided to try our luck in the casinos. We played for a bit, using the 'one arm bandits' or slot machines mainly and then later returned to grab a few more 'pull cart' rides. I really don't remember the details as to whether or not we had been successful in the casinos. I really don't believe that we were though. All in all, it was a truly awesome day.

*Cos Merlin, Esther, Morty & Family, Sonia, Paula, Erica.*

Our relatively brief sojourn in the US can be clearly ranked as absolutely amazing. We formed lifetime bonds with our cousins, especially Mortimer (Morty). He and his family went beyond boundaries to make us feel welcomed. This vacation was indeed one in a million, it opened our eyes and exposed us to the wonderful American ways of life. We returned to Cuba with a lot more dollars in our pockets than what we had initially taken to the US. In essence, Collin and I were both truly grateful for that golden opportunity that was afforded us.

# CHAPTER 31

# Packing To Go Home

I t was somewhere mid-August 1989, and it was time to go home. The race was well run and I had achieved and accomplished my goal, BSc in Microbiology, Cum Laude. I was also fluent in Spanish, French and well immersed with a wealth of knowledge in Medical Laboratory Science. It was an era filled with great experiences, of all kinds, very much like an amazing dream, one that will always be remembered. It was now time to come home; to hear the friendly sounds of English words caressing my ears. Strangely, we all spoke with a few Spanish words interwoven in our regular speech. 'I'm going to take my almuerzo' (lunch), sometimes simply because the Spanish word is more readily available to be spoken.

My luggage consisted of two old suitcases filled with articles of clothing, Russian wares (drinking glasses, tea cups, plates, and ornaments), an old microscope and lots of Microbiology text books in Spanish. The secondhand Olympus microscope was bought for three hundred US dollars, quite a good deal, in my opinion. I had to decide whether to choose between a brand-new silver alto saxophone and that microscope because I didn't have the luxury of additional funds. The rationale behind the purchasing of the microscope was to aid in the setting up of my own Medical Laboratory. Lots of saxophones could then be acquired at my whims and fancies after the lab starts to make a profit. Owning my laboratory was one of my futuristic dreams. Would this dream become a reality? In retrospect, this vision seemed so far-fetched and almost unattainable. My love for great saxophone music became more and more prominent as the years rolled by.

When the aircraft landed at Timehri International Airport I was super excited. Gosh, it seemed like only yesterday that I had initially left for Cuba. The sound of my native tongue was quite refreshing but somewhat strange. I had traveled home on two occasions, but this was the finale, the end of my studies. It was totally a fulfilling and successful venture, Glory to God. Mission accomplished!

# CHAPTER 32

# Claudia Antoinetta Bender-Boyle

If I had a crown of honor or medal, it would be a distinct privilege for me to present it to her, unconditionally. She is indeed a woman of integrity and a virtuous one too. Clauds, as we sometimes call her, is a one kind woman. This super woman raised her ten children like a Harpy Eagle would; she was watchful and caring, no one dared hurt her babies. She skillfully balanced the art of discipline and kindness. Over the years, she was a feared disciplinarian who never 'spared the rod,' but she became more lenient and relaxed for the smaller ones, probably as she mellowed. I, out of all of my nine siblings, might have been the major recipient of all forms of corporal punishment. Despite having to perform the unpopular role of the 'strict and no-nonsense Mom,' she was able to mutate into that loving, docile and caring Mom. It is a balancing act that she perfected very well with great efficiency that reaped dividends in the long run.

Both Mom and Papa only went to primary school but their tremendous instincts, experiences and tactful exposures have assisted in making them into very smart characters. Mom in particular knows all of her children very well, through and through.

I clearly remember that on one particular evening, I had not so long arrived home after spending some time in New Amsterdam. I was experiencing difficulties, in that I had wanted to spend some time with my girlfriend but couldn't because of work commitments at the shop I operated at Haraculi. As I lay down, listening to soft soothing music and reminiscing about those lovely moments we shared. Mom came up silently and put her arms gently around my shoulders and said:

"Son, are you alright?"

Even though I had attempted to mask my feelings, my psychologist Mom was able to see through me and was talented enough to realize that something was wrong with me.

My super Mom is an extremely caring individual, one who would go to the end of the world for any of her children. She had a book of home remedies or according to her, 'a doctor book,' which was used for guidance. Just imagine how busy Dr. Mom might have been over the many years of the upbringing of her children. Cuts, bruises, insect bites, vomiting, diarrhea, abscesses, skin rashes, fevers, tooth aches, headaches, colds, 'bête rouge' infestations (Trombicula sp), snake bites too, etc., were no match for my ever-vigilant and energetic wonder woman mother. She was quite versed in the use of local herbs to treat various ailments.

There were times when we either ate lots of fruits or perhaps consumed them too late in the evening. The resulting effect would be severe vomiting which was sometimes accompanied with diarrhea. During the bouts of vomiting, our ever-present Mom would be there with a glass of water to 'settle our little stomachs' as she would say.

Throughout our tenure at high school, we were given budgeted amounts of funds to last for maybe one or two months. These amounts were invariably not enough because of miscellaneous spending on un-budgeted items/activities. Our caring Mom would sneak in a few extra funds to alleviate the situation and this was done on countless occasions without the knowledge of Papa, who really didn't understand why we needed additional funds. Was that spoiling us? No, I really don't think so, she was simply being realistic. It surely didn't mean that we were furnished with our unwarranted needs and desires, surely not.

Strangely, this superwoman found the time to guide us in doing our primary school homework. This is quite a commendable feat that should be emulated by all parents and guardians, especially during the formative moments of the children's lives.

Mom, being the only child of her parents, was taught to do almost everything. Her dad (Daddy), taught her to shoot a shotgun. She was an extremely good markswoman in her younger days. There were even times when she shot Lukanani fish as they monitored their tiny off-springs near the river shore. In those instances, Glendon (Glenny) would plunge into the dark waters to retrieve the wounded and wriggling fish.

When on the farm, she would work toe-to-toe with Papa, to amazingly fetch bunches of plantains out from the field to the boat. Sometimes though, she would say some things that may be considered inappropriate, these are often simply disregarded.

*Mom and Papa (Younger days)*

*My Mom and I*

# CHAPTER 33

# William Fitzgerald Boyle Aka Willo, Smell the Rat

My dad was a phenomenal person and one of a kind. He had his shortcomings but his strengths most certainly outweighed his weaknesses. Papa was an industrious and such a brilliant man, one far beyond his time. Throughout my childhood years and even during my years of adulthood, I marveled at how he operated. He was outspoken and made his points and or arguments, whether it was for or against. His presence had to be felt and never would he sit quietly and not air his sentiments. Papa was a great father and husband, never once were we left wanting. This is quite unlike what happens in our real world today.

While others complained about the cost of living and hardships generally, he on the other hand never did. He used to say,

"You have to get up and get or the cat will eat your dinner." One of his favorite quotes was, "Time and tide wait for no man."

Papa was extremely influential in my upbringing and in the person I've become. It was his together with Mom's persistence that we, my siblings and I, pursued higher education. He often shared that his reason for not being fortunate to attend High school was because of his parents' inability to provide the means to send him to New Amsterdam.

Papa and his brothers worked with their dad on his timber grant called Kabiyaro which was situated at Bamboo Landing, upper Berbice River. From all appearances, it seemed to have been quite a relatively successful venture but I doubt whether there was proper paperwork and record keeping. He and his brothers were the best at teasing and making funny jokes. The late Brindley and Arthur Boyle Junior were the funniest when it came to teasing and making silly jokes.

If you ever visited Papa and after the transaction was completed, he would say in a nice way that it's time for you to leave. One of his regular notes would probably go like this…"Feddie (name of friend), hurry up and catch the tide or there is a storm coming, don't allow the weather to catch you." Very diplomatically said, to get rid of the visiting friends.

His Mom who was fondly called Maama did farming in the vicinity of their New Hong Kong, Berbice River home, just a stone throw from my village, just around the turn, up river. She did joint farming with my grandad, Menzo (Daddy) with whom she had developed a great friendship. Papa and his siblings were known to have a whale of a time, especially after selling timber. They were the 'sweet boys' of the river and were the talk of those riverain villages. The Boyle's siblings were some of the few privileged young men who moved around in speed boats.

When working on the lumber grant, Papa spent several months on each rotation, very much like what happens in the gold mining industry. The timber business in those days was very peculiar, in that, they only left the 'back dam' or worksite after they had completed a complete load. These logs were then transported to New Amsterdam on huge wooden punts, Balahoos (large wooden boats), sometimes on rafts (logs tied together) or a combination of both rafts and punts. These trips lasted for several days and were quite arduous and difficult at times. They were tied at the corner of the river when the tide flowed contrary to their direction of travel and then started to float as the tide changed and flowed in their direction. The rafts and punts were made of a woven network of timbers; the light woods floating on top and the heavier hardwoods strapped with bush ropes at the bottom. Huge wooden oars were used to guide these contraptions along the flowing river. At nights and during periods of rest they would relax in hammocks that were slung under a thatched covering for protection against the elements.

I'm told that Papa and Mom got married on May 30, 1960 in New Amsterdam and had a relatively quiet ceremony. His suit was borrowed from the late Mr. J.V. Jaundoo (aka Sydney) and his mother, mama, provided the marriage rings. Clearly, they were not at all ready financially but with love, determination and commitment, they made it work.

It was strange that on the following day, after they had gotten married, Mom lost her coveted ring which had fallen from her slender fingers and through the drain pipe of the bathroom. It meant that he had to break the pipes on the lower floors in order to recover the treasure. The very friendly and helpful staff graciously assisted and were successful in finding Mom's ring. Shortly after recovering the ring the newlyweds proceeded to travel up the river for their second celebration, the real one. Mom was only sixteen years old and probably about three months pregnant with their first child, Ken Nuffield. They were in the process of building their house and commencing their lives together, so it was quite understandable why they decided to be conservative. Mom was not in favor of his working on the timber grant, so after the first few years of marriage, which might have been when I was a little baby, he decided to find something to do around home. The decision was made to do farming near to where we lived. He liked to do things in a huge way; when everyone cultivated one-and two-acres farms, he did twenty instead. Papa taught me to think big, and to always keep striving for better.

Mom and Papa enjoyed a pretty decent married life and like most couples had their ups and downs. I clearly remember them arguing and Mom had made a decision to leave him. It so happened that she, Mom, had requested the late cousin Clifton Watson (Verna's father, who lived across the river) to drop her off to the passing steamer. Mom had already been seated in the canoe, awaiting the steamer to arrive. Papa quickly and silently asked me to steal her packed luggage from her boat. I cunningly managed to quickly remove it and handed it over to Papa. She ended up staying. Papa and I had scored a victory and it made me feel very happy.

His extreme weakness was that he couldn't hold his drinks. In other words, he became drunk a short while after imbibing alcoholic drinks. His tolerance level for rum and other alcoholic beverages was extremely low. Strangely, he drank mega shots whenever he imbibed, evidently, enough to do the damage. If it were only a case of him getting tipsy and going on to sleep early after being intoxicated, then that wouldn't have been any major issue. The unfortunate occurrence was that he often behaved badly and would say hurtful things about persons within his midst. The following day he wouldn't have the slightest clue of what horrible things were said and this led several persons to silently dislike him.

During the height of those imbibed states, sometimes he would say "When I talk, no lame dog walk." Despite all this spectacle, he never once ridiculed me as he would to most of the individuals who happened to be around him. It was as if he couldn't wait to get drunk in order to speak his mind. I'm told that during his younger days, he had been involved in numerous fist fights, especially after imbibing. It has further been narrated to me that he practically won most of those fights simply because he was a tremendously strong man.

On one occasion he nearly burnt our house down. I clearly remember that he had been totally drunk and couldn't walk upright as he shouted slurred obscenities. He threatened to burn the house and was heading with a box of matches to the drums of gasoline that were stored under the house. Tearfully I was the one, even though I was little, probably about eight years old at the time, who managed to beg, in tears, for him to reconsider his actions. Was he really going to execute those threats? It would have taken all of our lives, including his, in the process. During those episodes of drunkenness, he would only heed the advice of Verna Watson, now Bender, myself and my sisters, Valerie and much later Felecia. Verna was his Goddaughter, a term given at baptism when he became her Godfather thus making her my God sister.

Whenever there was 'church work' or parent teachers' activities, he was the first one in the line. So much so that he and Cousin Louise Richards (aka mother Richards) (Vin's grandmother) burnt wasps (maribuntas) nests on the old school during a clean-up exercise and didn't realize that they had left embers burning. The old school later that evening became engulfed in flames and was completely burnt down. Despite this being an accident, the two perpetrators were distraught.

He was scheduled to deliver the Good Friday message on the pulpit at the Reformation Lutheran Church on one of several occasions. This time however, he had been unfortunate to have taken a few shots of rum prior to the commencement of the three-hour service. Even though his preaching was generally quite good and coherent, he managed to say something out of the ordinary:

"If Jesus had smelt the rat that they were trying to crucify him, he wouldn't have allowed them to do so."

He was then given that false name "smell the rat" but no one dared to call him by that name to his face.

Quite interestingly, a visitor to our village stopped by and spoke to my cousin, Keith Boyle. The visitor was looking for a job and was sent by Keith to Papa but told to ask for Mr. Rat. Could you imagine how surprised and shocked Papa was when the potential worker turned up in front of him, inquiring for Mr. Rat? I'm told that Papa simply smiled and asked who had sent him.

During those intoxicated states, he would brag about how brilliant his children were and make unhealthy comparisons with several of our peers. He was extremely proud of his offspring but generally never showed his emotions and was not the lovey-dovey kind of dad.

Although I knew he loved us dearly, he never openly said it. Never once has he ever said the magic words "I love you." It might have been because of his upbringing; his feelings may not have been openly expressed.

Parents shouldn't show favoritism to their children. This can cause resentment and rivalry amongst siblings. Papa did have his favorite children and I'm pretty certain that this affected my other siblings. His preferences were clearly overt and no efforts were made to cover up.

I was offered, at the very tender age of eight years old, the very coveted opportunity to go hunting with my Papa. It simply meant me accompanying him on a hunting trip and entailed paddling quietly along the river bank while listening for sounds of wild animals e.g., wild boars and labbas (a very popular, large vegetarian rodent). There is an old Guyanese saying, really meant for visitors, that says, "If you drink creek water and eat labba, you will surely return to these shores." I sat in the front part of the canoe, all excited and happy that I was offered this golden chance to bond with Papa. I could only imagine how my brothers felt but I was still happy to 'rub their noses in it.' I don't remember the intricate details of our rendezvous but one particular incident lingers in my memory. We had been out for probably an hour when Papa whispered softly saying that he had heard something. As we moved closer, I could practically hear my heart pounding with excitement. I barely heard him mutter incoherently as he shone the three cells flashlight (a torchlight with three batteries), towards what appeared to be two shining eyes of an animal. The deafening sound of the blast from Papa's twelve-gauge shotgun was so overwhelming.

"You got it?" I managed to blurt out.

He calmly responded in the affirmative and proceeded to go ashore to pick up his trophy. He whispered softly that he was going to be back in a minute. What happened next was one of the most frightening experiences for me. When he departed with the only form of lighting, I was left in complete darkness. I was engulfed in pitch darkness and was extremely afraid and thought I was going to die. What if some strange creature managed to attack me in the dark? During what seemed like forever, I just sat there trembling, extremely terrified and wished and prayed for his speedy return.

When he returned with the huge Labba slung across his shoulders, which had run and stumbled away from where it was shot, I was so, so relieved but didn't want him to know that I was petrified. On our return and during the following day I had complete bragging rights and may have even added stories to the actual hunting trip. I never told a soul about how terrified I was during the period when I was left alone.

In those days in Cuba, it was indeed like a lost world for me; letters took on the average two to three months to reach their various destinations. It was practically impossible to make telephone calls from Guyana to Cuba and vice versa. While there, we were later told that Papa had had a terrible mishap. We felt helpless and sad; there was absolutely nothing we could have done. It was one of those half-expected incidents while we were overseas.

He was visiting one of his farms which was situated up the Manakuburi Creek and was paddling gingerly in his canoe well attired in his signature white hard hat or construction helmet. The time taken to arrive at that farm was roughly about one and a half hours.

Out of the blue, a huge dried branch fell from somewhere at the top of the forest canopy. Maybe he was not forewarned of the imminent danger because of its suddenness. The heavy branch struck him a violent blow to his poor head, knocking him unconscious to the floor of his canoe. Had it not been for his protective helmet, he might have been instantly killed. His brother, Uncle Lance Boyle happened to have been passing around the same time and found him lying in an unconscious state with his helmet smashed and bleeding through his nose. He quickly had him soaked in the icy cold water of the Manakuburi Creek. It is strangely inexplicable how cold the creek water gets, as if it's passing through a freezing chamber.

Thank God for the timely intervention of Uncle Lance who happened to be at the right place at the opportune time. He was rushed out to the health center at Ebini waterfront where he was attended to by a Medex (Dispenser) named Rorey. When the tragedy was being narrated to me, Mom said, the Good Dispenser called Rorey, did an amazing job before having Papa patched up and referred to New Amsterdam Hospital. Youngsters, it's so nice when you are highly recommended. Whatever you do, make sure that you are the best in your field, whether it is making concrete blocks or cassava balls. It was nice hearing someone being called the 'Good Dispenser.'

Papa was badly injured and it took a full day of being unconscious before improving somewhat. After regaining consciousness, he was delirious and kept saying senseless words. He was later transferred to New Amsterdam hospital where he spent about three months. Papa had survived this sad tragedy but his speech remained slurred for a while and he had developed a major stroke. He regained his balance somewhat and had to learn to walk all over again but annoying and piercing headaches plagued him for several years afterward. The slightest noise and loud music caused him to suffer immense pain and discomfort. This resulted in him being very fretful. He was indeed a very strong and resilient man to have survived that horrible accident.

My super dad's life had not been an easy one; generally, he grew up in hardship with constant and relentless work on the timber grant and then subsequently on the farm. His hands were rock hard, filled with countless calcified callouses, bruised and battered by the prolonged use of the cutlass (machete) and 4-5 lb. axe. He was a true leader in every sense, especially rolling up his sleeves and showing them how he wanted his farm bushes to be chopped. I feel so sad when I think of the countless moments of intolerable stress he might have endured. His feet were very much like his hands, disfigured by repeatedly walking without protective footwear. Prickly thorns were no match for his weather-beaten corned feet as he managed quite fine while working on the farm without boots.

It was about 3:30, one afternoon when I got a message from one of the guards at the New Market entrance to the Georgetown Public Hospital compound that my dad was looking for me and that he seemed to be injured. I immediately turned off the Olympus microscope that I was peering through and rushed through the two, or so, blocks that separated where I was at the Middle Street section of the Central Medical Laboratory. His left hand has a crude blood-soaked bandage and his arm was tied with a sling to support the injured hand.

"I was cutting a vine with my sharp cutlass and I got a bad cut," was his explanation after we had hugged each other. This had happened sometime the previous day and the gaping wound was still fresh and bleeding slightly. The tendons that controlled the movement of the fingers were completely severed as he couldn't move those digits. I took him immediately to the surgical department for instant attention. The surgeon, Dr. Francis Bailey, whom I knew very well, decided that Papa needed urgent surgery to re-join the severed tendons.

Nurse Rose, a gentle and caring individual, assured me that she was going to take special care of my Papa. She was an anesthesia nurse and a very close friend of my family. It was about 9:00 a.m. when the surgery commenced and I lingered around, not too far away, just in case I might have been needed. Just about half of an hour afterward I saw Nurse Rose rushing towards me; her face was expressionless and stared deep into my eyes.

"No, what happened? Is he alright?" By then my tears began to flow. I saw the look in her eyes, oh dear God, no, this can't happen to him!

"Your dad is fine now!" Those consoling words were like the gush of fresh morning breeze on a cool June morning. She went on to say that they had to stop the operation because he had a heart attack during the procedure but he is now okay. Thank you, dear Jesus, you spared his life! The dreadful feelings that gripped on that morning were inexplicable; Jesus Lord, he had almost died again!

We later decided that his surgery was going to be done overseas. Collin knew a good surgeon in St. Vincent who joined the damaged tendons using anesthesia that blocked the pain without putting him to sleep.

This was successfully done, and he regained the full use of his hands and fingers. To God be the glory!

My dear Papa suffered from hypertension (high blood pressure) for several years and he struggled to keep it in check. Not that he adhered to the doctor's prescribed treatment-he was not at all disciplined in this regard. It was therefore not unexpected that he suffered from a stroke.

*Papa and Mom (younger days)*

Etched in my memory are images of him that I would never, ever remove from my reservoir of pleasantries. The picture of him sitting at home, in the Eastern wing of our veranda, nicely powdered up after having had a cool evening bath, smoking a cigarette and relaxing, sometimes with his feet perched on the rails. That was his seat. No one dared occupy it, especially during the early evening hours. Sometimes I would sit there silently, in that very chair, reminiscent of those glorious days and allow my thoughts to wander. What would he have been like, had he still been alive? To picture him paddling in the 'bucket' (the long, curved part of the river called the bucket as opposed to the point head which was the other pointed curve) with his huge pram (boat made with sawn wood), well laden with hundreds of plantain bunches, almost totally obscuring him with his signature helmet at the helm, paddling slowly. The early morning vision of him, walking from the calf pen, without a shirt, again, donning his white helmet and fetching two, five-gallon containers filled with fresh cow's milk. His towel strapped high up on his waist as walked up after having had a refreshing dip in the river. Him, opening his black briefcase filled with all kinds of papers, receipts, cash wrapped with rubber bands. To hear him asking: "who used my razor? Or where are my spectacles", only to see him either having them already in his hands or on top of his head.

The sight of him writing a letter to catch the steamer-he loved to write and to give instructions. He somehow loved to do last-minute tasks, things that could have been done earlier, so that he could have been more organized. Several years later, it was one evening when I received a telephone call from his sister, aunt Norma, who lives in New Amsterdam. The sound of her voice was troubling; she might have been crying, she was very emotional.

"Andy, your father is sick bad," she said, "and I don't know what to do." Papa was really sick indeed. When I spoke to him on the phone he really didn't sound encouraging. He kept saying that this was it. Was he planning on dying? It was not normal for her to be so expressive and emotional. I assured her that I was going to come and get him the following day since it was already late and there was a closing time for the ferry that crosses the river.

We managed to get him into the front seat of my Hilux, surely not an easy feat. His arm was swollen and he just couldn't walk properly. I took him directly to the hospital where he was immediately admitted.

Later that day he was taken for emergency surgery, apparently, he had fallen into a clump of thorns that badly affected his arm. Papa had been battered throughout his life but prevailed. This time his prognosis didn't seem too promising.

After the surgery to remove a set of thorns from his left hand, I went to see him. He knew I was there but kept saying things about all of his children, some incoherent. After spending a few minutes with him I decided to head back to finish up some work that I was doing.

I was still at work when I got that dreaded call from one of the nurses at the hospital:

"Your father just died."

I was confused and disoriented. I managed to call Collin who immediately said that he was going to fly in the following day. Oh, what a tragedy, Papa was no more! He had developed septicemia as a result of the many prickly thorns in his flesh. He had fallen several days before finally being rushed for medical treatment. He only managed to live for sixty-four years but lived a tough life with purpose. I will always treasure my memories of him. He was truly a champion in every respect.

*My Papa*

# CHAPTER 34

# Central Medical Laboratory of The Georgetown Public Hospital

I loved the feeling, wow, Andy was going to commence working now, to showcase what he had learned over the years. These were particularly new and strange sentiments and I was extremely excited and eager to make a difference. When Alva Griffith and I returned to Guyana there were some clarifications with regard to our qualifications, they were not properly defined and everything was written in Spanish. I met Mrs. Audrey Moffatt, an official of the nation equivalency board. Audrey, an Indian national who is married to a Guyanese veterinarian and a very knowledgeable individual, was and still is one of the gentlest persons that I've ever met. She skillfully had our issues ironed out and we were assigned to commence work.

I was given a letter from the Public Service Ministry (PSM) and requested to report to Mrs. Trevelyn Smith, of the Personnel Department of the Ministry of Health. After meeting with her, it was decided that Alva Griffith and I would be assigned as Clinical Scientific Officers. We were then sent to report to the Central Medical Laboratory (CML) of the Georgetown Public Hospital. At CML we met with the

Director, Dr. Alden Chesney and Superintendent, Ms. Jenny LaFleur. I was beaming with enthusiasm and couldn't wait to start working.

My tenure turned out to be very good and extremely rewarding and self-gratifying. It was a very intriguing experience. I was able to implement new techniques while I was also privileged to learn from the existing staff. After a few years, I was appointed as head of the Tropical Diseases Laboratory which was situated in the same building that housed the Malaria Diagnostic Center. Not very long after commencing work, Dr. Roges, a Cuban microbiologist who lectured in the Health Sciences Department at the University of Guyana, announced that he was leaving Guyana. It was the end of his sojourn and I was asked to replace him temporarily as a part-time lecturer of Microbiology, Immunology, Laboratory Practice and Parasitology. It meant juggling work and teaching but despite having to travel back and forth between the Georgetown Public Hospital and the University of Guyana, I found it to be immensely satisfying and self-gratifying. I realized that I had developed a great passion for lecturing and did it with flair and purpose. Apart from being somewhat stimulating, it kept me current with new developments in the sciences as I had to make sure that I was updated with the latest technologies and innovations.

My lecturing style was somewhat formatted to simulate the Cuban experience. In these parts of the world, it was a sort of more casual learning system. I remember, quite embarrassingly putting out one of my medical students simply because he was, as I thought, very indecently attired in short pants. In retrospect, I now believe that that was totally ridiculous of me. Then again, in your opinion, was I wrong?

My tenure at the University of Guyana was extremely fulfilling and I did deliver personally from my standpoint.

It was somewhere around the second year after I had returned that I met this gorgeous specimen of a lady. I was in deep conversation with Dr. Debra Dye somewhere outside of the matron's office, in the compound of the Georgetown Hospital when she passed by. She raised her hands in salutation and smiled sweetly, our eyes met briefly, probably for a fraction of a second. I automatically raised my hands to return the greeting but little did I know that she hadn't even noticed me.

"Debbie, wow, who is that beauty?" I remember asking my friend with whom I was chatting.

"Oh, she is one of those returning doctors from Russia," was her brushing aside response. It was at that point that I expressed my interest in getting to know her and Debbie eventually obliged. So, I left it in Debbie's hands to organize because it might have been rude or rather pompous of me to make my acquaintance without knowing each other previously.

A few days later, during that same week, I was traveling in a mini bus in the vicinity of the Stabroek Market when I saw her again. She was wearing a light blue pants suit and was holding what appeared to be a shoe box. I waved at her but she didn't notice me once again. My heart throbbed frantically as I secretly vowed to myself that I was going to meet with that lovely lady. She seemed so happy as she walked gingerly to board another minibus. I briefly thought of disembarking in order to introduce myself but quickly retreated on that idea.

It so happened that I was busy reading an urgent differential blood count under the microscope that I didn't notice when the door was opened. I also might have been deep in my own thoughts while differentiating between the various cells, polymorphonuclear neutrophils, monocytes, lymphocytes, eosinophils, etc.

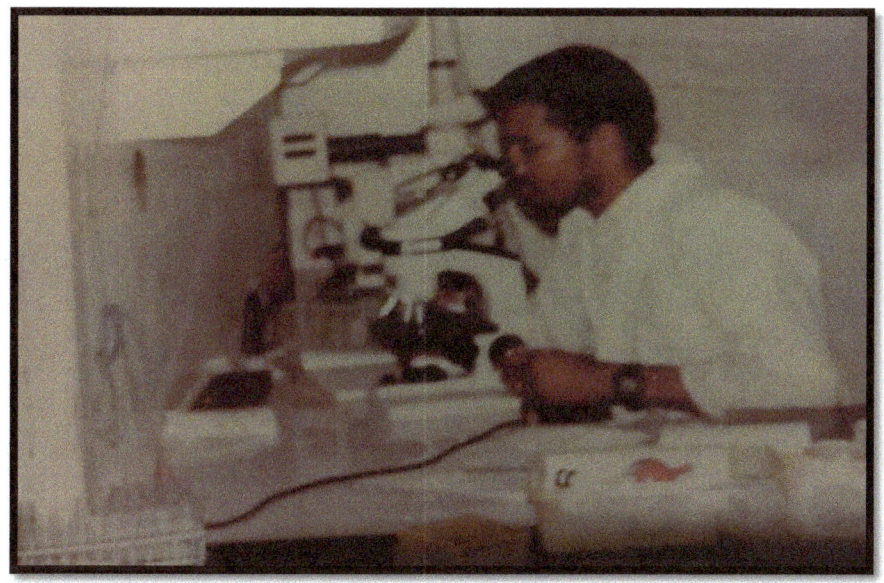

*A younger me at work*

"You seem to be too busy to meet my friend." It was Debbie's voice; she had brought her to meet with me. I continued to peer through my Olympus microscope as I counted the cells. Without turning I raised my hand and gestured that I needed a few more seconds as I didn't want to break my rhythm.

"Debbie, I have work to do, what's the problem?" I muttered as I turned slowly around from peering into the microscope. You could imagine the shock that came with this impromptu visit. I immediately peeled off my soiled gloves and got up shakily as I headed to wash my hands at the nearby sink.

"I'm Andrew Boyle, everyone calls me Andy." I managed to mutter these words nervously when being introduced. "I'm Karen," she responded. She returned my stare but I didn't detect any 'positive signs'. Debbie muttered something praising both of our characters and quickly offered an explanation and asked to be excused.

I had planned to steer our conversation in a certain direction but all of those strategies had flown through the window. My breath had been short and my poor little traumatized heart pounded with excitement. You bet I was super nervous and somewhat confused but nevertheless happy that we had been introduced to each other. We chatted briefly and innocuously but I was clearly impressed. She was brave and seemingly naïve but smart and drop-dead gorgeous. I managed to, sheepishly, let her know that I would be happy to see her again. She explained that she had a critical patient to check on and that it was her pleasure to have met me. If she only knew that the distinct pleasure was really mine and not hers. Or did we experience mutual feelings? When she left, I did an introspection into how I had conversed with her. Did I turn her off? Was my nervousness evident? Should I have offered her a seat? 'Oh, I probably blew it!' I told myself but she did express that she was happy to have finally met me. Was this just small talk?

Strangely, Debbie dropped by soon afterward to find out how it went. She came in as sneakily as she had done earlier, with a wicked smirk, very much like Collin's signature smirk, on her lips, "How did it go? You like my friend, eh?"

"I'm going to marry that girl," was my response. I had been involved with a lovely girl called Nelly-Angela (not her real name for privacy) but somehow, I don't think that we were compatible.

It happened once again! The following day I was playing chess in the Doctors' flats with Drs. Trevor Duncan, Francis Bailey, and Bro. John. This was a daily occurrence at around midday time and some afternoons. Those guys were smart and cunning chess players but we all shared mutual victories from time to time. Trevor and I were embattled at one of those chess sessions. Strangely I had difficulties beating him and found it harder than most of my encounters with Dr. Bailey and Bro. John. He, on the other hand, had difficulties winning while playing with those two guys. I casually looked up and there she was with Dr. Michelle Collins, another doctor with whom I was very familiar. My little heart began to behave erratically once again. I had met with hundreds of women but never was I this nervous and fascinated. Was I smitten? By then I had lost interest in the game and had stopped focusing. They came directly towards me and this time our eyes locked. I was about to stand to greet them when I barely heard Trevor exclaim, "Checkmate!" That was the end of the game, he had beaten me. It really didn't matter to me, who cared about chess, I was deeply concentrating on more interesting things now. Michelle made a gesture, "Andy, I want you to meet my friend, Karen."

"Karen, this is Andy."

I stretched out my arms and held on to her hand for a little longer than usual. "We met before but it's a distinct pleasure to make your acquaintance once again," I muttered, but this time a bit more positive and confident. This was, again, quite a coincidence, very strange that we kept running into each other's paths. Were we destined for bigger things?

Our running into each other happened more and more frequently and our friendship grew. We spoke very often on the telephone, almost every afternoon, and maybe early evenings. I stayed with Cousin Mary Lindie-Gibson at 134 Amla Avenue, Prashad Nagar and their telephone often gave problems. It meant therefore that I had to use the neighbor's, Elton Isaacs' phone. This must have been of extreme inconvenience to Elton and his family to have to shout out that I had a caller on the line, practically every day. I'm eternally grateful to them for allowing me to utilize their services without complaining. When I think of our first lunch date, I often wonder why I took her to eat in that crappy Chinese restaurant. It was situated on Middle Street, very close to Cummings Street, just around where those two streets met, not far away from the Georgetown Public Hospital. I guess my means were not up to scratch and that is what I could have afforded at that time. I'm not sure how it was perceived by her but all that mattered was the fact that I felt honored to be spending some quality time with this lovely lady with whom I was madly in love. Strange enough after several years of marriage we visited the rundown restaurant to bring back those old memories and we both had a good laugh.

Karen and I spent more and more of our free time together and our friendship blossomed. She lived alone with her dad who was rarely at home, so invariably I would spend extended hours at her place. It so happened that we had gone dancing at the Library Disco and came home at around 2:00 a.m. the following day. It was a really fabulous evening; we danced and had a couple of drinks. It began to rain after the taxi dropped us off at her place so we decided that I should stay over, after all, it was Saturday evening.

The following morning, probably around 10:00 a.m., we were still in bed when we heard the front door being opened. Geeze, her dad had come home. My fancy and shiny black shoes were left at the door. Oh, how careless of me, this was going to be awkward! Being an old soldier, he would have surely noticed my footwear sitting in front of the door. Colonel Clarence Gordon Retd. was a nice but very strict man and I didn't want to take advantage of his good nature.

*What to do now? Shall we both have a chat with him with an explanation that I decided to stay over because it was late? Or should I wait until he goes into his room and then disappear? Hell no! Of course not! I was the man here, and I will own up to my deeds.* I quickly slipped on a t-shirt and a pair of short pants. Over the past few months and weeks, I had left a few pieces of casual clothing at her place.

The Colonel was perched in his favorite chair while he browsed through the Sunday Stabroek News.

"Good morning, Sir!" I greeted him in a not too confident manner. We had met on several occasions and he knew that we were great friends but my sleeping over was not in the bargain. During those visits to his shop in Broad Street, we might have exchanged only a few pleasantries, more like 'brief getting to know you' kinds of exchanges. Karen was looking from the upper level as I approached her dad but she was quiet and didn't say a word.

"Good morning, Colonel, how are you doing?" I managed to muster some courage to greet him. He might have muttered a muffled response but I didn't notice. *What was I going to tell Pops?* I wondered to myself. I then bravely took up a seat on the sofa next to him and began to stutter my explanations.

"I know how it looks but we were out until late last night so I decided to spend the night. I love your daughter and we wish to have your blessings; I want to marry her, if you wouldn't mind."

*Phew! I finally got it off my chest.* He cleared his throat and gently lay his newspapers on the coffee table.

"I've been silently impressed by your mannerisms; you seem like a nice chap from good stocks. You have my blessings but you guys need to take it easy and not rush too much."

By then Karen had descended and was standing nervously at my side, "Yes dad, Andy is a great guy and treats me well." We chit-chatted for a bit about my parents and general things, then he offered an excuse that he had to go somewhere and left us alone. In reality, I actually hadn't asked her for her hand in marriage but instead had done the request through her dad. I meant to do it properly with an engagement and the full 'nine yards' but my funds were sort of on the low side, or rather non-existent may I confess.

# CHAPTER 35

# The Marriage

After a relatively short period of dating, we had decided to get married. We made that big decision to tie the knot on February 15, 1992, just a bit over two years since my return from Cuba. It was a major step but I felt ready to live a committed life. There was quite a bit of nervousness that began to creep in as the time grew nigh. *Was I ready for such a game changer? Where was Rosebud? What if it didn't work out?* Rosebud and I had seemingly grown apart and lots of stories were told to me and I really thought she had moved on. We had been apart for several years and the extended separation did not help at all.

I met Karen's lovely mother the week before our wedding. The mere thought of me meeting my mother-in-law was not comforting. My pals told me several horror stories and scary details of encounters with the mothers of their wives. What preceded Princess May Gordon, Karen's mother, was that she is a no-nonsense person who didn't mince her words and was clearly not intimidated to let her feelings be known. She was not afraid to call a spade a spade and was quite willing to give anyone a good tongue-lashing. I must admit however, that our meeting was truly magical and we got on like a wooden house on fire. I felt that we both liked each other and further, some people thought we actually resembled each other. Funny enough, my friends thought she was my mother and my mother was Karen's. You see, my mother's complexion is dark and her mother is lighter. I have also found her to be extremely supportive and totally unbiased in her wise and prudent modus operandi. Over the years our bond of friendship grew and we were able to discuss matters quite objectively.

*Princess May Gordon and I*

She took charge of our wedding preparations and did so admirably. This took the load off our shoulders and gave us some breathing space. Our big day was finally here! Andy was getting married! Dr. Maurice Edwards, a mutual friend of ours, offered to take me to the church. He, his wife, Yonette, Drs. Clement McEwan, Ronald Aaron, Trevor Duncan, Francis Bailey, Holly Alexander along with Pam, Ann Aaron amongst a few others, and I often partied together. Our get-togethers were frequent and we didn't need to have any sound reason to meet for a drink, music, a good gaff and dancing. We met at each other's houses and celebrated birthdays and other occasions, real or unreal.

Dr. Maurice Edwards drove me to church in his shiny, gold-colored car. I was on target to be prompt for my wedding. All of the finishing touches were made by my crew which included Mom, cousin Mary Lindie/Gibson, Big G, and others. Big G, offered me a double shot of Johnny Walker whiskey and said that it should settle my nerves. *Boy, was I nervous!* My curly hair was well-groomed and my white outfit was immaculate. I looked and felt like a million bucks. *Whew! My big day had arrived!*

Eddie and I chatted along the way to the Calvary Lutheran Church, on Alexander and North Roads. Before long, we had arrived, it seemed like the fastest ride ever. *This was it Bro, hold yourself together now, it's your show,* I whispered to myself as I stepped out of the open doors of my ride. Eddie said good luck as he opened the door; he is a very courteous fellow. It was really super nice of him to have offered to take me to the ceremony.

Dr. Gavin Peters and Mr. Warren LaFleur, our two groomsmen, along with bridesmaids, Dr. Marcia Chung and Ms. Dacia Robertson were all beautifully attired and waiting in front of the church. They stood there all elegantly clad and carrying a long-stemmed, fresh red rose. The groomsmen wore white tucks and gray tuxedos while the bridesmaids donned wine red dresses with silver gray trimmings and matching shoes. Oh, how gorgeous they looked!

This must be how presidents and celebrities feel when they step out to the sounds of cheering crowds. Warren and I were high school buddies and Gavin and I had studied together in Cuba. He was in the same class with Collin, my brother. They had both eagerly agreed to support me as my best men and I was extremely honored to have them serve in that capacity. Pastor Lochan who was also there amongst the crowd, all waiting patiently, quickly ushered us into the already packed church. Apparently, my lovely bride was already on her way and so, it was my duty to be on the altar while I awaited her arrival.

Everyone wanted to get a glimpse of the beautiful bride who was smack on time. It might have been a mere ten to fifteen minutes after I had arrived that I heard the cheering; she had just reached. Pastor Lochan beckoned and asked the congregation to stand and welcome my bride. I had already been up at the altar anxiously awaiting her arrival. We were finally married. Now it was time for the wedding reception and then the honeymoon.

The ceremony at the Country Pride was fabulous and colorful. Due to financial constraints, our guest list was certainly not as lavish as we would have hoped. It therefore meant that lots of our respective families were disappointingly left out. This phenomenon is not unusual in these parts of the world and it is as if people do not understand or simply do not want to understand. Two young couples venturing off into the unknown are often not financially endowed, therefore, it's suicidal to want to please everyone by having a huge reception. We captured loads of photographs in the lovely Botanical Gardens in the vicinity of the manatee ponds area and on the famous Kissing Bridge. By this time, it was somewhat tiring.

Dr. Alden Chesney was a fantastic and witty master of ceremonies who lightened the occasion with his jokes. There were many speakers and amongst those was my grandfather, Menzo. Daddy Menzo took the microphone and said some very pleasant words, including sound advice to us, the newly married couple. He closed quite nicely by singing a song, oh, how touching that was. Sadly, it was decided that Papa wouldn't be allowed to attend my wedding for fear that he was going to ruin the auspicious occasion. Papa might have found it extremely difficult to restrain himself from taking a few drinks to celebrate his dear Andy's big day. In retrospect, I'm so disappointed he was not able to attend, after all, he is my father but I do understand the rationale for not having him attend.

The Woodbine Hotel was the classical honeymoon spot, it was low budget and relatively decent. We spent one lovely evening there but were rudely interrupted by members of the wedding party. It was a bit surprising that our mothers along with some other relatives paid us a visit in our room. We shared some wonderful moments and raised three awesome young and bright children. Will they eventually take over and improve our thriving business? Now that's a question to be answered, hopefully when the time is right.

# CHAPTER 36

# Eureka Medical Laboratories Inc. (EML)

I t might have been sometime in 1994, probably towards the end of that year when it was unofficially commenced. March 5, 1995 was officially designated as the day EML commenced operations. My contract with the government had ended and I was preparing to venture out on my own. It was something I had always wanted to do but couldn't because of having been constrained by my contractual arrangements with the government. The decision was made to 'set up shop' but we had no name for the new entity. It's important to note that the most important steps for the realization of this massive project were to visualize one's dream, make a start and execute the plan accordingly. The name of the entity was coined long after the decision was made to commence operations. Finding a name proved to be a daunting but interesting and somewhat intriguing task. Possible suggested names like Boyle's Medical Lab and Family Clinic, The Lab and Family Clinic, Georgetown Medical Lab and Family Clinic, and Andrew's Medical Lab were made. The proposed names were numerous but none really resonated with me in the way I had wanted.

Then it happened on a lovely Sunday afternoon, Karen and I were relaxing in front of the TV, watching a movie. During the interlude, several ads came on as per norm and amongst them was one with an Eureka brand vacuum cleaner. As soon as the actor who was showcasing the device exclaimed "Eureka!" we both looked at each other. It was so automatic! We unanimously decided at the same time that our moment of glory had arrived! We had found it. Eureka was going to be the name of our medical facility.

Eureka is a Greek word which means "I've found it." Quite an appropriate name indeed! First and foremost, I've found my dream, Eureka! When we discover what's wrong with someone as in the case of finding the species of malaria that a patient has, we can say Eureka. When our patients/clients find us, they can say Eureka. This three folded concept is enough positive vindication for a perfect name.

We received positive vibes and great encouragement from almost all of our relatives and friends. My main cheerleader, Collin, was not in favor though. He thought that it would be difficult to compete against the existing heavyweights that are already in the healthcare industry. This time I decided to go against his suggestions and moved ahead with my dream. Sometimes in life you need to disregard naysayers. I always respected his judgment but this time my self-belief that this project was going to bear fruit was overwhelming.

The resources were pooled together and a plan was devised to bring into fruition this great concept. I was rather fortunate to have a combination of fruitful sources of initial funding for the eventual realization of EML. Kudos to my dear parents for the injection of a reasonable set of funds from the sale of some of their cows and all of mine. My lovely mother-in-law also contributed quite significantly to this urgent and incubating venture. Despite all of the support, it was felt that the financial resources were not quite adequate for the execution of this project. Ideally, some assistance from the banks would have been the 'icing on the cake,' but this was not to be. As a good family friend, Dr. Barton Scotland, skillfully arranged for a colleague to draft a very attractive project proposal. It was very strategically done and seemed like the perfect document. Surely, we were going to get the funds requested.

An appointment was made with the loan officer at a popular local bank and I felt elated that I was going to be granted the five million dollars that I was requesting. I donned my best long sleeve shirt and appropriate tie that matched my combination of clothing. My light blue shirt along with a matching striped tie, navy blue trousers and black, well-polished shoes were exquisite. After all, blue is my favorite color and I really thought I was smartly dressed for the interview. Interviews are a big deal, it's pertinent to dress properly and to be cheerful and polite.

*This is going to be my big day,* I thought to myself. "Be positive Andy, you got this!" I whispered. I approached the officer to whom I had previously sent an electronic copy of my supposedly strong proposal. I entered her office and stood there with a bright good morning and a smile. Daddy often taught us to be polite and await a request to be seated, whenever in someone else's office. She didn't offer me a seat and I just stood there. *Andy, this is not turning out as you had envisaged,* I thought to myself. She immediately proceeded to burst my bubble. It was as though I was being lumped with, 'you people without security to secure loans.' Maybe her day had been messed up by a previous customer because she simply ranted and raved about the common people who wanted to achieve greatness but didn't have the means to do so. She picked up my carefully drafted document and threw it towards me, not in a hostile manner but with some bit of disdain.

"Sorry, you have no collateral, we cannot take this risk." She quickly and unconsciously dismissed me while continuing to punch the keys of her computer. I stood there and waited to see if, perhaps she was going to add or clarify something else. I was completely nonplussed when she waved her hands as if to say, 'that's all, go your way.' I left the bank very dejected and extremely disappointed. Her painful words coupled with her strange smirk as if she gloated over my inadequacies kept swirling in my confused head. I felt so small and insignificant as I shrunk in front of whom I thought was a heartless loan officer. The ridicule I felt reminded me of when I was laughed at during my high school days when they made me feel insignificant because of where I came from. Strange enough, I felt the same way and deep down inside of me I made a similar resolution, just like I had done in those days.

"B--ch, I'm going to show you, just you wait and see."

I was upset and disappointed but left with a deep resolve to prove her wrong. That meeting might have been a distasteful one but maybe it was a blessing in disguise. In retrospect, I think that getting the loan and having to pay the hefty monthly installments might have been a burden to my newly initiated entity. I often advise and even caution my friends and those individuals who are in the process of commencing business ventures, not to take bank loans to start businesses. Alternatively, you can take a loan but have enough cushion to ride the starting up waves. On the other hand, when the business begins to earn profits and would have controlled its niche market, then is the time to seek assistance from the bankers for expansion. Otherwise, it's difficult to initiate a business and service a loan simultaneously. Of course, this also pertains to the type and magnitude of the business. There is a saying that banks give you an umbrella during the nice and sunny weather but take it away when it's raining. *Do you think that this statement has merit?*

Despite the odds, EML commenced operations and grew steadily. First, it was one patient per day then three and eventually seven. I was ecstatic! This was very encouraging and heartening. The level of support was admirable and surely, persons clearly desired Eureka to succeed. It was instilled in our few staff members to be super courteous and to treat our patients with decorum. EML, over the years, continually implemented new and innovative services and carved a very strong brand image. It might have been somewhere around our second or third year of existence when I clearly remember writing a letter to my parents.

Some of the writing went like this, "Dear Mom and Papa, hope this letter finds you in good health. As for me and my family, we are all doing fine. Tony is a big boy and little Andrew is becoming a chatterbox and indeed great joy. Eureka is growing nicely and today we had seven patients. I'm beginning to see the light in the tunnel. You know I'm now deeply convinced that Eureka will become so great, you will be gently surprised and proud of me."

When I look back at those humble days, I cannot help but reminisce on those moments, the formative ones of this truly amazing journey. I will never forget the gentle words of that grandmother when we discovered what was wrong with her ailing, 8-year-old grandson, "Thank you son, may God continue to bless you." The numerous thank you cards and countless words of gratitude from our many clients were like fuel to a hungry fire. These kudos and encouragement spurred me on to continue and strive to be as our vision now says, "To be the Caribbean's leading, state-of-the-art chain of medical laboratories, etc."

After operating for just about five years in the Waterloo Street location another opportunity presented itself. A piece of land, quite strategically placed in Thomas Street, was up for sale. It was a chance that could not have been ignored. The cost for that piece of land was $8,000,000 and this time the same bank that had shunned me, agreed to assist. Once again, a team of construction people, ably led by Colonel Clarence Gordon Retd. sprang into action. It was a joy to witness the transformation of the relatively narrow piece of land into our first building.

We have and continue to receive overwhelming support from our biochemical engineers (Lovell, Omesh, Aubrey and team) throughout the years. Notably also is the tangible and loyal support from Shundell Sampson, Kim, Vanessa, Wonica, Nazara, Aarti, Varsha, Kamini, LaLa, Peta, Christine, Jackie, Ren, Cheryl, Jason, Shawn, Dominic, Martina, Sybil, Bonny, Stephen, Germaine, Kurt, Bibi, Gabriel, Sophie, Colwyn, Fauzia, Karen C, Rouchelle, Shaundell, our doctors, the late Dawn DaSilva and countless others. Thank you for your amazing service.

During the evolution and growth of our laboratory service, I did a fair amount of traveling to visit sister labs and organizations overseas. These visits were done with the aim of improving our service and to keep ahead of the profession. I became a member of CASMET (Caribbean Association of Medical Technologists) and rose to the rank of Vice President.

Visits to the DNA Diagnostic Center (DDC), Center of Diseases Control (CDC), Caribbean Epidemiology Center (CAREC), Jamaican, Surinamese, French Guyanese, Brazilian, St Lucian, Bajan and Vincentian Labs were all quite fruitful and eye opening. I was also honored to be a part of several organizations namely, The Georgetown Chamber of Commerce & Industry (GCCI), Guyana Association of Medical Laboratory Professionals (GAMLAP), where I served as President on several occasions, The Guyana Kidney Foundation, Guyana Allied Professionals Council where I also served as President and the now defunct Guyana Association of Professionals (GAP) where I served as vice president.

*Andy*

Later I formed a few other companies namely, Caribbean Wind and Sun Inc. (CWS), Amazonia Farms Inc. Eureka Atlantic Offshore Medical Services Inc. (EAOMS) CWS is mainly involved in providing solar power services to our clients, particularly our riverain folks. This entity reminds me of my solar cooker project that was successfully done during my high school days. I had created a convex shaped foil-covered device that reflected rays of the sun to one focal point where a suspended dark-colored can with water absorbed the reflected solar energy. In the experiment, under the guidance of our Physics Master, Mr. Andrew Mancey, we were only required to show a 5-degree increase from the starting temperature. The water in my black can boiled instead, Mr. Eusi Rogers, the main man in CWS, continues to do an excellent job. As a result of this growing institution, my home in Felicity, Mom's house at Haraculi, EML Anna Regina and Amazonia Farms Inc., are all fully powered by solar energy. The two EML buildings and soon-to-be three in Thomas Street, Georgetown are 80% powered by energy from the sun.

Amazonia Farms Inc. was initially started as a collaborative effort among some of my siblings. Our first venture started at Haraculi but after a few months of operation, we noticed that it was almost impossible to operate from so far. The transportation difficulties were insurmountable. Eventually, I managed to secure a plot of land on the highway and there the company became a solid entity. Mr. Boodram, his sons and their families form the backbone of this egg production entity. I'm proud to admit that the nicely branded Amazonia eggs are now a household name and our eggs can be conspicuous in the major supermarkets of Guyana.

Our newly-found and booming oil industry in Guyana is likely to catapult our nation to higher heights. EAOMS is anticipated to provide services to that industry in occupational health and safety to our clients. Atlantic Offshore Medical Services our partnering company in Newfoundland, Canada is working along with us to deliver quality services in occupational health and safety to our clients in this industry.

Warren Buffet said, "Never depend on a single income, make an investment to create a second source." Bill Gates further went on to say, "Focus on more than one stream of income, the average millionaire has seven."

Youngsters, you have your work cut out. Start your businesses and dedicate your energies in fulfilling your dreams.

# CHAPTER 37

# You are Not the Father!

C ould you possibly comprehend how hearing this might have felt? "I'm very sorry, you are not the father!" DNA testing was revolutionized in Guyana by Eureka and the various scenarios encountered, vastly varied from person to person. These cases were mainly requested by the courts or by those persons who required peace of mind because of probable doubts. There were a few that stood out and are notable of mention. It should be noted that for confidentiality and privacy, the real names of these characters herewith have been changed.

## Case # 1

A policewoman, a probation officer, relatives, two supposed teenage parents, and a one-week-old baby boy all converged on my office. The young man who was barely eighteen years old was being accused of raping the now fourteen-year-old child. Even though, according to them, the sexual encounters were supposedly consensual, this could be considered to be statutory rape because of the age of the teen mother. His parents were very supportive of him and promised to adopt the baby, if proven to be his.

The police, on the other hand, wanted to enforce the law and to have him prosecuted in the courts. The poor, young Amerindian mother sat quietly and was adamant that the child was the young man's. I proceeded to do the necessary paperwork and take the required buccal samples from all three parties in question. It must have been a humiliating experience for these parties.

When the results came back, to our utter surprise, he was not the father of the child.

Time for regrouping! The relevant parties then returned to my office. The police and social services individuals now began to put pressure on the young teenage mother.

"Tell us who is the real father," the policeman angrily stated. "Yo wasting we precious time."

The young teenage mother had become the focus of their attention. After a session of threats mixed with some cajoling, she agreed to subject another individual to be tested for paternity. This was quite intriguing and indeed, hard to comprehend. A fourteen-year-old with multiple sex partners? Well, she was actually thirteen when she had apparently conceived.

This young lad, the second bloke, was not much older than she was. He was only 15 years old and had admitted to having had repeated sexual intercourse with the child. He too, like the former accused, was committed to taking care of the newborn if proven to be his. Once again, we proceeded to go through with the routine exercise of sample collection.

It usually takes one week or sometimes a little more to get back the results from the ever-efficient DNA Diagnostic Center of Ohio, USA. I imagine that this might probably have been the longest waiting period of their lives, especially for the clients being tested.

To all of our amazement, once again, he too was not the father. Yes, the second young man likewise, was not the real daddy. It was at this juncture that the police again began to apply more emotional pressure on the young mother. They again threatened to have her incarcerated and to put her baby into foster care. I was beginning to feel sorry for her. Clearly, she seemed lost and very emotionally affected.

The teenage mother held on to her story that the DNA was incorrect and that the last one was the correct father. She was even beginning to sound very convincing. So, what happened to the first accused? Was that an error too?

After about half of an hour of threats and harsh words, she eventually suggested that there was another possibility. She had clearly been cornered and didn't have any further plausible defense. The young mother asked to be left alone with her mother. We all left them in my office but we could hear them having a heated exchange of words. "You are lying! It's the truth!" These were some of the audible exchanges that we managed to decipher.

Finally, after their private moment together, it was finally and surprisingly suggested that another prospect was the girl's stepfather. It eventually turned out that the middle-aged stepfather was apparently having a sexual relationship with his teenage stepdaughter. Eureka! We have found the culprit! It turned out that he was indeed the father of the baby. Oh, what a disgusting and sad world we live in! This is one of the many instances when I receive tremendous satisfaction for being able to provide a good service.

## Case # 2

An appointment with two clients was made to have their chain of custody samples collected. An elderly señor wanted to test his alleged daughter for possible sponsorship to the USA. The eager 21-year-old "daughter" seemed so full of energy and was super excited to be sponsored by her alleged daddy. The strange thing was that they both had similar names for example Andrew Drakes and Andrea Drakes (of course, not their real names for confidentiality). The question came about because her name was changed by deed-poll and because Andrea was not signed for by her "father" shortly after her birth.

It was indeed quite a pleasant experience interacting and chatting with these clients. They seemed to be "into each other" and looked as though they were "making up" for lost time. They were seeing each other for the first time but had been in constant contact via the telephone and also social media. Why couldn't most clients be similar? On several other occasions, my pleasant office space became like a war zone with the hurling of insults and in extreme cases, fights and other physical altercations.

The required swabs, photographs and copies of the appropriate legal identifications were made. These very cordial and 'nice' clients left arm in arm, almost like newly found lovers. The following week when they returned to discuss their results and seemed even more 'chummy' and giggly. I wasted no time in opening the sealed package and proceeded to deliver the findings of these long-awaited DNA results.

"I'm sorry, you are not Miss Drakes' father."

Mr. Drakes' arm came immediately off Andrea's shoulder with such haste as though he had just been in contact with a live electric wire.

"What?" he blurted with his eyes bulging and darting about his clearly angry face. I carefully reread the results and he now jumped to his feet and began hurling angry and hurtful words at poor Andrea:

"You go and find your father, you little bitch."

By this time Andrea had curled herself into a small ball at the furthest corner of the sofa. I could imagine her whispering under her breath, 'Is this a crazy dream? What did I do to deserve this kind of life?' This was a total transformation. Were these the same two 'lovie dovie' father and daughter who came in earlier?

All my years of DNA collection I attempt not to become involved and try to stay out and act as the neutral party, as it should be. This one hit me very hard and I decided to intervene forthwith. I asked in a calm but firm voice that Andrea kindly step outside of my office momentarily.

As soon as the door closed, I pounced and it was at this point that I told Mr. Drakes how childish and totally out of place he was being. His distasteful insults that were aimed at Andrea were unfounded and baseless. Even though Andrea had practically gone past the tender teenage years to have been psychologically affected, it must be extremely painful and heart-rending for her. She didn't ask to be born and clearly, it was not her fault. There is no reason why he needed to be so obnoxious and self- centered. When I was finished counseling and telling him what was on my mind, he was in tears and seemed to be so repentant. He expressed deep remorse and regrets for behaving so insensitively. He further explained that he was very upset with her mother but indeed it should not be directed at Andrea. I then invited Andrea back into my office and watched as they held each other and cried like babies.

It was not surprising when, after a few weeks, I received a tearful call from Andrea. She had been allowed to be sponsored by her "dad." "Thank you, thank you sir." The U.S. Embassy had been lenient and they allowed Andrea to join him in New York.

Such testimonies are like wind beneath my wings and make me truly happy to be a contributor to the solution.

## Case # 3

Some mornings at our main office can be extremely hectic, especially those of Mondays, Tuesdays, and Wednesdays. It is as though clients cannot wait for their weekends to end before seeking medical assistance. So, in those instances steps are usually taken to deal effectively with the large influx of clients during those hours.

It was on one of those busy mornings when a couple, their one-month-old child, along with the maternal grandmother entered the waiting area. The grandma came into the filled waiting area in a rage and was hurling accusations like a mad woman. The scene created by this "mother-in-law" (grandma) was not dissimilar to a rowdy fish market scenario when two vendors are about to fight over a customer. The gist of the story is that she claimed that the man in question had raped her daughter and that the lab (my dear lab) was going to cover up because he (the alleged father) had lots (nuff) of money and was going to bribe us. She continued to perform at the top of her voice and in front of a packed audience. Strange enough, neither of the couples said a word. After entertaining the packed waiting area for a fleeting moment, they were ushered into my office for processing. This entailed the scanning of legal documents, taking of instant photographs, signing of chain of custody paperwork and of course the collection of buccal swabs from the appropriate parties. I cautioned her that her vulgar outbursts would not be permitted in my office. She then asked my permission to quietly tell me the whole story.

She claimed that her daughter had never been with a man before and comes from a decent home. At this time, the alleged father muttered something about how she should have had better control over her "#%>?<~ing" daughter. Well, it was at this point I had to ask the disorderly lady to leave my office. She lunged for and grabbed my letter opener and was going to stab her supposed son-in-law. With a quick maneuver I grabbed her arm and forcibly ejected her and asked my secretary to have security escort her out of the building.

We proceeded to do the process while I could still hear her ranting and raving outside of the building. The gentleman had his samples collected and he left hurriedly and while he was leaving his phone rang and he was deep in conversation while he passed near to his fretting 'mother-in-law.' By then some of my staff had peeped to see whether there was actually going to be another confrontation with her 'son-in-law.' Gladly, there were no further occurrences.

After a few days, they were all summoned to receive the findings of their DNA test results. She came in quietly this time but it was as though the "woman from hell" was prepared for another fight. Even though she seemed subdued, the look in her eyes spelled trouble.

I carefully opened the sealed envelope and then immediately disclosed the contents.

"Sir, I'm sorry, you are not the father of the child."

This time both of the female clients jumped up simultaneously,

"Fraud! You get paid! This is not right!"

The daughter started to cry uncontrollably while hurling insults. Strange enough, the mother said that she saw him (her 'son-in-law') on the phone while he was leaving the lab last week.

"He was talking to you and arranging for you to do your nonsense."

She then held her daughter's hand saying that she was going to take this to another level and that I was going to hear from her lawyer. They left hurriedly, but not before spitting a barrage of angry accusations.

Shortly after they left, I received a string of WhatsApp messages from the mother of the baby, requesting that I change the results and that she was going to make it worth my while (whatever that meant). I clearly explained that those kinds of practices were not done here at Eureka and that she should have a chat with her quarrelsome mother and explain that she was involved with another man. It must have been about an hour afterward that I received a call from an attorney insisting that I redo the tests or else he was going to write me a lawyer's letter with the aim of prosecuting me in the courts of law. I calmly explained to him how unprofessional he was being and that the tests were properly done and there is no way that those results could have been compromised. I further informed him that I was in possession of text messages from the mother of that baby asking whether I could alter the findings and that I should be the one pressing charges instead. He was now more confused and calmed down his rhetoric.

Wow, finally, at this point it seemed as though that saga had ended there. It didn't! About one month later the mother of the child brought in the real father for testing. Oh, how some parents can be misled by their children. Or was this simply a created drama?

Many of our DNA clients live in first-world countries. It is a fact that many of these male clients come home, especially during the summer and winter months and leave their offspring. In many cases, they are blamed to have fathered children during these vacation periods.

An elderly man who claimed to be a medical doctor scheduled an appointment and came for testing. He was nicely dressed and spoke with a deep Yankee accent. Let's call him Balram for confidentiality and his young partner, Kamini. This young subdued Indian mother appeared to be clearly not more than fifteen years old. She never looked up nor did she ever mutter a word and seemed to be ashamed and out of place. Balram bragged about the many properties he had and how he was going to sponsor Kamini and their newly born son. He talked throughout the collection exercise, offering compliments about the standards set by Eureka and the courteousness of my team. He further insisted that he alone be given the results and promised to share them with Kamini. He asked for her approval and she nodded in agreement. He was due to return to New York the following day and would commence the required documentation for sponsorship of the baby and later Kamini.

It is very common for those clients who pay for the tests to request exclusive rights to the results. I often caution them that that was not a transparent practice and it would be better to have the findings discovered at the same time by both parties. Balram did turn out to be that father and to my surprise and amazement, he told Kamini that the results were back and that he was not the father of that lovely baby. This wicked act was brought to my attention when I received a call from Kamini's mother saying that she was threatening to commit suicide because she knew that Balram was the father of her child unlike what was apparently discovered in our results. I was so upset and perturbed to even fathom that someone could be this devious. How could someone, especially a medical professional, who had a seemingly well-off appearance, be so callous and heartless. When I shared the good news with Kamini's mother, she was speechless and couldn't thank me enough. I provided her with the name of a lawyer from her village and promised to send her the relevant documents.

I then jumped on the phone and told Balram that he was the lowest being I've ever met in my life and that he had committed a fraudulent act by knowingly misconstruing our results. After listening to me for a while, he muttered "sarry maan" and eventually hung up the phone. I was fuming and extremely disturbed by this conman. I guess you live and learn about our fellow man.

I am told that he eventually agreed to pay child support because of the clever intervention and persistence of that crafty lawyer.

## Case # 4

When you think that you have seen it all, another surprise rolls through the doors.

A regular non chain of custody or peace of mind case was once again requested of us. The individuals seem to be quite innocuous and straightforward. The samples were discretely collected in the confines of my office and all seemed fine and routine. It had not been a mere five minutes since they left when my secretary asked me if I was willing to take a call from the 'mother' who was here a moment ago. I readily acceded to her request and took the phone.

"Good afternoon (Mrs. No Name), how can I be of assistance?"

It was strange receiving a call so quickly afterward.

"Doc (like is customarily said), can I come to see you?" Now, that was not normal and my red flags were immediately raised.

"But you were just here and I repeatedly asked if you had any questions or concerns; Now, what's bothering you?"

"No, I need to see you in person," she reiterated.

"Is it something in connection with the test that we just did, if it is, I would be most happy to have these discussions with both you and (Mr. No Name)," I insisted.

She was persistent that she needed to discuss a development. Knowing what or rather suspecting that she had wanted to do some underhand deal or make unethical offers, I replied that I would be most happy to have a discourse with both adults and at the same time.

"Could we work something out? You know what I mean, just call any amount," she finally confessed.

"Are you for real, are you offering me a bribe? Listen, I will have none of this," I retorted in a very polite but firm manner.

"Okay, okay," she conceded, "please call me first when the results are ready."

"Ma'am, this is not how we operate, you both need to come in at the same time to prevent any misconceptions," I clarified. I was upset and disgusted, why in the world do some people think that they can bribe their way through life? Very disturbed and disappointed, I ended the call by hanging up the phone.

I thought it was over and that she was simply going to accept the chips where they fell. It must have been three to four days after the initial sample collection when I received another call from her.

"I did something wrong, please don't be upset with me," she blurted out.

I was shocked and didn't know what to expect. "What clandestine move could she be up to this time around?" I questioned. Before I could have responded she said, "I've falsified your results."

"Are you mad?' How could you? Do you want to go to jail?" At this time, I simply couldn't figure out if she was crazy or so desperate and foolish to perform such a heinous act.

"Look, I'm not going to have any more discussions on this matter with you."

Shortly afterward I then got a visit from Mr. No Name who was seeking my clarification on whether or not a crudely typed result was authentic. Clearly, he was upset and confused and was genuinely seeking expert guidance while she, on the other hand, seemed embarrassed but with a pseudo-angry face. The crumbled word document, very unprofessionally written, had these words typed, "DNA Result-Positive."

"Are these your results?" he questioned nervously.

I really couldn't understand why someone would go to those lengths to lie and misrepresent our report. Of course, that was very far from what a DNA result looks like.

"Your partner is a fraud and is either not right in her head or is stupid," I exclaimed.

I then calmly showed him copies of what authentic DNA reports look like. All along she kept holding on to her lies that the faulty report was given to her by my staff.

A few days later I received an email from DDC requesting that we retake the samples. They gave no explanations and I figured that we might not have collected enough samples. So, we rescheduled another collection and I apologized for the inconveniences caused and offered that we may not have collected sufficient samples from the parties in question. It was quite a tense and awkward moment, Mrs. No Name seemed more embarrassed and very distracted. I tried to lighten the encounter by explaining that sometimes the buccal swabs are not rubbed with the required firmness.

This was the second collection of buccal swabs from the same patients. *Why would they request a retaking of those swabs,* I wondered. *Was there something sinister going on?* Strange enough, a third set of samples was requested by the DDC because they suspected 'switching.' This phenomenon rarely occurs in large hospitals where babies are switched at birth, sometimes erroneously or deliberately. It seemed as though that might have been the thinking of the DDC officials. When a third rejection was conveyed to us, it was suggested that a chain of custody sample be taken, thus ensuring that the samples collected are from their rightful and respective origins.

On the fourth occasion, absolute care was taken to once again ensure flawless specimen collections. It was not surprising when the fourth submission turned out in the test being finally performed. Yes, you guessed it; he was not the father. Not unexpected at all! I was really not expecting to see what was written on the other side of the coin. She too was not related to the little child, yes, she was not the mother. This strange twist now required some professional help. My team strongly advised me to contact the 'Child Services Ministry' for expert guidance.

This was done and the officers advised me to call in the delinquent 'parents' so that they (Child Protective) can properly investigate this strange and bizarre case.

The advent of DNA testing has brought light to life. It is similar to the effects of lighting a flambeau (a crude bottle and wick lamp) in a pitch-dark room. Many problems/ crimes have been solved as a result of this relatively new and innovative science. At Eureka, we are grateful to have been partnering with the DDC. This has afforded Eureka the privilege of being labeled as the DNA lab. Our confidential DNA stories are numerous and we pride ourselves with giving authentic answers.

# CHAPTER 38

# Mark Anthony Boyle

One word to describe this gracious and handsome son of mine would probably be "solid." Tony as he is fondly called is super dependable, extremely obedient, exuberant and yet at the same time, gentle and loving.

He excelled at the Alphabees playgroup and his graduation ceremony from that kindergarten school at the Pegasus Hotel was befitting of a prince. His fellow classmates, including Ashley and Dwight Archer danced their little souls as they sang joyfully, "Alphabees, Alphabees, I love Alphabees." Now they are all grown young men and women.

As Tony grew up, he mastered the sport of playing table tennis, particularly during his tenure at Maes Under Twelve schools. He later went on to do his secondary schooling at Wadleigh High in Harlem, New York. Under the watchful eyes and guidance of the principal, Dr. Karen Watts, an old friend of Karen's, he excelled. I would marvel at how efficiently he handled waking up, getting a snack, then off hurriedly leaving the house before 6:00 a.m., every morning, whether it snowed or rained. This form of discipline was certainly commendable. Apart from regular support, Grandmas Gordon and Levy, who both live in New York, played a pivotal role in his development. After high school, he went on to attend Marist University where he pursued studies in Marketing/Management. According to him, those were truly amazing years of his life and it is where he met with the love of his life, Grace.

I clearly remember his graduation from that prestigious Marist College of Poughkeepsie, in upstate NY. I've never seen the dude so excited and it was truly an honor to witness my big son graduating. Chuck Todd, host of Meet the Press and Meet the Press Now; NBC News Political Director was the keynote speaker. We sat there beaming as proud parents and grandparents as Tony strode up to receive his coveted first college degree. Reflecting, was this not the same youngster who gave us hell in the Barbados airport?

Mark Anthony Boyle later studied at Regis University in Denver Colorado for a master's degree in Organizational Leadership. Our big son then graduated with academic honors, well done champ. Tony became a vibrant member of the internationally renowned Rotary Club and his passion to assist and work with the needy is quite evident. Maybe this trait was learned from his parents, since we have been involved in much charitable work during his upbringing. During the Christmas holidays of 2016, he came up with the bright idea that he wanted to sponsor breakfast for the orphans of the Joshua House. Oh, what a joy to see him and his siblings with smiling faces as they served the happy residents of the orphanage. I discovered that it was particularly touching when they sang their signature song, "You are my sunshine, my only sunshine. You make me happy when the skies are gray, please don't take my sunshine away," which brought tears to my eyes.

Young Tony is now gainfully employed by the internationally renowned Google and seems to be enjoying every minute of it. He recently graduated with a Master's degree in Organizational Leadership and is contemplating reading for his Ph.D.

It was a familiar display of wonderful exuberance when he and Grace finally tied the knot. Their big day was postponed because of Covid-19 but was eventually realized in July of 2021. Their wedding was truly awesome in every sense of the word. It was very dramatic and pronounced when this happy couple and the bridal entourage danced their way into the reception hall. Further, during the frenzy of one of the dancing sessions, without identifying the culprit, someone, while dancing, actually dropped to the floor and did a few pushups. We all had a blast as we celebrated with Tony and his gorgeous wife, Grace.

Mr. and Mrs. Mark Anthony Boyle had done it with class and style; may God continue to shower them with profound blessings.

*Tony becomes a Rotarian*

*Tony and Grace's wedding*

*Andy, Andrew Jr. and Tony*

# CHAPTER 39

# Princess Andrea Boyle

Karen had been about two months pregnant when we got married and we were exceedingly excited to welcome the young Princess. She was born on August 25th, 1992, and was a gorgeous little lady with dark curly hair and pink lips added to her awesome beauty. Oh, what a darling baby she was!

Strangely though, during her delivery, which was extremely difficult, an injection to quell the pain was given to Karen, just prior to little Andrea's birth. After several hours of agony, discomfort and horrendous pain, Karen eventually delivered.

Andrea took a long time to cry as she was born "flat out," a term used to describe her limp state. It took rapid suctioning of the fluids from her upper orifices to clear her airways. When she finally cried it was several moments afterward and it was felt that she might have been affected by this delay. In retrospect, it was clear that something was wrong with her; she had a strange way of clasping her fists with her thumbs tucked under the other fingers and had vomited more often than normal. As parents, though medically oriented, we didn't notice these shortcomings or simply refused to even consider that something might have been wrong with our child.

She developed slowly and melted my heart with her gorgeous smiles; she was truly a gem. We had her Christened in the Calvary Lutheran Church and was privileged to have her visit the land of her fore parents. Though the trip to go there was an arduous and difficult one, I'm happy that we did manage to take her for a visit. She was just about four months old when we were preparing to celebrate Christmas and we had all gone to church that day to catch the early morning service. A day, as Karen reminded me later, when she had strangely developed an urge to go to church.

After attending church, which was only for just over an hour, we returned home. It was now shaping up to be a pleasant day as we celebrated the birth of Jesus. We both played a bit with Andrea before Karen retired to the kitchen to prepare some goodies for the afternoon, while I entertained my brother-in-law, Anthony Beaton, who had dropped in briefly. He is married to my sister, Ellenore and was originally from a sister village, Mariah Henrieta, of the Berbice river. Not very long into our session, Karen passed us as she quickly went to check on Andrea who had not so long ago dropped off to sleep.

"Andy come," I heard her say but we were engrossed in our conversation. "Come now!" she screamed. I jumped up and ran upstairs to see what she was shouting about but was not prepared for the horror that I saw and the image is forever etched in my mind. Andrea was dead and lying face down in a pool of vomitus. She had already died and my futile screams and efforts to revive her did not make any difference whatsoever. Her life had already been snuffed away and we tried in vain with CPR to no avail.

It baffles me how I mustered the courage to take her to the mortuary after visiting the police station. Karen was even saying that she should have left an additional blanket because she was going to be cold in the refrigerator. It was all like a bad dream and for years I had actually blamed myself for not having her constantly in my eyesight. The day of her funeral came and went; we managed to float through the ceremony all dazed and in shock. I'm told that I had to be held back from trying to give her one last kiss as her little body lay in the coffin. This was clearly one of the worst days of my life. I was numb for years afterward and the outpouring of support and show of sympathy from our friends and family members was truly amazing and comforting. I used to pass by her tomb and just sit there, I had felt so well connected with her; how in Heaven's name could this have happened to my little Princess? It was several years afterward that we realized that she had been severely affected during her birth. She obviously had brain issues and this was later pointed out by how she used to clasp her hands with both of her thumbs held inwards. The mystery forever remains though and I sometimes ask myself, *but why, oh why? Why me? Why us?*

She is still, very much like those other lost souls, constantly in my dreams. It took me several years to 'get over' her death. One never forgets or completely 'gets over' the death of a loved one but the pain becomes less severe over time.

*Princess Andrea, Karen and Andy*

# CHAPTER 40

# Andrew Yanick Boyle

A ndrea's fleeting life on Mother Earth left an indelible mark on our lives and Karen and I made a conscious effort to quickly have another child. It was not quite two months since her tragic death that my dear wife became pregnant once more.

I remember hastily driving towards Medical Arts at about 4 o'clock in the afternoon of November 6th, 1993 with Karen in the back seat, grimacing with pain. She was almost ready to give birth and the sharp pains were like clockwork, every five minutes. According to the nurse who examined her, she was not quite ready but was getting there. She further stated that the obstetrician was not there as yet and asked whether I was willing to go pick her up. I hurried and made sure that Karen was well accommodated at the hospital then immediately rushed off to pick up Dr. Irene Quandie from her South Ruimveldt home.

After returning to the hospital, I decided that I was going nowhere and made the decision to wait and look and listen out for the outcome of the delivery while several nervous and silent prayers were offered. *Dear God, let all be well this time around, please Dear Jesus!*

It was probably around 5:00 p.m., not very long after we had rushed to the hospital when the nurse peeked out of the delivery room:

"It's a boy, you have a son!"

He was already screaming, making a strong statement that he was here to stay.

Very much like Andrea, he had long curly hair and oh, how gorgeous the little man was. He was too busy crying while he looked around the labor room and I desperately fought to hold back the tears of joy. Still in pain, Karen queried in a whisper whether he was alright. This time around no pain injections were used. We had given clear requests to the obstetrician and her staff. God had given us back our child, thank you, dear Jesus!

During the ensuing months and even the early years of little Andrew's development, he was always under our watchful eyes. One can only imagine the magnitude of care and attention that was given to our newborn baby boy. It was quite understandable why we would have been this way.

Andrew grew up to be a bold and positive young man with a very strong will. When he was barely able to talk, he would awake very early and firmly insist that he wanted his 'tea tea' (porridge) now. Impatient he was, especially during his younger days and seemed to have been born with natural leadership tendencies and there were times when he behaved as though he had lived here on Mother Earth before. There are quite a few of his striking developmental episodes that I clearly remember.

His maternal Grandma had scolded him for leaving his toys all over the house. She was holidaying from the USA during one Christmas season. Her visits at Christmas time were like clockwork, especially after the tragic death of our Little Princess Andrea. Grandma is a disciplinarian and quite strict but this trait didn't go down very well with the kiddies at that time. So, in the evening while she packed her suitcase, Andrew stood at a safe distance, pointed his penis and urinated into her nicely folded clothing. Of course, he was punished but the damage had already been done and he had made his statement and rebelled.

Somewhere in the late 1990's, my old school (New Amsterdam Multilateral) had a BBQ and informal karaoke, Andrew Jr. was probably about five or six years old. Karen and I both sang a few well-known tunes. "The Green, Green Grass of Home" by Tom Jones and "Endless Love" by Lionel Richie were amongst our favorites. Before we knew it, the little man was on the stage with the microphone singing The Backstreet Boys' song, "Quit Playing Games With my Heart." The crowd of my peers went wild as he danced and sang the song word for word, without fear whatsoever.

His entrepreneurial skills became evident when he and his fellow five or six-year-olds pals picked fresh cherries from our trees and then walked from house to house in the neighborhood and sold them. How could the residents have possibly refused to buy cherries from those innocent young smiling entrepreneurs, skillfully led by Master Andrew?

It was the weekend of November 6th, 2009; Karen and I were required to attend a Rotary InterGuiana's (IGM) meeting in Suriname. So, we asked Mom, my mother, to spend those few days taking care of young

Andrew and Tony, while we were away with our then ten-year-old daughter, Keziah. At that time, we had a live-in helper whose main responsibilities were to prepare our meals and assist with the general tidying of the home. Mom was therefore only expected to have watchful eyes on Andrew and to ensure that he was properly taken care of. It so happened that it was Little Andrew's 16th birthday and he, together with his pals, decided to have a grand party at one of their homes, situated just about three houses up the road from where we lived. Later we were told that it was a fabulous birthday party with lots of food and drinks. He had actually signed, earlier that day, to collect a sizable amount of cash from my staff. Strangely, even the popular and extremely attractive Guyanese singer, Ms. Tamika Marshall had graced it with her presence. Earlier during that afternoon, Andrew's explanation to Mom was that he was going up the road to the neighbors to spend a few moments but he had his party gears unknowingly tucked in, under his arms.

It was getting late in the evening and he had gone for some time so Mom sent our helper to go and bring him home. It was later narrated to us that he offered the helper a lavish amount of food and drinks and put her in a nice and comfortable corner to wait until the celebrations were over. After all, it was his sixteenth birthday that had to be celebrated in grand style.

He later pursued undergraduate studies in Psychology but not before finishing secondary school at Olympia High School in Orlando, USA. We thought that he stood a great chance of excelling in life if he continued school in the US after taking CXC's. After all, he also probably wanted to follow in the footsteps of his big brother, Tony.

This period overseas was quite rewarding to him and he evolved into a fine young man who is well-rounded. Young Andrew developed tremendous fighting and self-defense techniques in the Brazilian Jiu Jitsu martial arts.

Andrew is currently pursuing a Master's degree in Psychology; he is about to graduate with a grade point average of 4.0 from Rollins College, Winter Park. Isn't that amazing? Our second son works with trauma and sexually assaulted victims. Sometimes he tries to psycho diagnose me by asking me questions as though I'm his patient. "So, how does it make you feel?" "Tell me about your feelings." Sometimes I simply smile and say to myself, *wow, he has really learned well.*

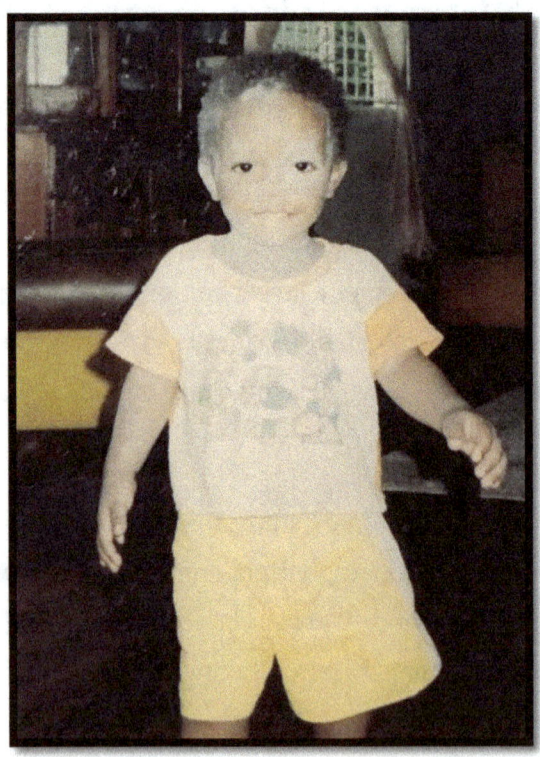

*Little Andrew*

# CHAPTER 41

# The Big Day

The plan was for us to leave Orlando at 2:00 p.m., even perhaps half hour later would suffice. The journey to Tallahassee would normally take four steady hours of driving. It meant heading northwards, away from Miami and towards Atlanta as Orlando is situated between Miami and Tallahassee. Andrew's graduation was slated for 7:30 p.m. at Florida State University (FSU) in lovely Tallahassee and we needed to get moving if we were ever going to arrive on time. We sat in the rented van, some eleven of us, all awaiting my nephew, 'Rocky' Alphonso.

Rocky lived a mere stone's throw away from our house in Vineland Oaks Blvd. but was taking forever to get to where we were waiting. It was past 3:00 p.m. and his mother, Valerie, my sister, was becoming very agitated and angry. She screamed on her cell phone, "Rocky, where the hell are you?" We were all beginning to become worried that we were not going to arrive on time for 'Oldman's' graduation. Oh, what a terrible shame that would be!

"I'm at the traffic light, Mom," was Rocky's answer. After all, if he was merely a couple of minutes, just up the road, surely, he would arrive any minute now. This news brought some relief and comfort. They made us feel a bit more relaxed but it took exactly 30 minutes later when he and his lovely wife, Nicole, finally arrived.

"Mom, the traffic light was jammed with cars," was his lame excuse.

He further consoled us that he was going to get us there on time, and that we shouldn't worry. My other sister, Camille, suggested jokingly that we should name that traffic light, the Rocky's stop junction. He took charge of the wheel and began his quest to take us to FSU. The ride was smooth but long, as we meandered along the lovely pathway towards the university. It was amazing how many beautiful endless fields of farm lands were passed along the way. Our vehicle was only equipped with a radio which kept us company with nice soothing music and a bit of chatter from time to time. Rocky redeemed himself as we carefully sped along the road. It turned out that we made it in a mere three and a half hours to our destination. All along, Andrew kept enquiring of our location as he gave us directions for our GPS.

Just prior to our arrival, around 7:15 p.m., merely a few minutes before the big occasion, it was announced that it was expected that the temperature would drop from 82 to 38 degrees Fahrenheit. We hurriedly found appropriate parking and rushed to find the reserved booth, ably guided by the man of the moment, the young graduating student, on the phone. To our pleasant surprise, we were nicely accommodated in one of the booths that was strategically placed for easy viewing. We couldn't see him but learned of his approximate location which was situated way below our VIP booth.

The guest speaker was quite eloquent as she spoke of the importance of remaining grounded, humble and simple. She, being an 'old student,' captivated the majority of the guests but I rather doubt that the graduating students actually heard a single word. It was surely their moment of glory, their huge evening; they had weathered the storm and are now about to reap their dividends. Then they began calling the names of some of the graduates but from another faculty. Our hearts began to pound harder and harder as he prepared to receive his accolade. My Samsung phone was poised to capture this glorious moment.

"Get ready now, he is in the line," I managed to hear Karen excitedly whisper as she clutched my left arm. "Now, now, there he comes," she further stated as she couldn't contain her enthusiasm.

He skipped gingerly across the stage with a confident swagger and shook the professor's hand along with a fleeting hug. "Yaaay!" The sound of the thunderous screams of my entourage was deafening. I felt the rush of emotions and fought back the tears of joy that managed to sneak down my smiling face. I felt immensely proud and happy as though I was the one graduating. It was truly an overwhelming feeling. This was clearly one of the proudest moments of my life. *Oh, what a feeling!* With a swift brushing movement, I hastily wiped away the trickling remnants of my tears so that no one would notice. It might have only been a mere minute or two after he had made his graduation walk, then he appeared in our VIP booth, all beaming with ecstatic joy. Still dazed, we snapped numerous photos and showered him with congratulatory kudos.

I gave him the biggest of embraces and the rush of emotions returned as if to reiterate, "You did it Oldman, I'm very proud of you."

*Karen, Andrew Jr., Keziah, Andy and Tony*

# CHAPTER 42

# Keziah Renée Boyle

It was the birth of our baby girl and this time around I was privileged to have witnessed her birth and oh what an awesome experience it was. It is just sad that women have to endure such a painful and unforgettable experience.

Her little yet powerful cries were very marked and pronounced as she signaled her arrival. My nervous hands mustered the courage to remain fairly stable as I clipped the umbilical cord with honor and pride, severing the tube that connected little Keziah to her mother. It was just about 3:00 p.m. when our marvelous little miss was born into this wonderful world. She is truly a gorgeous, lovely, and adoring little lady.

I clearly remember the days when, as I drove into the driveway after a long day's work, hearing her thundering little chubby footsteps as she ran to welcome me. "Daddyyyy!" It was the most refreshing greeting a father could ever ask for. She would then leap into my arms and it was as though nothing else in the world mattered. A flurry of sometimes incoherent, probably pent-up words followed her extravagant welcome. I would ask her:

"How much do you love your daddy?"

She would stretch out her little arms to full length and say with a bright and happy smile, "Oneeee," clearly signifying that she meant a whole lot. Those lovingly kind gestures were indeed worth looking forward to, especially after having toiled all day.

Lionel Richie sang a very touching love song, "Tender Heart," which contained the following words, "we don't stand a chance in this wild romance." Keziah simply loved this song and each time she heard it being played, she would rush to the telephone to hurriedly call her daddy and we would sing along to those beautiful words. I was so moved and touched by this classical demonstration of love from a little four-year-old child.

It was also with immense joy and pride that we watched her evolve into a smart, beautiful, and caring young lady. It often appeared that she played a lot and seemingly did not dedicate enough time to her precious studies but strangely, she always excelled at her studies when it mattered. Her ability to prevail was not only evident in her academic studies but in other areas as well. The first time she rode a jet ski or drove a car, it was as though she was in quite a comfort zone and did so fearlessly. By age seventeen, she had her own car and had aced her driving exams with very little or no effort. It was therefore not surprising to hear that she drove around when she and her cousins visited St. Vincent. It should be noted that in that beautiful country, the roads dangerously cling to the hillsides and are very narrow and seemingly precarious.

Kez sings beautifully and also plays the keyboards, guitar, and steelpan with gusto. Oh, it is such a joy to watch her play and move in time with the rhythm of the music. I was exceedingly excited to witness the fiercely fought steel pan competition at the Cliff Anderson Sports Hall. Bishops High School, her alma mater, placed second with North Georgetown Multilateral taking top honors. It was at that event that Kez and her peers exhibited class and sheer talent as they danced and played. It was a marvelous display of great talent and resilience.

How quickly time flies! Eighteen years had gone by so fleetingly. Kez started her undergraduate studies at the University of Central Florida (UCF) in natural sciences with the aim of pursuing a career in Medicine. The day of her departure arrived before we knew it and the scenario reminded me of when I was heading off to Cuba.

It was the July 21st, and the weather was quite overcast. It was already past 11:00 a.m. and their flight was scheduled for 2:30 p.m. I felt very sad to see her board the aircraft. Our scenarios are quite different though, I could have easily hopped onto a plane and flown to the US.

The years flew by very quickly. After completing her undergraduate studies in Natural Sciences, she moved on to pursue studies in the Emergency Medical Technician course and then later the Emergency Paramedical program. These are all in preparation for studies to become a doctor or a Physician Assistant. Keziah continues to blossom nicely and has evolved into a very focused and responsible 24-year-old young lady.

I happened to be on a business trip to Orlando and popped in to relax in my daughter's condo, on that lovely evening, Kez and I shared pleasantries and she later retired to bed. Josué, her boyfriend, and I talked about little things here and there. After chatting for about an hour I started to feel sleepy and kindly excused myself. It was then he muttered that he had something to discuss in private, I ushered him into my bedroom where he nervously jumped straight to the point. He seemed somewhat afraid as he stared into my eyes and said the following, "I wish to ask your permission to marry your daughter." I was not surprised but taken aback. Not that I saw anything wrong with his sudden and wonderful proposition, I was touched by his sincerity and genuine demeanor. Young lovers, this is exactly how it should be done! It reminded me of the tales of how Papa proposed to Mom. He had actually written a letter to Daddy and Gamma but first passed through, according to Papa, Police Headquarters. Great-grandfather Henny's home was labeled as such.

"Josué, I'm honored to have you as my son-in-law but please treat her nicely." Further, I stated that she was still studying and needed to complete her goals. He quickly responded that it will be his duty to treat her like the queen she is. We later shared a few shots of 15-year-old Demerara Rum and retired to bed, both feeling happy and over the moon.

*Kez and I*

*Tony, Andy, Andrew Jr. and Kez*

# CHAPTER 43

# Letting My Hair Down

It is clearly established that a bit of play is good for the soul. The batteries can be recharged and you return to your routine fully energized and ready to take over the world.

I have habitually used Friday evenings and most weekends to relax and to forget about work. I also strongly believe that one should have family time, especially when young children are involved.

My cousin Ava, her husband Terrence Seaforth (aka 12), and their children, Christopher, Kyle, and Kurt, together with Dr. Colin and Nadira Lee and their children were our regular camping buddies. We would take off on Saturday early afternoon and head for either the Colonel's, Sparkie, and Joan's farms on the Linden Soesdyke Highway or simply remain and camp in our yard. Camping, in my opinion, takes away the monotony and literally adds a bit of fresh air to one's life. We would cook using an open 'fireside' then play cards using the camp fire and gas lanterns to illuminate our surroundings. Terry and I were pretty good at cards and won most of our games. Our tactics were not always above board though, as we mastered the uses of signs and signals, much to the annoyance of Nadira and Colin. Cold beers together with sometimes Absolut Vodka and ginger ale were usually the accompanying drinks of our choice. The children were fully involved, especially in the setting up of our tents and the airing up of our beds. They too would become engrossed in catching up with their cousins and friends.

Sometimes there would be a bit of sing along sessions to Sparkie's melodious guitar music. Most memorable was his favorite rendition of "Yoda Lay Hee Hoo," an old cowboy song. There were funny episodes that made the camping experience very memorable. One night, our dinner which happened to be a lovely, well-seasoned trout, fell into the fire and was covered with ashes and filth and was not fit for consumption. We tried to clean the half-cooked fish but this proved to be an impossible feat. There was another one of those very laughable moments which happened while we were making our breakfast around the fire. A heavy gust of wind came and blew Sparkie and Joan's little tent away. It was quite funny to see their 'home' rolling away with the wind.

Camping at their farm at Loo Creek, on the highway, was quite a regular occurrence. We did that practically every weekend. There was an occasion when Kez, who was just about five years old, had a near-drowning experience. We were all walking towards the fast-running waters not very far away from our camping ground. Kez had become accustomed to swimming in our domestic pool but with the aid of a floating ring. So, she probably believed that she could swim. It happened so suddenly, she let go of my hands and darted towards the water, and plunged into the beautiful dark creek water. Her little body quickly disappeared into probably six to seven feet of blackness.

Instinctively, I jumped after her and managed to grab her as she screamed and cried with her eyes bulging. Oh how terrified she was as she grabbed her daddy with a never-ending bear-like hug while she sobbed. This near-drowning experience caused her to stay away from water for quite a few months. She had to be cajoled into risking even going near the water again.

A good Friday evening drink after work at the Red Shop was another priceless means of relaxing and bonding with good friends. At these so-called 'boys' night outs,' we would have a good time while discussing topical issues. These subjects included Donald Trump, girls, the local Guyanese elections, oil, solar energy, and all kinds of interesting topics. Sometimes the arguments would become very heated, depending on who formed the audience. A good gaff with refreshments and the sumptuous taste of plantain fries and curried iguana or Labba are certainly worth looking forward to.

On a few occasions, I was privileged to spend priceless moments on cruises. One of the most unforgettable ones was organized by Ms. Neglas Brandis and her crew. Karen, her dad (The Colonel), Colwyn (my cousin), and I made up my entourage. Our group spent most of our time together with Rawle (aka Gino) and Iolanda Jordan who also formed part of our Elite group of cruisers.

We all danced in the silent party where we wore headphones which were equipped with various musical tunes. So, if you were not synchronized with your partner's music, it appeared as though there were all crazy people dancing to different and silent tunes. Dining, having breakfast, and playing mini golf were all activities which were done together.

ASPIRE: DARE TO DREAM

It was on one of those lovely evenings after dinner we stopped by one of the many bars to have a few more cocktails. The night was progressing nicely and we were really having a blast. Not far away from where we were, there was a Spanish band playing some good old Latin tunes. With our drinks in hand, I encouraged my team to go closer to where they were playing. It might have been the effects of the strong beverages we were consuming that might have influenced my next move.

The band began to play 'Besame,' one of my favorite Spanish songs, and they were doing a fabulous job. I'm not sure what got into me. The next thing I knew was that I had approached the singers and politely requested to take over the microphone, Andrew Boyle was on stage singing 'Besame' with a Spanish band. "Besame, besame mucho, como si fuera esta noche, la ultima vez. Besame, besame mucho, Que tengo miedo perderte, perderte despues." In my opinion, I sounded pretty good and people were dancing. I thought to myself that I must have been doing a good job. But later in the tune I just couldn't remember the rest of the song. Luckily, the lead singer was just at my side and he continued and no harm was done. My team cheered and we all had a good laugh but later I was ridiculed for not knowing the entire song. It added some spice to our mini vacation. My hair had been truly let down.

# CHAPTER 44

# The Accreditation Journey

I t was February 12th, 2016, one Friday evening, just around half past six, when my cell phone rang.

"We got it!" blurted the caller on the other end of the line. "What are you talking about?" I questioned. After all, I was confused, since I was not even sure with whom I was talking. Who could this be? I wondered. With a frenzy or incoherent words, the caller, obviously super excited, continued. Was this a prank call? Maybe it was the wrong number. Should I simply hang up the phone? I have had numerous mistaken calls as my GT&T cell numbers are similar to those of the former Minister of Home Affairs, just one digit different. "Clement," "Comrade Rohee," "Minister Rohee," or sometimes "Rohee!" Those are the possible utterances of the mistaken calls. Was this another of those mistaken telephone calls?

"Accreditation, accreditation, JANAAC!" He managed to shout once again, "we got it!" This reminded me of my younger fishing days. When one of us would exclaim, "got one bai!" Obviously, super excited about the catch.

Shawn Manbodh, my quality control manager was the breathless and jubilant bearer of fabulous news. He and his team had really worked diligently over several years and it was not easy work. We were half expecting this since before Christmas 2015 but had to await the full decision from JANAAC (Jamaica National Agency for Accreditation).

After several attempts, he finally was able to utter coherently and that he had just forwarded me an email outlining the massive achievement. Eureka Medical Laboratories Inc. was now internationally accredited to the ISO standards.

Today I was ecstatic! Team Eureka had delivered! It was no ordinary achievement. We had become the first and only medical laboratory in Guyana to have achieved this coveted accolade. Thank you, Almighty God!

EML has also been certified repeatedly over several years, on more than eight occasions by the Guyana National Bureau of Standards (GNBS). Initially, the staff thought it was a pain. "Why did Candelle and Mr. Hooper have to ask all of those questions?" She, Ms. Candelle Walcott-Bostwick was one of the most thorough and efficient managers of the Guyana National Bureau of Standards, the entity responsible for the certification of Medical Laboratories in Guyana. Mr. Dickson Hooper was one of those thorough and knowledgeable auditors of the GNBS. Then afterward, our staff members got accustomed to the rigors and documentation requirements. The many impromptu visits were truly sudden and without notice. We were caught off guard on many occasions but managed to prevail because of our systems that were implemented. The thought of becoming accredited was totally remote and seemed out of reach.

*Certified by GNBS again*

Around 2010, I had pitched the idea of the possibility of having EML accredited to an old Rotarian pal, Past President, the late Dr. Leslie Chin. It might have been over Rotary lunch at the Pegasus on a Thursday midday. He suggested that the Canadian Executive Service Organization (CESO) be written to and to have them provide assistance via a suitably qualified person. This was exactly what we did and they, the CESO, responded instantaneously. This resulted in them sending a warm and meticulous professional to our assistance.

Dr. James Dalton, a former Laboratory Director in Canada, seemed like the perfect scientist for the job. The fleeting week he spent with us was most invaluable and priceless. After some 15 years of existence, we, for the first time, did a five-year strategic plan for Eureka and created our Vision and Mission statements, etc. The managers of Eureka did two, three-hour training sessions at the Campbell room, Georgetown Club.

It was the commencement of our quest for international accreditation. These sessions were greatly beneficial for our internal growth as an entity but we had hit a brick wall because there was no clear pathway to accreditation. His guidance, however, paved the way to having us increase our awareness of strategic thinking and to be more focused on our futuristic goals. It was projected that we expected to be internationally accredited at the end of five years. Wasn't that great strategic planning? Or was it prophetic? Or maybe simply a coincidence?

The last two years were phenomenal in regard to the urgency and purpose that were dedicated towards the accreditation process. Under the guidance of the Guyana National Bureau of Standards led by Ms. Bostwick and Mr. Hooper, we made tremendous strides. They, in collaboration with Caribbean Regional Organization for Standards and Quality (CROSQ) and Physikalisch- Technische Bundesanatalt (PTB) created a national focal point to work specifically with labs who wished to become accredited. We hired a proficient HR guru who incidentally was one of the lecturers of the MBA program I had done. His intervention offloaded me of a sizable chunk of administrative duties which helped me to be more strategic and futuristic in my thinking. Action Coach Guyana, Dr. Vishnu Doerga, also did some work with us in creating systems for the marketing of the EML brand.

Shawn Manbodh and his Deputy, Domnick Russel took over the helm of leadership of the quality system from Shondell Thomas, the former QC manager and dedicated team member, who was seconded to head our EML branch in St. Vincent, W.I. Shawn and Domnick are thorough, exceedingly efficient, and almost annoyingly persistent.

We initiated discussions with JANAAC and an audit of our facilities was arranged somewhere around July 2015. The CEO of JANAAC met with a few managers and me during the early days of 2015 and outlined the process and various challenges. We were hoping to schedule a 'mock' audit in preparation for the real deal but for some reason, it didn't materialize. When the audit team from JANAAC arrived at the lab on that July morning, we were nervous, tense, and apprehensive. "The day of reckoning had come. Hopefully they can get beyond this" (Erich Merkle). Ms. Bostwick and Mr. Hooper, our two "advisors" were present for the opening meeting but they were not allowed to answer questions. It was one of the most anxious days of my life. All of the members of my team had been prepared but were all tense as if they were writing an exam. The four assessors selected different departments where they questioned and chatted with the various team members. They were extremely professional and their approach was somewhat friendly and accommodating as if they expected us to be nervous. Their mannerisms might have been learnt during their vast exposures and experiences in the industry.

It was probably the longest and never-ending day of my life but we had done it. The many but minor non- conformances were read and explained to us. It was further pointed out that we were required to have these addressed and corrected accordingly. But it was the uncertainties of measurement which proved to be somewhat challenging. Thank heavens for the kind and timely intervention of CROSQ and PTB, that we managed to have Shivanna, a consultant from Trinidad, work us through those intricate details.

Clearly, my lifelong dream was beginning to unfold. This reminds me of the words of Rene Descartes "I think therefore I am." Perseverance was the order of the day. People tell me that I might have some inner driving force within me to succeed.

"No matter where you're from, your dreams are valid." Lupita Nyong'o.

The road to accreditation was costly, rough, and long but today we have reaped the benefits of our hard work. The saying "Teamwork makes the dream work" by John Maxwell is totally true. Eureka has the best team and this is not just lip service.

So, on that Friday evening when Shawn made that breathless and bursting with exuberance call, it took me right back to those initial struggles. I made a conscious note that we were going to continue to improve our service with humility and empathy.

What a lovely, profound feeling of satisfaction that was!

This significant event makes me remember one of my many motivational songs that I enjoy listening to. One of such songs is by Busy Signal, a renowned Jamaican reggae artist. "Out comes the sun, shining on my face again, dreams of brighter days again." These songs remind me that even when things are dull and bleak, the sun will come up again. Lou Rawls', "The sun will come out tomorrow, you bet your bottom dollar there will be sun." This was our moment of glory, our sunlight and you know what, we'll now bash in its radiance and enjoy every second of it. The lesson learned here was that one should expect to succeed in the future, even though the odds may seem to be against you. Our task now is to ensure that we upkeep these high standards.

It seems like just yesterday when Eureka started, that was more than 28 years ago. On March 5th, 1995 we commenced operations with two individuals and today we are a team of one hundred workers including medical technologists, technicians, doctors, laboratory aides, administrative and security personnel, and 10 centers and satellite stations in Georgetown, Parika, New Amsterdam, Linden, Rosehall, Bartica, Anna Regina, Diamond, Skeldon, and St. Vincent.

Eureka is now internationally accredited! This is huge, it's massive, but what does it mean? It means harder work for our team, yes, higher salaries and general improvement in the quality of our various services. Now, the work has really started and I can assure you that you have not seen our best just yet.

Innovation, in my humble opinion, has been the hallmark of our organization. Soon, very soon, probably within another month, our main office will be fully powered by solar energy, the first of its kind in Guyana. There is another exciting service that will be launched simultaneously, so you may need to stay tuned. You bet Eureka will continue to be accredited, to innovate and to give of our best.

These young Scientists, Medical Technologists, Doctors, and collaborators, I promise you, will continue to make your lives and those of your families better.

Eureka Family, let's continue to give the best service, let us serve with humility and dignity. Gosh, I felt like crying, shouting, screaming! I am not sure you can manage to experience this truly overwhelming sensation of joy and happiness.

Kindly raise your glasses to "Great service!"

I thank you Almighty God, team EML, stakeholders, relatives, and friends.

*Eureka receiving accreditation*

# CHAPTER 45

# The Opening of EML'S Second Building

The weather forecast for Saturday, April 30th, 2016 was not encouraging. It was predicted to have steady downpours during the day with a 100% chance of thunderstorms in the evening. It was just the beginning of the rainy seasons in Guyana and it had poured buckets during the evening of Friday, the 29th. The patio paint, we had painted during the course of that day, had been almost completely washed away, leaving streaks and spots of discolored greenness. Was today, our big day, also going to be like this? What if the weather forecast was correct? We had planned to have the western half of Thomas Street closed to vehicular traffic and to cover the entire area in front of the two EML buildings with tents. In the past, flooding of Thomas Street was not uncommon. Were we going to have floods today? I asked two of our 'praying' sisters, Felecia and Camille to pray for good weather. In fact, at around 10:00 a.m., during the early morning downpours, and I mean serious and heavy rainfall, I received a call. Dr. Gansham Singh called to see if we were still going to have the launch. He thought that there was no way we could have possibly had a successful event because it appeared so bleak and dark.

We decided to proceed as planned, come what may. How could you tell the president of the country that you were going to postpone the event because of the inclement weather? That day, even while it rained, we spent time putting in the finishing touches. The Northern side of the older of the two buildings was power washed. We were racing against time, as Eusi Rogers and team connected and tested the solar system.

The rains abated and the afternoon became very pleasant and mild. The rains had simply disappeared from the horizons. Where did they go? Was this a Divine intervention? All of a sudden it was 5:30 p.m. and only a few guests had arrived. We were aiming to start promptly at 6:00 p.m. come hell or high water. My already pressured mind was playing games with me. Shall we start the programme with just a few people in the audience? Then, on the other hand, it would not be prudent to have the President waiting. Colonel Gordon Ret'd. was in the thick of things; afterall, he had supervised the entire construction. We quickly decided that we were going to take him on a quick tour of the new facilities while we bought some time for our guests to arrive. I was never happier to see Mr. Ronald Robinson, fondly called Ron. He was our designated Master of Ceremonies for the evening. He arrived at 5:45 p.m., by which time I had decided in my mind that we were going to ask HR Manager, Mr. Ren Gonzales, to do the honors and deputize as the stand in MC if Ron didn't show up. It was surely refreshing when he did turn up!

At 6:00 p.m. sharp, we heard the loud sounds of the sirens blaring, announcing the arrival of our President. It all felt like a dream when I approached the arriving convoy. I stretched out my nervous right hand.

"Welcome Mr. President, my name is Andrew Boyle, it's truly an honor to have you here with us this evening."

"Madame First Lady, good to see you again."

My heart pounded, "Oh Lord, let it go smoothly." As soon as the presidential party entered the tents, Ras Camo and his musical arrangements skillfully played the National Anthem. It was one of those occasions when our anthem sounded very much like sweet music to the ears. Invariably like when you are overseas and the anthem is played and you are just a few who can identify with the lyrics. Normally it sounds quite routine and straight forward but this time it was emotional. I guess it's simply because it was an honor to hear it being played at our ceremony. This was precisely a magical moment; or was it just a dream?

The members of the media appeared from all angles as we entered the new building. There was nothing to show on the bottom floor because the offices were not quite furnished yet and Dr. Joseph's offices were all locked. I shyly explained that we were not quite ready as yet and led him on a detour to climb the stairs to showcase the exercise machines and the lovely conference facilities.

I began to climb the stairs with the President and First Lady and numerous media personnel, all trying to get good snapshots. My smiles for the cameras were genuine, as I felt extremely privileged, humbled, honored, proud and happy.

I heard in a distinct voice: "This is really a lovely building."

In mid strides, I glanced towards that familiar voice. *Oops, she got me!* Felicia Mariam Candacy Boyle-Bazard (my sister) had succeeded in surprising me. She had come all the way from The Bahamas to share our joyful occasion. I was honestly shocked! I wanted to turn back and give her the biggest of hugs but it would have been inappropriate and very disrespectful to his Excellency. *Wow, she really got me good this time!*

I chatted with the first family about the second floor, en passant, explaining that the Caribbean Heart Institute (CHI) was hoping to establish an outpatient department. When we got to the third floor, I explained that the exercise area and machines were going to be used by our members of staff and friends to keep fit. As we entered the conference room, I pointed out that I had brought the wood for the table from the Berbice River. The First Lady correctly suggested that it was Wamara, a very lovely and exotic local hardwood. This two-colored marvel looked exquisite against the mild gray curtains of the cool and comfortable conference room. I felt overwhelmed with happiness! It was frankly an exhilarating feeling.

While descending several photographers began shouting instructions. "One minute Mr. President!" "Mr. President! Mr. President!" After we posed halfway down the stairs for appropriate shots, we shook hands and the touring party was guided to their seats.

By then, the crowd of well-wishers and friends had gathered and we were ready for the show to begin. Ron Robinson, in his usual elegance and flare, captivated the audience with his wit and charm. He steered the programme like an experienced captain. The honorable Minister of Health, my dear and eloquent baby sister, Felecia, Dr. David Singh (representative of the Minister of Natural Resources), Karen, Keziah, myself, and President Granger all made glowing presentations. The second EML building was commissioned with pomp and ceremony and it felt good. Glory to God!

*First two Eureka buildings*

*Team Eureka during emancipation celebrations*

# CHAPTER 46

# Freemasons Lodge

My neighbor Dr. Lennox Applewaithe, Mr. Stanley Wills, and Capt. Egbert Field agreed to pay me a visit one Sunday afternoon, to discuss the possibility of my becoming a member of the English Freemasons' Lodge. It was indicated that this was a customary practice and a prerequisite for someone to be considered for membership into the organization. During these visits, it's normally expected that various questions, answers, and the general clarification of gray areas would be the main items on the agenda.

Actually, I had heard about Lodges before but never gave it any serious thought or consideration. There were strange stories circulating, e.g., about men escaping prosecution from the law by secretly indicating that they had some affiliation to this clandestine body. It was said that both of my grandfathers had been members of Lodges but there was little or no discussion about it, maybe they were probably inactive members. There was certainly an air of secrecy and mystery that accompanied discussions about this topic, as if there were something sacred and prohibited occurring.

There are many types of Lodges in the world and these various types are generally segregated by classes or one's position in life. The Mechanics, Foresters, English, Irish, Scottish Freemasons and the Prince Hall Masons are some of the Lodges found in Guyana. However, the Irish Freemasons and Prince Hall Masons are practically non-existent. The Foresters and Mechanics do include women in some of their institutions but the other Lodges previously mentioned do not.

Our conversation hovered around the basics and was rather cordial and impersonal and maybe used as a sort of "getting to know you" session. I offered them a few strong drinks while they tried to explain to me, and later Karen about the advantages of becoming a Freemason. They outlined the important role played by the institution in bringing relief to the underprivileged in our society. That becoming a Freemason was a voluntary decision and that there were no illegal nor unholy practices involved. They further intimated that the veil of secrecy was simply geared to protect and enhance the exclusivity of this grand institution. I was very encouraged by these discussions and immediately made the decision to become a member of this very coveted organization. This visit took place during the first year of our marriage and Karen too had no objection, therefore the way was set for me to assume the relevant steps for membership. The information meeting lasted for about two hours during which time the visitors outlined all the details that I was allowed to know. All of my questions were answered and misconceptions clarified.

I was proposed to join the Roraima Lodge, an affiliate of the English Freemasons, a Lodge that had been around for almost one hundred years in Guyana. Their meetings are usually held on the evening of the third Friday of every month. On that lovely August evening, I arrived at 6:00 p.m. for the ceremony that was due to commence at 6:30 p.m. I was told to be early on this, the night of my initiation. My new black two-piece suit was worn with pride and my well fitted white long sleeves shirt and black tie gave me an air of confidence but deep down inside I was a bit nervous. I was about to join an organization that is clouded by secrecy and mystery. This was further compounded when the late Albert Butters, the Secretary at that time, passed and said to his peers "He looks like he could tek it," and they in turn rolled with laughter. He has got to be joking, I said to myself with a sheepish and nervous grin. Clearly, I thought, these grown men couldn't all be involved in nonsense, then I remembered the assurances that were given to me by the senior brothers who had visited me.

The ceremony turned out to be a very brilliant and impressive one, where I was simply marveled by the articulate speeches and addresses. Oh yes, I was going to enjoy this august and ancient institution. The after-proceedings were even more gratifying as we all were privileged to partake in a sumptuous dinner and exquisite beverages. It was an enlightening experience for me in every respect, especially in the observation of various speaking protocols.

Over the many years that followed I thoroughly enjoyed Freemasonry and was fortunate to become friends with stalwarts like the late Albert Butters, Michael Elliot McLean Davis, Neville Peters, Melvin Austin Sankies, Edward Garnett Hopkinson, Cecil Norman Murray, Lloyd Piggott, Sydney Edwards, Bramanand Prashad, and Eon Caesar; may God rest their souls. These individuals have made positive impacts on my life because we were more than simply Lodge brothers but rather, great friends and comrades. Worthy of mention also are the living brothers whom I hold in high esteem, Egbert Field, Ivor O'Brien, Mark Bender, Erwin Chapman, Gary Hall, Aubrey Roberts, Dr. Lennox Applewhaite (my proposer), Fr. Clifton Elias, Dickson Hooper, Dr. Barton Scotland, Terence Seaforth, Rawle Jordan, Dr. Terrence Joseph, Dr. Clement McEwan, Andre Kellman, Flash, the Vandeyar brothers and the entire crew of the Guyana Wheel of Service, Roraima, and Kara Vander Lodges, amongst many others.

As I spent more time immersed in Freemasonry, I became more intrigued and learnt all the intricacies of this wonderful organization. My deep interest in the craft resulted in my being elevated to several high positions. After about five consistent years I eventually became the Worshipful Master (as the Chairman is known), then later elevated to join the District membership. Yes, it was and continues to be a distinct honor and privilege to be a Freemason.

*Brethren of Roraima Lodge with our district Grand Master, Roysdale Forde*

# CHAPTER 47

# Rotary Club of Georgetown Central

It was probably somewhere in 1999, during my first year as a Freemason when I met the late Mr. Melvin Austin Sankies who was also a member of Roraima Lodge. He was also a Senior Lecturer at the University of Guyana and a prominent mechanical engineer. Mel invited me to have lunch at the Guyana Pegasus Hotel where The Rotary Club of Georgetown Central held their weekly meetings on Thursdays at 12:00 noon. I indicated to him that my life was very complicated, and that my free moments were few and far apart. Mel kept saying that Rotary is for busy people and he thought that I would make a great Rotarian. I had heard about Rotary but my image of the persons in Rotary was that of aged, rich men or a "rich boys club."

I decided to give it a try, after all, I wanted to make a difference in the world and Rotary might just be that avenue. So, after visiting the club on three consecutive Thursdays, I was interviewed by senior Rotarians who explained all about Rotary. They explained the financial obligations, attendance requirements and all basic rules about Rotary, in a synopsis. My first impression of the club was surely not different from my initial perception. At 35 years old, I was definitely the youngest but I was made to feel at home even though there was no overt welcome per se. Rotary turned out to be so enjoyable that I would feel awkward whenever I didn't attend lunch meetings. It became a part of me and I grew nicely and rose up along the ranks. I was made Director of Community Services a mere week after my induction. It so happened that the previous director resigned and I was voted in to take up that very important position. I took my role seriously and gave it my all, after all, I was enjoying every minute of Rotary. Later that same year, I was selected to be the Rotarian of the Year, a distinct honor and privilege.

I took the bull by the horn and executed my task as a director with zeal and enthusiasm. I clearly remember how great I felt when I had given an oral of a monthly report. I was quite nervous but stuck to the issues and outlined my findings and suggestions. It was a thorough and very informative document that covered issues about the mobile dental unit. Though I was trembling like a leaf, I gave the discourse in front of those respected "elderly gentlemen." Some of them had strange ways of blurting out funny and sometimes unnerving comments, often unrelated, for lightening the atmosphere. Past Assistant Governor Ivor O'Brien was the chief culprit for these sudden interjections.

After one of my presentations, the late Terry Holder came up to me, patted my shoulder, and said, "Well done young man."

This simple gesture made me feel ecstatic. It reinforced the notion of how important kudos are for one's self-esteem and general well-being. Incidentally, I was also charged as the liaison officer with encouraging and supporting our Rotaractors, our younger service group. Because of my age, I was considered to be an honorary Rotaractor and we worked well together. Rotaractors are known for their enthusiasm and wild partying exploits. Oh, what an awesome bunch they are. Vibrant, hard-working, innovative, and fun-loving are all words that can be used to describe these progressive youngsters.

Rotary, particularly my club, was instrumental in being involved in sending and hosting students on exchange visits. I'm reminded that our current Vice Chancellor of the University of Guyana, Dr. Paloma Mohamed-Martin was one of those fortunate recipients. This particular foreign student exchange was done under the Presidency of one of our founding members, Past President, Randolph Choo-shee-nam.

The Rotary Club of Richmond Virginia of the USA had been collaborating in areas of dental health with our club over several years before I joined Rotary. Under the astute leadership of Dr. Julian Metts, it managed to bring much needed relief to the Guyanese children.

The Rotary Dental Bus, as it is called, is an old Greyhound bus that was retrofitted with five complete dental chairs, sinks, and all of the main comforts of a mobile dental unit. This is taken to various primary schools where children are offered free dental care. Digicel, Colgate, Palmolive, Banks, DIH, John Fernandes Ltd., Hand in Hand, and the Ministry of Health play a major role in financial support of this entity. At one point a few Rotarians and I were invited to visit our overseas partners and I relished that opportunity.

*Rotary's Mobile Dental Unit*

Past President Heather Johnson and myself, along with the late Past Presidents Mike Davis, Lloyd Piggot, and Mel Sankies, made this unforgettable trip to Virginia. It was truly an awesome journey, one that I will remember for a very long time.

It might have been sometime in October or November, the temperature was quite cold, and I was fortunate to have borrowed a coat from my brother-in-law, Terry Gordon, from New York. The thick furry coat served me well during my stay in Virginia. We attended several dinners and even met with President George Bush Sr. The fox hunting and bass fishing added excitement to this wonderful trip. My host, the late Russel Jones and his lovely Russian wife treated me like royalty and made my stay a super enjoyable one.

Our trip had ended and we left with a tremendous resolve to work harder and to improve our service to humanity. As we assembled to go through security checks as are the stringent requirements of international airport security, we bade farewells and wished each other well. An officer swabbed my coat that had served me ever so faithfully during my stay, he then placed the swab into a machine. I was caught by surprise when he muttered something that sounded like "code red, code red" to a hidden communication device on his shoulder. With guns drawn about six or seven security personnel appeared out of nowhere. Well, I was dumbfounded! I attempted to grab my carry-on bag and was immediately cautioned not to touch anything. *Dear Lord, was I going to be arrested?* In the meantime, my hosts automatically backtracked as the military men surrounded me, some with guns drawn. It was not long after 9/11 and they were very vigilant for security threats. They proceeded to search my belongings and asked me several searching questions like if I owned a firearm and to whom my faithful coat had belonged to.

"Do you have explosives strapped to your body?" was one of the interrogation questions. It turns out that the coat I was wearing had traces of gunpowder since my dear brother-in-law had been a member of the armed forces. *Whew! This was a scary end to a wonderful trip.* I happily and hurriedly returned the piece of proverbial clothing to my brother-in-law when I arrived in New York.

In Rotary, we were involved in, and successfully executed several striking and impressive projects. Doing these exercises were not only satisfying for the recipients but it brought personal satisfaction to us all. I had developed a very deep friendship with some of those elderly

Rotarians. I clearly remembered that day when Past President Mike Davis (PP Mike) came up to me and asked "Who is William Boyle from Kimbia to you?" After I responded that I am his proud son, he explained that Papa was his good friend. He reminded me that my Papa had supplied plantains and ground provisions to Bermine (the Kwakwani operation) and he felt that he owed him, Papa, a debt of gratitude.

The late PP Mike Davis took me under his wings and taught me. He was a genuine, amazing and powerful fellow, a Rotarian to the bone who had actually resigned because they were not allowing females to become members. This majestic leader only returned to rejoin Rotary when women were finally allowed to enter the halls of this prestigious organization.

Following the sad passing of PP Mike, the management of this bus eventually fell under my care as head of the dental project. I took up the challenge and it was really an honor to emulate such a great leader. I have found being a member of this wonderful organization to be one of my best decisions. Later, I was privileged to serve as President on three occasions. I learnt from the stalwarts; the massive Rotarians like PP Randy Chooshenam, PP Ron Robinson, PAG Keith Williams, PAG Ivor O'Brien, PP Claudette Harry, PP Gail Robinson, PP Heather Johnson, PP Judy Semple, PP Charles Woon A Tai, the late Rotarians PP Mel Sankies, PP Richard Berkley Fields, PP Terry Holder, PP Mike Davis, Rot Phillip Allsopp, PP Leslie Chin, and many others.

It was Rotarian Phillip who also remarked, in open meeting, that "PP Andy was the best president ever of our dear club." It was indeed heartwarming to hear one of the no nonsense and well-respected

Rotarians utter such kind words. Though I didn't believe it myself, it really felt good. I became a 'Paul Harris (PH) Fellow' on two occasions and I'm also a member of the Paul Harris Society. One who contributes $1,000 US to Rotary International (RI) can become a Paul Harris Fellow and one who donates $1,000 US annually to RI qualifies as a PH society member. These funds are used for various humanitarian projects including the fight against Polio.

Kudos to you, my fellow Rotarians, keep up the amazing work. It's not going to be easy but trust me, you are touching lives in no small way and people are honestly grateful for your efforts.

*Past Presidents of Rotary Guyana*

# CHAPTER 48

# Colonel Clarence Maurice Gordon

There are few people in this world who have golden hearts. Colonel Clarence Maurice Gordon Ret'd. is one such individual. I've learnt a whole lot from him during those almost three years of knowing him. He was a man of class in every way including being an accomplished ballroom dancer. He stuck to his promises and delivered on them, just like my Grandad did. He might not have been as timely as was expected but still managed to deliver on those promises. I suppose he was busy fulfilling other needs. This good gentleman would leave his farm on the Soesdyke Linden Highway at 8:00 a.m., a one-hour drive, and eventually, get to Georgetown at roughly around 2:00 p.m. and that was on an early occasion. The fact that he was so well known and liked by many, both near and far was surely a contributing factor.

Pops or Dada, as I used to call him, was an overtly generous and genuine fellow. He was given that name because Andrew Jr. couldn't come to say grandad but instead called him Dada. My team members used to say, "That man didn't know how to say no." He obviously had lots of needs but he took pleasure in giving. He was not a Rotarian but clearly, he was one at heart.

During the construction of Eureka's first two buildings, he was the main advisor, quantity surveyor, architect, and consultant and insisted on the collection of zero fees. When my father died, Dada came up to me and said, "I'll now be your father." I did cherish those kind and generous words; they meant the world to me. We had lunch together for several years, mainly at the Rasta Vegetarian restaurant next door to EML. Dada was also a permanent member of our Friday night hang with Rawle Jordon (Gino) and Terence Seaforth (12). During these 'boardroom' sessions his drink of choice was Absolut Vodka and soda water (sometimes plain water), he never backed down from drinking a few bottles of beer.

His early life was intriguing! He would frequent the trenches on his way home from school to get a good swim and play. On one such occasion, he hid his school clothes nicely in the bushes and proceeded to have a blast with his buddies. A massive problem was created when he simply could not locate them afterward. He had to end up going home with his hands covering his private parts, without school books and garments. You could only imagine the amount of licks he got. Despite his 'Tom Sawyer' like youthful escapades, he turned out into a fine gentleman.

Dada and his wife, May, raised Karen, Terry, and Ato. Lawrence, Dr. Ramon (uncle Rambo), Samantha and Dorian (who lived with us for several years), are his children too. This faithful son of the soil lived a good life and his glorious legacy will certainly live on with us. Thank you, Dada, for touching our lives in a significant and profound way. Let's raise our glasses to the Colonel!

*The late Col. Gordon and I*

# CHAPTER 49

# Paho's Recognition

It was May 14th, 2016, on the evening of our daughter's seventeenth birthday when it happened. I had also, just a few days before, quietly celebrated another milestone. She had reluctantly agreed to accompany us to the PAHO/WHO's 50th anniversary awards dinner at the Marriott. Keziah was not too keen on formal events, but loved going to the movies or having breakfasts at Grand Coastal, The Hermandstand Lodge, Cara Lodge and the Marriott.

The elegant Marriott ballroom was splendidly decorated with the colorful drapes of our national flag along with bright 50th anniversary logos placed at strategic points. It was a classy affair, one nicely done with pomp and ceremony. We were ushered to table number 3 but not before stopping to greet the Ministers of Health and Agriculture, and a few acquaintances along the way. My inner hunch told me that I was going to receive an award or was probably in for a little surprise.

The Anniversary celebrations began with a very tasteful flare, with our homegrown and good vocalist, Jackie Jazz singing her heart out, 'The Guyana Song.' It's such an amazing pleasure to hear her in person. Guyana is truly blessed to have Lisa Punch, Tamika Marshall, Juke

Ross, Terry Gajraj and Jackie Jazz, all young local singers who should be supported and given opportunities to go to that next level. They are truly marvelous. *When was the last time you listened to one of their songs?*

Several deserving companies and individuals received various awards for their sterling contributions. Karen's name was also called and she copped a trophy for her dedicated service to Guyana's Health Care industry. Quite deserving indeed!

It was surprising to hear my name being called to collect another prestigious award.

"For sterling and valued contributions to the Health Care of Guyana," were the words on the plaque given to Eureka Medical Laboratories Inc. It was truly another joyful moment to be recognized by PAHO on that glorious evening.

# CHAPTER 50

# Anthony Sabga Award of Excellence

"Hello, good afternoon," echoed the very cultured voice in the unmistakable Trinidadian accent.

"Is this Mr. William Andrew Boyle?" she continued in a very purposeful, businesslike tone. Being totally unaware of the nature of the call, I responded appropriately:

"Yes, good afternoon, this is he." I further added, "How may I be of assistance?"

"This is Maria Superville-Neilson, from the Anthony Sagba/Ansa Mcal Laureate awards," the very calm and cultured voice continued.

By then my heart was racing almost out of control and thoughts running wild. Was this a prank call? A prank? What is she going to say next? As I listened carefully. By this time a bubble had formed in my throat. The split second between her introduction and the real reason for her call seemed like a lifetime.

"I wish to inform you that you have been awarded with the Laureate for Entrepreneur of the Caribbean, 2018!"

The muffled scream that thoughtlessly escaped my quivering lips was quite uncharacteristic of me but the announcement clearly warranted it. She continued to say that it's an official decision and that I should not make any public announcements as they were going to make the necessary statements at a press conference scheduled on the following Tuesday, at 10:00 a.m. She further said other things like congratulations and something about Sir. Shridat Ramphal writing me an official letter. They were clear and concise words but somewhat incoherent at this time.

"Would you accept this award?" she questioned me finally.

My 'yes' was not firm and convincing and slightly muffled from the deep sense of excitement and positive confusion. My wide, beaming smiles and half chuckles coupled with my pleasurable thoughts prevented me from capturing and digesting all that was being said. *Oh, Heavenly Father, I had won this prestigious and coveted award!* When she eventually hung up, I felt the freedom to scream and not be contained.

"Yessssss, Yaaay, Yepeeee, I did it!" were screamed from my trembling lips as tears of joy rolled down my cheeks.

Dominique and Germaine who were in my adjoining secretariat had heard the commotion and came knocking.

"I won, I won!" I simply couldn't contain myself as I tearfully hugged them both.

*Was I in a beautiful never-ending dream? Oh dear God, did I really win it? Am I a Laureate?* After the sting of my signature journey up to cloud nine had subsided and my beaming team members finished conveying their congratulations, I said a quiet prayer to the Almighty;

*Thank you dear Lord for your infinite blessings. Dear God, you have blessed this humble river boy beyond measure. You are my Lord and I thank you wholeheartedly.*

The days that followed, my amazing story was amply covered all over social and print media, along with various press conferences and TV appearances. I was treated like a celebrity; Oh what a wonderful feeling of accomplishment! I, however, remained humble and grateful to God and all of my team and family members who made this a vivid reality. I had a mere four months to prepare to receive my grand award. On May 6th, 2018, in Kingston, Jamaica, with pomp and ceremony, I was going to be crowned as the Entrepreneur of the Caribbean, 2018.

Preparations were in train and some of my immediate family members had journeyed with me to Kingston, Jamaica. My dear Mom, Ken, Glendon, Valerie, Camille, Felecia, Colonel Clarence Gordon Ret'd., Tony, Andrew Jr., and Keziah all formed part of my entourage. Glendon had flown for the first time and was, like everyone, super excited. We all flew in a few days prior to the evening of celebrations. Maria, Raymond, and Sharon, the extremely efficient organizers took charge of the rehearsals and eventually, the evenings proceeding.

That evening of May 6th was arguably the most colorful night of my life. The pomp and flare were immense and lavish. My fellow Laureates and I were made to feel truly special. When it was my turn to go on stage to receive my coveted award, I was a bit nervous but ecstatic and soaring on cloud nine. During my acceptance speech, I kindly asked my mother to stand and paused as they gave her thunderous cheers of appreciation. I was later told that there were people in the audience who were emotional and awed at my story. After the ceremony, we took dozens of photographs with my fellow Laureates, Mr. Norman Sabga, Sir. Shridat Ramphal, Major General Joe Singh Ret'd., Prof. Harris and other members of the eminent panel.

The evening and all of the after proceedings were truly awesome and unforgettable. One that I will always cherish and hold dear to my heart. To God be the Glory! I was awarded almost $20,000,000 (Twenty million Guyanese dollars) for that amazing accolade. A part of the funds were used for 'Inspire Kimbia.' This exercise was created to provide tangible assistance to my alma mater, Kimbia Primary School. Two concrete rooms were constructed below the existing school building and were furnished with seven computers and printers. Team members for the Caribbean Wind and Sun Inc., one of my other companies, skillfully installed a solar PV system big enough to power the project.

On Sunday, September 1st, 2019, The Rotary Clubs of Georgetown Central, Stabroek, Demerara, and New Amsterdam along with our Rotaractors, Eureka Medical Laboratories Inc. and Caribbean Wind and Sun Inc. did an amazing job at launching Inspire Kimbia. This was simply my way of giving back to my river people. My plan is not to stop with this single project but to continue to provide tangible assistance to my old school in the future.

**Thursday December 14, 2017** — *Kaieteur News*

## Eureka Labs founder nominated for entrepreneur award

Founder of Eureka Labs, William Boyle, is the latest Guyanese to be nominated for the Anthony N Sabga Caribbean Awards for Excellence.

Boyle, a microbiologist who built Eureka into a respected, accredited lab that is one of the top facilities of its kind in the region, would be among persons when the four awards in different categories are given out next year.

Boyle's nomination would see him join the likes of turtle conservationist, Annette Arjoon-Martins and Professor David Dabydeen.

According to a release from the awards committee, Boyle is a medical services entrepreneur.

The committee explained that he is the founder of the Eureka laboratory which provides state-of-the-art ... the country and

Information System (LIS) services, whereby test results can be accessed by doctors online, and in real time."

It was explained that in the late 1980s, working for the University of Guyana, and at the Georgetown Hospital Tropical Diseases Lab as a medical microbiologist, Boyle noticed the lack of adequate and high-quality medical laboratory services in his country.

"To meet this need the EML was formed in 1995. From a start with a limited range of tests, performed manually by two staff members, EML today consists of a main laboratory in Georgetown and eight smaller collection/minor test branches within Guyana. He has subsequently introduced a wide range of the latest tests, over 1,000, as well as up-to-date laboratory equipment."

... average of over 20,000 per year, as well as sixty major companies. Senior citizens are also offered a 10% discount. The lab serves an ...

... added to the Eureka serv...
His innovative prov... merely directed to ... business. In 2016 Boyle ... his Georgetown and A... laboratories and his lo... power. And in Marc... founded the Caribbean... Sun Inc. of which he ... director, to help pro... energy installations na...

"Entirely away fr... and technology, Mr ... diversified into an ega... and supply business... Farms. His 'Produ... Berbice River' brand b... source of pride and em... persons from the area...

He is the recipie... awards, inclu... PAHO/WHO for i... contribution to pub... leadership from th... Chamber of Co... innovation, in re... recorded bre... achievements in ... processes, market... and development...

*Nominated for an entrepreneur award: Eureka's founder, William Boyle*

*Newspaper clipping of the Prestigious Award*

*Proud Laureate for Entrepreneur of the Caribbean, 2018*

*Congratulations*

To

*Past President William Andrew Boyle*
*from the Rotary Club of Georgetown Central*
*on being conferred with the*
*Golden Arrow of Achievement*

*President Granger conferring me with The Golden Arrow of Achievement*

*Being featured in the INC Magazine*

*Thank you, Republic Bank*

*Relaxing in my office*

# CHAPTER 51

# Menzo Collin Boyle Aka Balram/Pado/Governor

Zack Alphonso, my sister Valerie's third son, was going to graduate in the field of theatrical arts. Yes! our first actor in the family. Mom and I left Guyana on an American Airlines flight on Thursday, February 6th, 2020. On this well-coordinated trip, we arranged to meet with six of my ten siblings. This was going to be another mini-family reunion. We were all super excited even though it meant a whole lot of flying. It meant us, Mom and I, traveling from Guyana to Miami, then to Orlando. This first leg was surely not as long as the next one, which took us all the way to Los Angeles, California. Our trips to Miami and Orlando were uneventful. I tried without success to have my dear Mom stop rubbing her hands on the rails of the escalators while in the airports.

"Mom, you can infect yourself with something if you keep on doing that." I gently warned on each occasion.

It must be awkward and maybe a bit tiring for the elderly to desist from touching those supposedly contaminated surfaces. When we arrived safely in Orlando the weather was very pleasant and invitingly comfortable. It was as though we were back in Georgetown. The temperature was comparable and perfect.

Keziah picked us up from the airport. Oh, what a joy to have her do the honors. These children do grow up quickly and before you know it, they are no longer babies. She is now twenty years old and heading to twenty-one in a matter of months. Kez had also grown into a lovely, courteous, well-mannered, and gentle little lady. She drove very efficiently to our destination as she clearly was very familiar with the route. After spending one night in Orlando, it was time for us to make the flight all the way to Los Angeles. Different flight itineraries were chosen, probably being cautious or because of the various passengers' availability and schedules. In essence, it took five different flight arrangements for our traveling family members to get to LA.

The flight to LA was a relatively long and tiring one. I was worried about Mom. Was it too much for her, after having flown all the way from Guyana? It was quite fine initially but after a few hours, we began flying in turbulence. During inclement weather or sometimes with seemingly nice and sunny conditions, the air turbulence can make flights very uncomfortable and scary. I often wondered, *suppose the plane crashes?*

I held on to my seat and said a few quiet prayers. It was as though we were all riding wild and bucking horses. At one moment, the aircraft made a sudden drop and continued with several up and down movements. Some of the passengers screamed and the pilot, with a very calming voice, indicated that we were experiencing a little bumpy patch and that we should adhere to the seat belt rules. Pilots are trained to remain calm. Their usually soothing utterances tend to have a calming effect on the worried passengers. It was terrible! *Was this going to be our premature end?* It was quite a frightening experience. After a few more jerky, up and down movements it subsided. Mom and Felecia were sitting somewhere in the middle of the aircraft and I was in one of those seats at the back. I couldn't see their reactions and facial expressions as we were hit by those turbulences.

I was later told that Mom had developed a coughing frenzy during most of the almost six hour flight. The Covid-19 pandemic has not taken root as yet but many persons were very cognizant of the dreaded disease. Persons who coughed were frowned upon as they feared contracting the same. I could imagine how badly Mom must have felt. The sudden and drastic drop in the temperature when we arrived in LA might also have greatly contributed to her discomfort.

We arrived safely after a pretty rough flight. As we left the airport, I noticed that Mom appeared tired and haggard. She started coughing uncontrollably once again. We gave her sips of water which worked temporarily. Oh, she must have been having a terrible time. There was obviously a cold front in LA on the evening of Friday, February 7th, 2020. The place seemed mercilessly cold! Leaving the warm climates of Georgetown and Orlando makes a drastic contrast to cold LA. This shock affected Mom as we boarded the shuttle and headed for the hotel. I felt sorry for her as she took regular sips of water in an attempt to ease her annoying coughing. A few passengers took searching glances at her. Maybe they wondered whether she was afflicted by the dreaded Covid-19.

The ride to the hotel was relatively short and uneventful. I wanted us to get to the hotel quickly so that she could get some rest. It must have been a horrible traveling experience for our poor Mom. Later that evening, we got her some cough mixtures. Felecia, our little sister, along with her son, Kalen and I were chosen to share a room with her. The three of them shared one bed and I was privileged to have my own. It was therefore not surprising when later that night I also started to cough horribly. Maybe the rigors of two days of long flights, coupled with drastic changes in temperature might have gravely contributed to us developing this flu. That night was quite a miserable one for us as we both coughed our heads off. Later that night, Collin and his wife, Rose, arrived from Miami. Their room, 511 was just next to ours, 509. They arrived very late during the night so we didn't see each other.

Zack's graduation was scheduled to be held at 10am, on Saturday, February 8th, 2020. It should be noted that 10:00 a.m. in LA can be equated to 2:00 p.m. Guyanese time. We decided to sleep a little longer than usual since we were afforded time. Suddenly, there was a loud banging on our door. It was almost 9:00 a.m. Mom and I looked at each other. Maybe they will simply go away if not attended to.

"Bang! Bang!" The person or persons persisted, with deep urgency. With a sheet wrapped around me, I mustered the courage to go see who was being so obnoxious and persistent.

"Come on, open the damn door!" Collin exclaimed as he and Rose entered. Our seemingly annoyed impromptu visitors pushed and forcibly entered as I barely opened the door to see who it was. This forced entry was jokingly done.

"Why is this room so hot? Good morning, Mom, how you feeling?" He greeted us with a wicked smirk.

Felecia interjected, "Quiet maan, you gon wake up da puppy (referring to little Kalen, who was fast asleep)."

"Bal, you not getting ready for Zack's graduation?" Collin again made his presence felt.

I was honestly not in the mood for small talk. I then interrupted in a frenzy of uncontrollable coughing.

"No bro, we can't make it, we sick like dogs here. You guys go and please give an explanation to the folks." I managed to blurt out, in the midst of my coughing. By that time, I was back wrapped up in my bed, nice and cozy.

"Rose, let's get out of here before we catch Bal's nasty bug."

"Okay Bal, I'll tell you about it later."

A few years prior, I was the recipient of a massive blow to my scrotum when one of my nephews hit me. While playing, he jumped and accidentally struck me with his knee with a massive "thump" to my scrotum ('balls'). The blow was severe and I was even forced to use ice to soothe the pain. After a few months, one of my testes began to swell uncontrollably. I had also been struck there on many occasions in the past while wicket keeping, but on those instances, I wore a scrotal or seed guard. I ended up having surgery to remove the affected testes and made a full recovery shortly afterwards. I had it tested for malignancy and was given a clean bill of health. My dear brother Collin, with his jovial self, started to call me one seed Balram. Now, it's usually difficult for false names to stick on me because I turn the tables and call the perpetrators those same names. I started calling him Balram and he ended up with the name instead and I was left with a shortened version in Ram. He insisted on calling me Bal though and rarely, Ram. Hence an explanation of those funny false names.

They hurried out and were on their way. There is no way we could have made that journey to Zack's graduation. It was most likely extremely cold outside and our coughing had not subsided by much. It would have been almost suicidal to have gone out in that miserable coldness. So, Mom, the puppy and I stayed in bed with the hope of us beating the flu. We both took fruits for breakfast as we had lost our appetite. Felecia got us oranges, apples, sliced pineapple and melon. Those worked fine and I recommended taking fruits when there is little or no appetite. We slept for most of the day and our coughing subsided somewhat. Before we knew it, it was already early evening.

I was in a deep and peaceful sleep when my phone rang. "Bal, wake up u R--s! I'm going to take everyone to dinner." It was Collin again. He then added:

"How you feeling bro? How Mom?"

I responded that we were still somewhat under the weather and it might have been too risky to venture out in our present condition. I further insisted that they carry on the sporting exercise without us. He seemed somewhat disappointed but I guess he understood because he didn't persist.

A few more hours of sleep, while intermittently taking medicine for the cough, took up the entire afternoon and later that evening. This extended rest did us well and we were already on the way to a full recovery.

It might have been about midnight, LA time when someone banged at the door. I was jolted from my pleasant dreams once again. I don't recall the details but my dreams were rather pleasant. They thumped on the door as though they lived there and had overwhelming rights. Clearly, that could only have been Balram. The impatient banging continued unabated.

"What's your problem, Balram, let me sleep nuh," I angrily muttered as I opened the door.

"Ram, u still in the same clothes that you had on since yesterday!" Balram exclaimed as he and sister Rose brushed past me. I could smell the whiffs of alcohol on his breath as they pushed themselves into our room.

"Come on Ram, time you have a bath! Rose, he does the same thing when we go up the river, would you believe it?"

His ridicule was relentless. Clearly, he had consumed quite a few drinks. By then I had snuggled back under my covers but my socks-covered feet were slightly exposed. He proceeded to snatch off my socks and threw them across the room.

"Come on Ram, don't go back to sleep now, you really missed out on a good lime. We had dinner at one of Kurt's friend's, a peace corps dude. The man is a frigging beer connoisseur, he had nine kegs of amazing flavors. He is a frigging zythophile bro." What the hell is a zythophile? I didn't bother to ask him. I got up to go get my socks and as soon as I wrapped myself under the cozy covers, he again tried to remove them but couldn't.

"Mom, how are you feeling dear? Haven't you noticed that your son is still in the clothes that he traveled in? He has not had a bath, no wonder why this room is so hot and smelly."

"Leave the boy alone, he is not feeling well," answered Mom.

"Careful, don't wake up your nephew with your noise," she added.

Kalen, aka puppy Shark, Felecia, and Kent's one-year old child were left in our care during the day and night.

"Ram, so you gon bathe now?" Collin seemed not to want to let go of this juicy discovery. Sister Rose, who was quiet all the time, jumped in.

"Collin, leave your brother alone now, he is sick." Collin shot back, "Of course he must be sick not to bathe, it's the third day now, Rose. He does this all the time when we travel, he must be sick indeed." She pushed him out of the room while he continued to mutter, "Go bathe bro, go bathe Ram."

The rest of the night was uneventful and we all dozed off once again into deep slumber. The flu was practically gone, maybe the copious amounts of rest along with heavy and regular doses of liquid Tylenol cough suppressant, together with large amounts of water probably did the trick. I was almost myself once again and felt much better. Mom, however, was still a bit under the weather and though on the road to recovery, was not quite there as yet. I figured that with meds and a few days more of rest she would be back to her bouncy self.

Sunday morning my other siblings insisted that we take a trip to Hollywood. It was quite a reasonable suggestion as I had been practically shut in for the entire previous day. It really felt like a lot longer than just a day. Maybe it was because I had missed the graduation and later, that much talked about dinner. This time I gave myself a nice and refreshing bath. I felt good about it.

The LA midday weather was no different that Sunday from the previous day. In my almost recovered fragile state, I felt the cold temperatures down to my bone. My head was now covered with a knitted beret that didn't look nor fit as fashionable as I would have wished. We gathered in the hotel's lobby before taking off. "Where is Balram?" I inquired from my other siblings. I was informed that he and Rose were fast asleep and that he had now started coughing. He was also due to travel to Las Vegas later that Sunday evening. I decided against harassing him like he did me; perhaps he was indeed feeling miserable.

We had quite an enjoyable afternoon and I took the opportunity to bond a bit with Keziah. Her flight back to Orlando was that same Sunday evening. We walked gingerly along Hollywood's star-studded streets. A short distance of about 8 ft. apart, on the pavements, had the names of famous actors, musicians, and other individuals who would have won Oscars. I saw several popular names engraved on those shiny gold-colored stars. Maybe one day, who knows, my name will be engraved as one of the stars. You know what? Today, February 9th, 2020, I'm speaking it into being!

We were hoping to see the celebrities in person but some of the roads were blocked as scores of police prevented passersby from walking anywhere near where the Oscars were being presented. The weather was not very pleasant but this time I was properly attired with a matching LA soft hat that also covered my ears.

We returned from a very pleasant walk in downtown LA and I proceeded to pack. My flight to NY was early on Monday morning. Collin and Rose had already left for their 'getaway' in Las Vegas, Nevada. They owned a massive timeshare program which afforded them the luxury of enjoying absolute pampering once every year. They both loved the casinos so their vacations in Las Vegas were befitting of their mutual desires.

It was later confirmed that he (Collin) had contracted an annoying bout of our coughing disease. Indeed (Mom and I) obviously gave him that infection when he frequented our room.

My flight that early Monday morning to New York was uneventful, it was long and tiring though. My annoying cough had practically subsided and it was no longer of any major concern. It was another five-hour flight and there was a rollback in the timings again. So, in essence, my flight from Los Angeles commenced at 7:00 a.m., arrived at 12:00 midday but that was really 4:00 p.m. in NY. Despite the time difference and unstable and fluctuating weather, flying to various destinations is an exciting and rewarding experience but can also be a very tiring one too.

Tony was there at the JFK airport, waiting for me and had brought a very thick winter coat. I had just planned to spend one evening with him. The next day, I was hoping to spend time with the Colonel, who was receiving treatment for pancreatic cancer in NY. Tony and I had planned to make a surprise visit to him. I love to give surprises, in my opinion they add flavor and spice to life. I always look forward to seeing the reaction of the people being surprised.

We spent most of the night chatting about Tony's upcoming wedding which was slated for July 17th, 2020, a mere few months away. Even though my entire day was practically spent traveling, I was not very tired, probably because I had slept during the flight and I had my full share of rest and relaxation in LA. We talked about almost everything until it was time to hit the sack.

The following day, Monday, February 10th, 2020, as we were on our way to visit his grandparents, my phone rang a few times. It was probably around 8:30 a.m., who could be calling me at this time? I purposefully didn't answer because I figured it might have been an unimportant call, but when the caller or callers persisted and called again, I decided to answer.

"Collin collapsed and was rushed to the hospital," My brother-in-law, Kurt Alphonso, was almost incoherent.

"Is he okay? What happened?" I managed to question, while holding back tears. Strange how one's emotions can affect his or her demeanor. This was very shocking. He didn't seem to have all the details.

"They managed to get his heart beating again."

"Oh dear God, let him recover," I prayed silently.

"Tony, pull over, stop the car, Uncle Collin is unconscious and in the hospital."

I tried hard to hold back from having an emotional breakdown. How could this be? He was there monkeying around only a few days ago. I then frantically called Valerie to have her book an available and realistic flight to Las Vegas and make reservations for a hotel not too far away from the Desert Springs Hospital, the institution to which Collin had been taken. I then messaged Annique, his daughter, who was in St. Vincent but got no answer. Rose, as was expected, didn't answer, perhaps she was too busy at the hospital and coming to grips with the recent occurrences. Tony continued along the way to visit his grandparents. We still had enough time to pay them a quick visit before heading to the JFK International airport. Having telephone contact is truly amazing as all of the flight and hotel arrangements were skillfully coordinated. My dear sister, Valerie, worked like an efficient secretary to have all the kinks and rough edges sorted out for my return flight all the way to Las Vegas.

My check-in time for my flight to Las Vegas, Nevada was 5:00 p.m. NY time which was equivalent to about 1:00 p.m. there in LV. My mind kept racing and my imagination ran wild. Was this a serious and life-threatening situation? Is Balram going to recover? I hurriedly checked in for my flight; all along I was in another world. One security officer actually asked me if I was alright, and that I had seemed dazed. My flight was uneventful and I might have slept a bit during that never-ending journey.

Las Vegas airport was, like most airports in the U.S., quite classy. My wondering and worried mind did not permit me to absorb the surrounding beauty of the airport and the well-lit city of Nevada. It was sometime around 10:00 p.m. or there about when I arrived, my very first time in lovely Las Vegas. My immediate goal was to check in quickly at the hotel Valerie had booked, drop off my baggage, and head straight to the Desert Springs Hospital. My hotel was located a mere ten minutes away from the hospital. I had the taxi wait for me to check in and drop off my baggage.

The hospital was a huge and quite modern one. The taxi driver dropped me at the main entrance. It was almost midnight and there were not many people hustling and bustling about. My mind was racing. Is Collin going to be sitting up with his wicked smile or was he still unconscious? What was it going to be like? I had finally arrived at the hospital after a very long and tiring journey. Are there going to be surprises? Strange enough, there was no one at the front desk so I wandered around in search of someone to direct me accordingly. There was absolutely no one in sight. Then suddenly an elevator door opened and out popped a pretty little nurse; she seemed like a Filipino. I approached her and told her that I was there to see my brother and needed direction. She asked for the name of the patient. She surprisingly indicated that she had just finished attending to him and graciously offered to accompany me to see him. We rejoined the elevator and she pointed out that he was on the fourth floor. She walked quite quickly and we moved through some intricate twists and turns until we finally arrived. During our walk through, I tried to find out how he was doing but she cleverly gave me diplomatic answers.

"He is being attended to and is unconscious," she managed to say while we walked quickly along the corridors. He was in a private room and from the view box in the middle of the door I recognized Rose sitting at his bedside. He was on a ventilator and hooked up to machines. The friendly nurse gave me a disposable gown and masks to put on. I don't think I managed to properly thank her enough for her kindness because there was absolutely no way I was going to easily find him.

As I entered, Rose held on to me and cried her heart out. "How is he?" I managed to ask from under the yellow surgical mask while fighting back my tears.

"I thought I had lost him." She managed through her sobs.

I held his hands and tried talking directly to him.

"Wake up star, you got this, come on bro." His expressionless stare was heartbreaking. Jesus Lord, save my brother I prayed silently while Rose cried unabated. It was as though she had it all pent up. We both cried as she explained what had transpired.

He had developed a terrible cough shortly before leaving for Las Vegas which most likely he had picked up from our sick room. He had coughed on his way to and in the airport and also on the airplane. They had arrived safely on Sunday, February 9th. He had taken cough meds and felt better. The following day was their 30th wedding anniversary, quite an interesting occurrence. They had thoroughly enjoyed those 30 years of total bliss. Here is a classic example of true love and togetherness. Collin had confessed to me on several occasions that he had thoroughly made the right choice in marrying his best friend. Indeed, he and Rose were tailor-made for each other.

She further narrated that they had had a pretty good breakfast after sleeping late on their anniversary morning. It was customary for them, while holidaying, to sleep up to some ridiculously late hours, sometimes up to midday.

"All was so good with him; he was recovering nicely." She confessed. They had spent practically the entire day of their special day relaxing in bed. Later that evening they both decided to go downstairs to the casino to 'try out their luck.' This is a subtle weakness they both enjoyed. They relished their annual pilgrimage to the welcoming arms of the Las Vegas casinos. Their yearly voyage was therefore something for which they yearned. They both worked extremely hard hence these trips were quite deserving.

Even though he, Collin, was not in tip-top condition, they had decided to go downstairs to the casino in Planetarium. As the games became sweeter and encouraging, they both became engrossed in their individual worlds. They might have been there for a couple of hours. It's amazing how time flies when one is enjoying the moment. After playing for perhaps a few hours and she noticed that he was nowhere near to where she was playing the slot machines, she glanced at her phone and noticed that he had messaged her. His note read that he was going up to the room as he was not feeling too well. Immediately, she decided to end her game and hurry to go check on her husband. On arriving at the bedroom, she noticed that he was fast asleep so she quietly crawled into bed, hoping not to disturb him.

Around 5:00 a.m. the next morning, she was jolted from her sleep by his cries of anguish. While clutching his chest and sitting on the bed, he exclaimed that he was having difficulty breathing. He then suddenly collapsed on the bed, still holding his chest in anguish. She immediately and tearfully jumped up and switched on the lights. Collin indeed was not responsive and had urinated himself, he appeared to be dead. My dear sister-in-law told me that she did try to offer him CPR but was unsure of how effective she was. Dear God, was he dead? She tried desperately to revive him but panicked and screamed out loudly. Rosemary is a doctor, but she is also a human being too. That is why it's usually advisable, as a doctor, not to self-treat or examine and attend to one's family members. One's judgments are usually clouded and impaired.

During all this time his face was expressionless and had begun to appear blue, probably from the lack of oxygen. She finally managed to get into contact with the front desk. Paramedics were in the house and they scrambled to get to their room. It was a race against time because some time had elapsed from when he had lost consciousness and stopped breathing. They eventually restarted his heart and hooked him up to an oxygen source but he remained unconscious. "Dear God, save his life, oh holy Jesus," Sister Rose prayed as they whisked him away to the hospital. Even though he remained unconscious, at least he was breathing, aided by oxygen that was being supplied via a mask. Even though the situation seemed relatively stable, she couldn't stop herself from crying. With blaring sirens, they rushed through the streets of Las Vegas. The ambulance ride to the Desert Springs Hospital was not a long one, probably around fifteen minutes. Collin was immediately rushed to ICU for urgent treatment. It was then that Rose managed to alert the other family members of this tragedy via telephone.

Having learned the minute details of what had transpired, I gave Sister Rose some reassuring words that all was going to be well. I also insisted that she went to the room in the waiting area to rest and that I was going to take over the vigils. There was a couch there that served for this purpose. She must have been tired and clearly needed to take a break.

When she reluctantly left, I proceeded to tell him all kinds of subtle words of encouragement, then a few harsher ones.

"Get up yuh backside nuh bro, come on yuh r--s."

It is normally said that one, even in an unconscious state, usually hears when people converse in their close environs. All throughout this one-sided discourse, I was partially expecting a response from him but absolutely none came forth.

During that first night of vigil, I might have dozed off a few times. The nurses were back and forth, ensuring that Collin was cleaned and that all was in order. Sitting next to him, I could see the nurses hustling and bustling in their station which was situated just outside. Later, I was told that he was diagnosed with having both Influenza A & B in addition to having suffered a cardiac arrest.

The room was relatively small but allowed for two simple chairs and his many gadgets. One monitor on his near right indicated his temperature, pressure, heart rate, etc. That on his left was hooked up to his ventilator and assisted with his breathing. It also displayed his oxygen levels and his breathing strength. His eyes were slightly opened but were gazing without any emotions whatsoever.

This scenario continued for a few days and we rotated our vigil. I did the days and Rose did the evenings. Collin remained in a coma but my presence was very supportive, especially to her. During one of the subsequent days, we noticed that his eyes would open for a bit and then close again. This occurred in fifteen-second intervals. Was this a glimmer of hope? We looked for subtle signs of possible improvement but none was forthcoming.

The doctors seemed to think that his brain had suffered irreparable damage and that the prognosis was bad. He was not improving; his kidneys had practically shut down and he had to be dialyzed several times. His sugar levels remained over 300 mg/dl and kidney function levels were also abnormally high. His hemoglobin level was also frighteningly low and he was transfused on two occasions to boost his blood levels. So, there were a few components of his body functions that were not up to speed.

When their daughters, Ayesha and Annique Boyle arrived it was heartbreaking. He had loved them dearly and the father-daughter bond the three of them shared was beyond anything I'd ever seen. It was a classic example of profound love and friendship. Annique had confided in him and would even discuss things that she would dare not tell her mother. I knew because we, Collin and I, shared an extraordinary bond and friendship.

"Wake up daddy, please don't die, I love you so, so, much."

My heart was torn into multiple pieces when I heard Annique's overt expression of love and grief.

It took a herculean effort to have their two daughters join us in the United States. Annique's visa had expired. The renewals of visas usually take no less than two weeks. The appropriate appointments had to be arranged and a visit to the US embassy in Barbados also needed to have been made. A letter, outlining the gravity of the situation, from the Desert Springs Hospital was sent to the St. Vincent and the Grenadines' government. They in turn then sent another one to the US embassy requesting that Annique's visa be expedited. Two horrible things happened - the letter was not immediately dispatched to the relevant persons in SVG and sat on someone's desk for a few days. Then a rumor was hatched, I suppose as a result of that bit of correspondence, that he had died.

Rumors in villages and countryside are often dispersed like bushfires during the dry weather. They are spread with impunity and are often changed and spice added. Someone went on to post on his Facebook page. "Sleep well Dr. Boyle, rest in eternal peace and rise in glory." I happened to notice the baseless post and quickly requested that it be removed forthwith. He eventually did but by then the damage had already been done. Calls began to pour in, some even went on to express deepest condolences. Now, during all this drama, we were trying to keep the news of his illness from our mother.

Mom is a very special person, one who worries and becomes totally depressed even with the slightest bad news about any of her children. Collin's chances of recovery seemed to be slowly fading away. It had already been a few days of anguish, not only for sister Rose but also for his siblings.

Annique's and Ayesha's presence augmented mutual physical and moral support for Rose. Annique kept noticing positive signs of physical changes in Collin's demeanor. An occasional whisper in his ears, "Love you daddy" or "'You got this dad, let's do this, wake up please." Ayesha, on the other hand, seemed to be in a trance and did not show any emotions whatsoever. Some people do react differently to adverse situations. This was clearly her way of operating.

"Nurse, his pressure is dropping considerably!" exclaimed Rose to the attending nurse. It was probably around 8:30 a.m. on Sunday, February 16th. Indeed, his pressure kept tumbling downwards and he felt colder than how he was earlier. His pressure had initially been stabilized at around 135/85. It started to plummet to 120/70, 120/65, 110/60, all within a duration of 15 to 20 minutes. The nurses quickly covered him using an electric warmer / blanket and injected his drips with epinephrine. Then his pressure began to climb remarkably. In retrospect, I think that's the time when he actually died.

Later that day, they did an EEG and a CT scan, and then the neurologist requested to have a word with us. He was a relatively young doctor of Indian descent who seemed to be cold and expressionless. When he came in, there were no greetings or messing around. The neurologist looked directly into our faces and blurted the most inhumane and unemotional words.

"He is brain dead and there is no use keeping him on these life-supporting machines," he callously pointed out with no sense of pity whatsoever.

"Legally, he is dead." He then said, "According to the laws of Las Vegas, he will need to be disconnected from the life support instruments within 24 hours."

The neurologist then muttered something which sounded like: "Do you have any questions? and I'm sorry," but we were no longer on his page.

This sad and sudden news hit us like a ton of bricks dropping on our heads. We knew that he had gone but deep inside, we were hoping for a miracle that Collin was going to snap out of the coma. He was too young to die so prematurely. Thank God I was there to hold on to Rose, Ayiesha, and Annique. They once again began to cry their hearts out as they received this shocking and sudden news. Good lord! We now had to tell Mom what was happening. How would she react? Was it wise to fly her up to Las Vegas and to see her second child in this state, and according to this 'frosty' doctor, brain dead? This was turning out to be the worst day of my life. I tried to be strong for Rose, Ayiesha, and Annique but in the midst of their crying, I received a call from my son, Andrew.

"How is Uncle Collin?"

Suddenly I was jolted into reality. God, he is dead, my buddy is no longer with us. I felt weak and my usually sturdy legs could no longer support my weight. Thankfully, there was a vacant chair nearby. I slumped into the chair and cried and cried. I can't remember if I had continued the conversation with my son. At that moment, nothing mattered, I was lost and my ship floated with no purpose, no direction with no gust of wind in my sails. I felt empty and beaten. During all this ordeal, Collin remained the same way, all hooked up to the ventilator and monitors, with his eyes slightly opened and his stare blank. His breathing, ably assisted by the devices, was rhythmic. *Was he really dead?*

The fact that they were going to 'pull the plugs' in 24 hours made it more difficult to comprehend. After the unsympathetic doctor left, one of the very caring nurses came into the room and tried to comfort us.

It's truly amazing to see how human beings could be so strikingly different.

Later, after careful discussion among my siblings, we managed to relay the news to Mom, that he was critical and that the prognosis was not good. Mom said that she knew that something was wrong with him, that she had felt it. That same night she had dreamt that he had visited her and had kept reassuring her that he was alright. We thought that it would be the best thing for her to travel to LV to see her dying son. Camille and Valerie volunteered to accompany her early, the following day, Monday, February 17th. We spent most of that day and night at the hospital, trying to console each other while we hoped and prayed for a miracle. It was probably the longest night ever and I kept replaying the blood-curdling words "legally he is dead," and found it hard to come to grips with the situation at hand. The next day commenced and he continued the same way. His temperature had to be maintained with an electric blanket and he was given epinephrine to regulate his pressure as his body had lost the ability to regulate itself.

It was probably around eight that morning when a call came through from Orlando saying that Mom was taken to the hospital. While they were preparing to make the journey to LV, they discovered that she was not moving. That she was not responsive and seemed to be in a coma. There, a popular quote which says that "when it rains, it pours" immediately came to my mind. In the hospital, they found out that her sugar level had dropped to a scary number, maybe she had taken too much insulin. Was this a deliberate act? Maybe she took it twice without realizing it. Who knows! This ordeal ruled her trip to LV completely out of the picture. God always finds ways to deal with scenarios.

Mom quickly recovered after having been given a bit of rehydration and dextrose to raise her glucose level. This bit of confusion caused them to postpone their flight to LV. Another flight reservation was made and my two sisters, Valerie and Camille had proceeded to journey all the way to the land of the casinos. All the while, my dear brother was breathing rhythmically in a comatose position in the Desert Springs Hospital. Clearly, it was not our intention to have her see her second child in this state. That would have been disastrous. Valerie and Camille finally arrived in LV and their presence was tremendously supportive. These were trying times, moments that were never ever experienced before.

Suppose he was not really dead! This theory was now being put forward by my two sisters. I've never heard of persons recovering after being pronounced brain dead. Being comatose is totally different from being declared as brain dead. They, my sisters, suggested that we get an injunction from a judge to have Collin stay longer on the life-supporting devices, in the hope that he would eventually recover. It was therefore a mad scramble to secure a possible injunction. After discussions with a lawyer who charged us $2,000 USD, it was finally agreed that this exercise would have been futile. The laws governing similar scenarios were quite stringent in LV.

It was already late in the afternoon of February 18th, 2020. Preparation was being made to cease the resuscitation efforts later that evening. We all felt as though we had lost a massive battle, drained and weak we were as we attempted to support each other. He had lived a good life; he has kept the faith; now he is no more.

Strangely, according to Glendon, on the afternoon of Collin's demise, a wild pigeon (Weeruu), similar to the ones we used to trap, appeared on the back porch. This was strange because in his life at Haraculi, this has never occurred. The bird was there for about 30 minutes on the porch of the backstairs at our Haraculi house, before flying away. In his words, he knew that Collin had just died. Similarly, on the evening when Mom fell ill, she too had felt that something had gone wrong with him. In her dreams, she heard him knocking on her door and then she heard him say that all was well and that she should not worry. Quite strange occurrences indeed.

It was decided that he would donate his organs and was to be honored by the famous "walk of fame." That must be similar to the final walk when someone is being taken to the gallows to be executed. His organs, thankfully, managed to save people's lives. Thank you, Balram.

The walk of fame was like a bad dream. He had another dialysis done to clean his organs and while hooked up to the various life-support systems was wheeled to the operating room. This walk was only about fifty feet to the elevator but seemed like one mile. The healthcare professionals lined the walkway and cheered in honor as we sobbed and moved slowly, following him as he was taken to the gallows. It was something you would never wish to experience.

Later, he was cremated and the ashes transported to St. Vincent and Guyana. They were then sprinkled in the waters of Kingstown and

Berbice River. In Guyana, this exercise was done particularly in front of the Haraculi creek and around the 'waterside' at our house.

My brother, you lived a good life. Thanks for all you have done, I truly love you.

Rest in peace Governor Balram, I salute you.

*Health Minister, Dr. Frank Anthony and I opening "Dr. Collin Boyle's Virology Lab."*

*Balram and I*

## Oh, What an Honor!

Sunday, November 20th 2022, mid-afternoon was very pleasant, it had just rained and a sense of freshness prevailed in and around the "Ram." I would usually go to my log cabin situated on the Soesdyke Linden highway (The 'Ram', named after my deceased brother, Collin) to recharge my batteries on weekends. It's a concrete, two-bedroom structure with a bar made of Demerara Distillery's refurbished rum barrels. Greenheart slabs were nailed on the external walls thus giving it a wooden cabin appearance. This fully solar-powered 'Ram' is the perfect place for rest and relaxation.

My mobile phone rang and I wondered who could be calling on this lovely Sunday afternoon. "Hello Andrew, how are you doing? Sorry to intrude on your weekend." It was the pleasant voice of Dr. Paloma Mohamed-Martin, the University of Guyana's Vice Chancellor. "Hello Madame VC, no, not at all, all is well and hope you are too."

"Andrew, the Special Conferral Committee of the University of Guyana met and considered offering you an honorary degree in recognition of your work, will you accept this honor?" At this time, I was speechless. Oh dear Jehovah, you have done it once again. Clearly Andy, you are indeed God's protégée. He continues to honor and bless you beyond measure, you are truly blessed. When I reflect on my humble upbringing, tears come to my eyes.

"Yes, yes, of course." was my response, which might have been delayed, to the VC, as my mind raced and I wondered if it was a dream.

"Andrew, she went on, we would also like you to be the featured speaker at the graduation ceremony." Now, Andy, it's time to say another prayer to Almighty God for his endless blessings and favor. I was ecstatic. My sentiments were not dissimilar to when the news of my two previous awards (The ANSA Award of Excellence and the Golden Arrow of Achievement) were communicated to me. The feeling of disbelief, and euphoria, one that is absolutely amazing. Later during our conversation, she kindly asked me not to have it broadcasted to the world. I then informed my immediate family members and requested of them that they keep it confidential.

My children, Tony and Andrew agreed to fly in from the USA to attend this auspicious award and graduation ceremony, which was slated for December 9th, 2022. Keziah expressed her desire to attend but stated that she was too busy with classes and work to actually make the journey. Little did I know that she had planned to pleasantly surprise me. It was a perfectly orchestrated move; she skillfully coordinated with her Mom, Germaine, Sophie, and Reuben, our driver, to execute the surprise visit.

The 9th of December seemed to come at a snail's pace. This happens when you are eager and excited to get to a special date. I donned my nicely tailored black suit, the same one that I wore at Tony's wedding. This was combined with a striking light blue shirt and bold red tie. I felt confident as I practiced my speech, I was going to blow them away. A slight variation of a speech that I had previously delivered at a graduation ceremony in Barbados a few months prior.

The hour had come and I was ready for the big stage. The traffic to get to the cultural center was terrible and it took roughly about an hour for us to get there. The procession of the members of the hierarchy of the University of Guyana was a sacred and revered tradition. Yes, I was included as we trod through the main aisle of the packed cultural center and made it to our seats on the front stage.

It was just around 4:00 p.m., practically at the commencement of the ceremony, when Professor Lucus read out what sounded like my generous curriculum vitae. The way he delivered the contents made me sound like an accomplished superstar, The Esteemed Chancellor, Dr. Edward Green along with Vice Chancellor, Prof. Dr. Paloma Mohamed-Martin presented me with the impressive accolade of Honorary Degree of Letters and enrobed me with the distinguishing graduation gown and cap. I felt super excited. Oh, what a euphoric feeling, thank you Holy Jesus!

My discourse centered on advising the graduates to know who they are, give service and create and follow their goals and dreams. I further added "You are special, be a paragon of virtue and uprightness. Your vision and goal need to accompany your purpose."

Thanks be to God, The University of Guyana, my family members and the various hard-working members of my various teams. My gratitude is profound and I'm truly grateful.

The day of graduation, Friday, December 9th, 2022.

*Andrew Jr., Andy, Keziah, and Tony*

# CHAPTER 52

# An Inspiration

It is said that all good or not so good things must come to an end. It was quite an exhilarating experience putting my life's journey on paper. Before I close, I would like to expound on a few areas which I think can serve as catalysts for a better life. They have served me well, and I am absolutely certain that they will have a similar effect on you. I am not a perfect human being, by any means, but I do feel satisfied that I am living a good and fruitful life. If ever these writings resonate with you, then I would have accomplished one of my many goals; that is, to positively influence you.

Firstly, I encourage you, my dear reader, to inculcate an attitude of gratitude. Carve out a few minutes daily to list at least three things in your life for which you are grateful. It is my personal belief that this simple act reprograms what we focus on, and after a while, it manifests in almost every area of our lives.

I admonish you to recognize that you are the pilot of your life and you decide the path that you should take. Coupled with guidance from our Creator (whomsoever you perceive him or her to be), there is absolutely no way you can go wrong. Of course, there will be hurdles and bumps along the way, but those can be surmountable and teachable moments. After listening to all the voices around you, take the time to be quiet, self-introspect, and then feel the next right move to make.

Be positive! A positive outlook on life is important to attract good vibes and repel negative ones. Try as much as you possibly can to eliminate words and phrases like, *I can't, I'm poor, I'm stupid, I'm tired, I'm a failure, I will never succeed, I always lose.* When you utter those negativities, your subconscious being is influenced and the outcomes are usually not satisfactory. Start your day with positive utterances. Speak positivity into your expected journey. Always consider the glass as being half full instead of being half empty. It is a process, let it become a habit, before you know it, you will become a positive, influential person. Being positive can be amazing and provide positive tools for success.

Pray and believe daily not only when you face issues, but reach out to give praise to Almighty God or to whom you consider as your supreme being. Conversations with the supreme being can be done during your quiet moments, when you are paddling, driving, walking, or simply sitting quietly somewhere. This can be simple songs of praises or gratitude; or muttering discreetly your desires and your deepest thoughts. Let prayer become a habit.

Teamwork is important and can prove to be most beneficial. Work in teams, there is strength in numbers. An old African adage captures this concept very well: "If you want to go fast, go alone, if you want to go far, go together." You do not have to do it all alone; partnerships, collaborative efforts and so forth, can work wonders. In order to have these alliances though, trust will be a key factor. Bonds formed with untrustworthy persons, may not last, be trustworthy! My grandfather

(Daddy) used to say that "your word should be your bond." In other words, whatever you say, you should stick by. Your word is your honor, as much as possible fulfill it; however, if the human moments arise and you are caught between 'a rock and a hard place,' have a discussion around why you have to deviate. Joyce Meyer sums it up nicely: "If you say you are going to do something, then you need to do it."

Be humble. Stay humble, act with integrity, and inspire others. "Being humble is one of those ingredients to make you into a person with integrity and hence into a great and effective leader." says Hei-Ran Park.

Never give up…perseverance is the name of the game. Do you know how many people failed at their first attempt? The great Thomas Edison in his attempt to create the first light bulb, failed 2,774 times. Suppose he had given up on his 100th attempt? And justifiably so. I have not succeeded at many of my first tries. I failed miserably at my first attempt at one of my sports competitions. I returned to the drawing board and trained desperately and prevailed eventually.

I remember that song by Lou Rawls, "The sun always comes up tomorrow, you bet your bottom dollar." I find that to be inspirational and a reminder that despite how tough the goings get they will not last forever. That famous quote also says, "This too shall pass." (Unknown)

Press on, my friends, hang in there, tomorrow will be a better day. Busy Signal sings about absolute optimism in dreams of brighter days. For those of you who are considering throwing in the towel and even some with possible suicidal thoughts; giving up is not an option, I promise you, this too shall pass, tomorrow will be a better day. Things will turn around, they have to. The only way to go would be upwards.

Steve Harvey, one of the influential persons to whom I listen, has had a tremendous impact on my life and I hope that his positive utterances in the foregoing will do likewise for you. Two things in particular Steve purports which resonate with me: The first is "to write the vision and make it plain." Steve encourages us to write the things that we would like to see/achieve in the future. One way of doing this is to create a vision board; this act will help in the visualization of one's wishes and desires. Write even the minute details of your desired vision. For example, the color and make of the car that you dream of having. Life is surely not only about dreaming; but of working diligently to achieve one's goals; however, everything begins as a thought. This concept is based on a verse from The Holy Bible, in the book of Habakkuk.

Habakkuk 2 [1]: "I will stand upon my watch, and set me upon the tower, and will watch to see what he will say unto me, and what I shall answer when I am reproved. [2] And the LORD answered me, and said, Write the vision, and make it plain upon tables, that he may run that readeth it."

This mechanism also underscores the importance of positive thinking or simply being optimistic of your future endeavors and visualizing them.

The other profound thought of Steve is to ask God for what you want. Also found in The Holy Bible, James 4:2-3 "You have not because you ask not." Ask God for what you want and then go after it.

I would like to wish you well in your life's journey. Go bravely and grab the world by the scruff of her neck and take charge. Make a difference with your service to humanity, take calculated risks; don't be afraid to take that leap of faith. My friends, "go, don't just go where the path leads but create your own path and leave a trail for others to follow." (Ralph Waldo Emerson) I survived because the fire inside me burned brighter than the fire around me." (Joshua Graham)

All the very best.

Thank you
Merci beaucoup
Veel dank u
Muito obrigado
Danke
Grazie
Blagodaryu vas
Muchisimas gracias
Fēicháng gǎnxiè nǐ

**-The End-**

*Banner of the 'Inspire Kimbia' project*

# Acknowledgments

Praise God from whom all blessings flow! (2 Corinthians 13:14)

My siblings are truly an amazing bunch, I'm exceedingly grateful for their love and never-ending support.

Thank you to my hardworking team members, all of the various teams, Eureka Medical Laboratories, Caribbean Wind & Sun, Amazonia Farms, and Eureka Atlantic Offshore Medical Services Inc.

My friends Gino (Rawle), Twelve (Terence), Denise, and many others are truly an inspiration.

The late Dr. Menzo Collin Boyle, your influence and guidance in my life were beyond comprehension. Thank you, wherever you are; I'm indebted to you and I'm truly grateful for all you have done. May your soul Rest in Peace and rise in glory.

Thank you, our bouncing octogenarian Mom; you are genuinely an amazing mother. My gratitude to you is magnanimous.

Deep and sincere appreciation is also extended to Dr. Janice Imhoff, Dr. Paloma Mohamed-Martin, Mr. Dickson Hooper, and Major General Joseph Singh (Retd.) for their guidance.

Tony, Andrew Jr., and Keziah, you are the oxygen that I breathe; thank you.

# About the Author

Dr. William Andrew Boyle or simply "Andy," started to define his purpose at age nine. Growing up in the pristine forest of an Amerindian Village, Kimbia also called Haraculi or Good Hope, located in Berbice, Guyana, South America. – and challenged by lack of technology. Since then, like a canoe forging against the Berbice river, he set forth his destination towards his motto "the sky's the limit." Soon, he would graduate from the New Amsterdam Multilateral Secondary School, become a scholar in Cuba, earn a degree in Microbiology and an MBA in Business Administration. He is now a PhD candidate.

Dr. Boyle was selected as The Caribbean Entrepreneur of the year 2018 and awarded with Guyana's Golden Arrow of Achievement in 2019. In December 0f 2022 he was conferred with an Honorary Doctorate by the University of Guyana.

From nothing, he and his wife, Dr. Karen L. Boyle, established Eureka Medical Laboratories Inc., now a premier medical health care institution in Guyana and St. Vincent, W. I.

"Aspire: Dare to Dream" an Autobiography, is his first book and there is no turning back for Andy. His story is now being written.

www.ingramcontent.com/pod-product-compliance
Lightning Source LLC
Chambersburg PA
CBHW070903120626
46546CB00001B/119